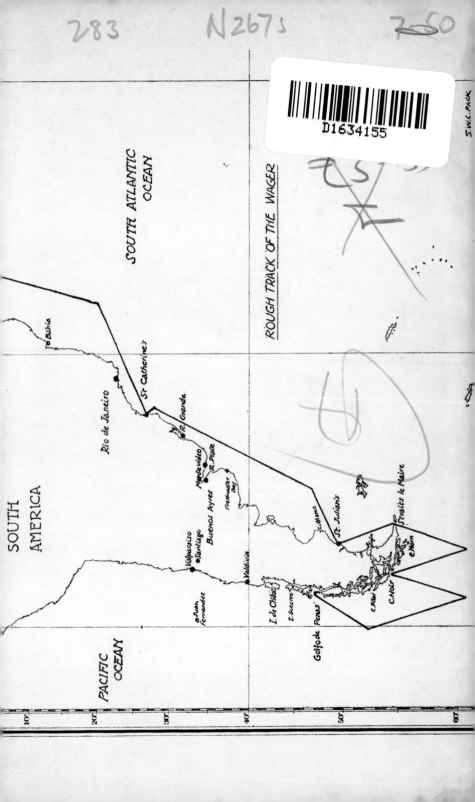

ROUGH TRACK OF THE WAGER

THE *WAGER* MUTINY

Other works by S. W. C. Pack:

WEATHER FORECASTING

ANSON'S VOYAGE

ADMIRAL LORD ANSON

THE BATTLE OF MATAPAN

WINDWARD OF THE CARIBBEAN

THE *WAGER* MUTINY

by

S. W. C. PACK

ALVIN REDMAN
LONDON

First published by
ALVIN REDMAN LIMITED
17 Fleet Street
London, E.C.4
1964

PRINTED IN GREAT BRITAIN BY
BRISTOL TYPESETTING CO. LTD.
BARTON MANOR - ST. PHILIPS
BRISTOL 2

To

My Own Beloved

Mutineer

ACKNOWLEDGMENTS

The author's sincere thanks for willing help are due to:
Commander Peter Kemp and Miss Vivienne Heath of the
    Admiralty Library,
Mr. Ian Thomson of the Edinburgh University Library,
Mr. G. H. Draper of Ilford, for information on ship's boats,
Miss P. Sichel, Messrs. J. Munday, G. Naish, and B. Patton of
    the National Maritime Museum,
Messrs. W. Best Harris and C. A. J. Smith of the Plymouth
    Central Library,
Mr. A. K. Timings of the Public Record Office,
The Librarian of the Southampton University Library,
Captain T. E. Jackson of the Victory Museum, Portsmouth,
Miss Freda Busby

The illustrations 1-11 are reproduced by kind permission of
the National Maritime Museum.

PRAYER
TO BE USED IN THE
ROYAL NAVY EVERY DAY

O Eternal Lord God, who alone spreadest out the heavens and rulest the raging of the sea; who hast compassed the waters with bounds until day and night come to an end; be pleased to receive into thy almighty and most gracious protection the persons of us thy servants, and the Fleet in which we serve. Preserve us from the dangers of the sea, and from the violence of the enemy: that we may be a safeguard unto our most gracious sovereign lady, Queen Elizabeth, and her dominions, and a security for such as pass on the seas upon their lawful occasions: that the inhabitants of our Island may in peace and quietness serve Thee our God; and that we may return in safety to enjoy the blessings of the land, with the fruits of our labours, and with a thankful remembrance of thy mercies to praise and glorify thy Holy Name: through Jesus Christ our Lord.

Amen.

CONTENTS

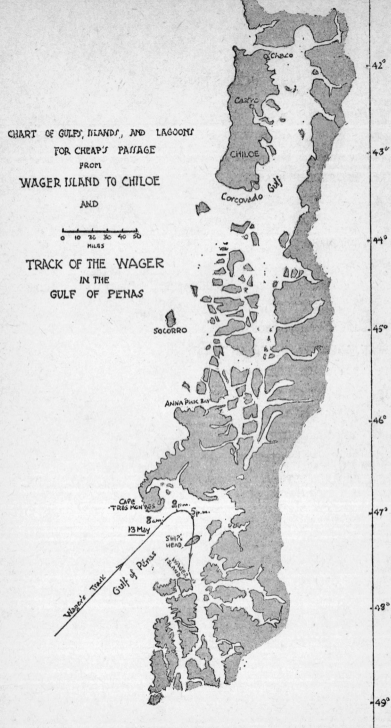

CHART OF GULFS, ISLANDS, AND LAGOONS

FOR CHEAP'S PASSAGE

FROM

WAGER ISLAND TO CHILOE

AND

0 10 20 30 40 50
MILES

TRACK OF THE WAGER

IN THE

GULF OF PENAS

Q. Chaco

Castro

CHILOE

Corcovado Gulf

SOCORRO

ANNA PINK BAY

CAPE
TRES MONTES   2 p.m.

8 a.m.   5 p.m.

13 May

SHIP'S
HEAD

WAGER
ISLAND

Wager's Track   Gulf of Penas

S W.C. PACK

LIST OF ILLUSTRATIONS

CHAPTER I

WAGER SAILS WITH ANSON

" MY END is near." The speaker gasped the words as he lay dying in his cot in the captain's cabin of H.M.S. *Pearl*.

" Take heed. Remember the curse which spells the doom of the little *Wager*."

Lieutenant Salt bent close, clutching the captain's cot with one hand to steady himself against the ship's motion. It was difficult to hear the captain's feeble words above the shriek of the gale in the rigging, the thrash of the seas, the creak of the timbers, and the great thumps which accompanied each violent lurch.

" You shall take command of the *Pearl*," continued Dandy Kidd, the captain. " But remember the curse on the *Wager*— my old ship." He winced with pain, and was silent for a while. A great sea struck the *Pearl*. She shivered, momentarily stopped, then recovered. Kidd continued speaking.

" All our company are cheerful. They hope to sack the Spanish towns. Every man sees himself rich and prosperous . . ." Kidd's voice faded away again. A whole minute passed, and the turmoil of the storm seemed to emphasize the silence of his voice.

" But not those in *Wager*," Kidd continued excitedly.

" They shall know poverty, vermin, famine . . ." He hesitated,
and then resumed. " And absolute ruin . . ."

These were his last words. On the 31st January 1741,
Dandy Kidd died.

On the 18th September 1740, Commodore Anson's squadron had sailed from St. Helen's roads off the Isle of Wight.
There had been months of delay in assembling the squadron.
Even when it was eventually assembled, contrary winds blew
for a long period and further delayed Anson's departure. The
delay was regarded by many as an ill omen. In addition to
Anson's squadron of six men-of-war and two store ships, there
was a large convoy of 150 merchant ships with escorts, carrying trade to the Mediterranean and to Britain's American
colonies. These ships were to be escorted safely out of the
English Channel. Britain was already at war with Spain. War
with France was impending.

During a long peace Britain had suffered many indignities.
There were frequent reports of ships being plundered by the
Spaniards. This raised great indignation. Finally an event came
to light which fired the public mind and precipitated the
declaration of war against Spain. The master of the brig
Rebecca of Glasgow had had one of his ears cut off by the
Spaniards of a guarda costa, and had insolently been told to
take it home to his King, George II.

Anson's squadron was under orders to " arrive on the
Spanish coast of the South Sea " . . . (now Chile and Peru,
and at that time a place of great wealth) . . . " to annoy and
distress the Spaniards . . . by taking, sinking, burning, or
otherwise destroying all their ships . . ." Anson was further
instructed to take any base belonging to the Spaniards on that
coast which he deemed worth while; Panama was specifically
mentioned. This latter enterprise had the purpose not only of
" annoying the Spaniards " but of establishing a " proper place

for careening of the ships, and for supplying them with provisions either for their voyage homeward or for their continuing longer abroad." How few were to return homeward could little be foreseen at that stage. In the event, only one ship of Anson's squadron, the 60 gun *Centurion,* was to survive, and it was to be four years before Anson and his small band of survivors sailed homeward up the English Channel with the biggest booty that had ever returned to England in a single ship.

Anson's squadron consisted of six warships, recently refitted, ammunitioned, and provisioned:

Commander	Ship	Guns	Tons	Men
George Anson (Commodore)	*Centurion,* 4th Rate	60	1,005	400
Richard Norris	*Gloucester,* 4th Rate	50	866	300
The Hon. Edward Legge	*Severn,* 4th Rate	50	853	300
Mathew Mitchel	*Pearl,* 5th Rate	40	595	250
Dandy Kidd	*Wager,* 6th Rate	28	559	160
The Hon. George Murray	*Tryal,* Sloop	8	200	100

There were also two store ships, known as pinks or victuallers: the *Anna* and the *Industry.*

In this story we are mainly concerned with the *Wager* and her crew, but we may picture the beauty and grace of this concourse on a September day in the Channel, and imagine the thoughts of each man in this vast assembly, many of whom would never return. Many were unwilling victims of the press gang. In addition to the ships' companies, there were 470 marines and soldiers; quite a few were sick or old and unfit for the rigours of an expedition. Following many years of peace, neglect and corruption had entered the administration of the Navy, and ships were unsound and provisions unwholesome. Nevertheless the spirit of adventure prevailed, and in the majority dwelt the prospect of fortunes to be made at the expense of the Spaniards, and interest and curiosity in the next port of call.

Before standing to the south-west with his large assembly, Anson hoisted his Commodore's broad pennant in the *Centurion,* and received a salute of thirteen guns from every man-of-war in company. He then made a signal for all captains of men-of-war to repair on board *Centurion,* to receive fighting and sailing instructions. By the 29th September he was well clear of the land. The last of his tenders had parted company, and his own particular squadron were standing for the island of Madeira. Again they met contrary winds, and it was not until the 25th October 1740, five weeks out from Spithead, that they anchored in Madeira roads. Of those captains listed above, not one was destined to stay the whole course with Anson. Norris was already ill, and on arrival at Madeira was given leave to return to England. On the 4th November, Anson ordered a number of transfers among the commanders, Mathew Mitchel relieving Norris in the *Gloucester,* and being himself relieved in command of the *Pearl* by Dandy Kidd of the *Wager.* The Honourable George Murray transferred to *Wager* and thus left vacant the command of the small sloop *Tryal.* This vacancy was filled by the promotion of Cheap, the *Tryal's* lieutenant, one of the leading characters of this book. With Murray from *Tryal* to *Wager* went a midshipman, Alexander Campbell, destined to acquire fame for his extraordinary adventures in this story.

The squadron spent a week at Madeira, watering and replenishing with Madeira wine, and on the 3rd November 1740, weighed and proceeded southward for Brazil. Important news had reached Anson when calling on the Governor of Madeira, for he learnt of the existence of a Spanish squadron of six men-of-war seen off-shore to the westward of the island for three days at the end of October. A search by the fast sloop *Tryal* revealed nothing, though it is clear that the information referred to a Spanish squadron commanded by Don Joseph Pizarro; a squadron superior in number of guns and men, and having on board a Spanish regiment intended for the reinforcement of Spanish bases in the South Sea. The news of Anson's expedition had reached the ears of Spain months before. It was to be a race round Cape Horn. Pizarro was anxious to get to the Pacific before Anson, so as to prepare for and frustrate all assaults. Anson was determined to evade Pizarro and forestall him in the South Sea, so as to maintain the initiative. St. Catherine's Island off the coast of Brazil was ordered by Anson as the next rendezvous. Here his squadron, with one exception, arrived safely in late December.

The exception was the storeship *Industry*. Two weeks out of Madeira her master had requested that she be unloaded and released, as his charter was approaching its termination. The ships of the squadron were deeply laden, nevertheless Anson did not wish to detain *Industry*, particularly as she was slow. All ships brought to, and for three days their longboats were employed in transferring casks of brandy from the *Industry*. The other pink, the *Anna*, still heavily laden, was compelled to remain with the squadron, and was destined to put up a splendid performance with her small crew of under a score. By the evening of the 18th November, unloading had been completed. *Industry* parted company, bound for Barbados where she was to embark freight for England. With her went many letters written by the officers of the squadron. Unhappily, she was taken by the Spaniards soon afterwards.

Scurvy had broken out in Anson's squadron after leaving Madeira. By late November it was rife in every ship. Rapidly it spread through the mess-decks. Many men died. All ships were now very heavily laden and so deep in the water that their lower gun ports could not be safely opened. As a consequence, no fresh air could penetrate the mess-decks, and these now became foul and unhealthy. The three days of lying-to in the tropics, while brandy was being transferred from the *Industry*, augmented the foul conditions, and on the 20th November

captains reported to Anson that many men were confined to
their hammocks, some past hope of recovery. The Commodore
immediately ordered scuttles to be cut in each ship, to allow
the entry of air into mess-decks. He was well aware of representations that had long been made to ship constructors that
ventilation should be introduced into the mess-decks. Perhaps
owing to an obsession for stoutness and durability, there had
been considerable opposition to such representations.

On arrival at St. Catherine's the sick were landed and
accommodated in tents, while the ships were scrubbed and
fumigated between decks. Their condition had become abom-
inably foul and nauseous. Many men were dying. The cause of
scurvy was still unknown, but it was believed that the foul air
and filth of the mess-decks were largely responsible for its
onset. Many of the sick recovered after being brought ashore,
but their recovery was at this time attributed to the benefits of
fresh air rather than to anti-scorbutic fruits, whose value came
to be realised at a later stage of the expedition. The *Wager*, in
common with all the other ships of the squadron, buried about
a tenth of her complement while here: one-fifth were still sick.

Anson was anxious to proceed as soon as possible. Because
of the possibility of an encounter with Pizarro he was determined to be in fighting trim, and ordered the proper securing
of masts and overhauling of rigging in all ships of the squadron.
It was found that the *Tryal*'s mainmast was sprung, and her
foremast in such a sorry condition that a four-day search in the
woods took place to find a suitable tree. The search proved
unsuccessful, and it became necessary to fish the masts; that is,
to provide a three-sided casing for strengthening. *Tryal*'s main
top-mast and fore-yard were also found to be decayed and
rotten. This condition in the King's ships was common, following years of neglect and corruption in naval yards, and it was
to contribute greatly to the loss of nearly all the squadron. It is
questionable whether the *Wager*, an East Indiaman freshly

purchased from a merchant in the previous year, 1739, was in any better condition than the rest. In later years, when Anson served as First Lord of the Admiralty, he took great care that warships' masts and yards should be of a standard size and pattern, so that spares could be made quickly available.

It was necessary that the *Tryal*, being the eyes of the fleet, should retain her speed. Anson otherefore ordered her to be hove down and her bottom cleaned. Her refit lasted nearly a month. But worse than the delay was the fact that information about Anson's squadron at St. Catherine's was being passed to Pizarro. The latter was at this time at Buenos Ayres in the River Plate, about 750 miles away. The informer was no less than Don José Sylva de Paz, the Governor of St. Catherine's who, although a subject and representative of the King of Portugal, and therefore nominally friendly to the British, was so deeply committed to illegal commerce with the Spaniards, and the smuggling of gold in return for silver, defrauding thereby both the revenues of his own sovereign and those of the King of Spain, that he was compelled to ingratiate himself with the Spaniards. Not only did he oppose the free purchase of goods and provisions by the Englishmen at St. Catherine's, but he dispatched news by express messenger to Buenos Ayres, giving details of the British squadron particularly in relation to their condition and the number of men and guns in each ship.

St. Catherine's Island had hitherto enjoyed a splendid reputation among English sailors. Fresh water was good and plentiful, and there was an abundance of fresh fruit and vegetables, fish, and even pheasants. Nevertheless the squadron now found the place humid and infested with mosquitoes and sand-flies that bit them furiously and raised itchy swellings. There was growing suspicion concerning the Governor's duplicity, despite the utmost respect and courtesy shown to him by Anson. Little regret was felt therefore when on the 18th January all the ships of the squadron weighed and put to sea. Anson was still

uncertain of the exact composition or location of Pizarro's
squadron. He was, however, well aware of the possibility of his
own ships becoming disabled and separated as they approached
the stormy latitudes of the South. Before sailing, he named St.
Julian's Bay (latitude 49° south) as the next rendezvous, and
directed all captains to exercise the utmost care to avoid separation. If ships became separated or missed the first rendezvous,
they were to continue southward and proceed through the
Straits le Maire, round Cape Horn into the South Sea, and
then rendezvous off the island of Nuestra Señora de Socorro
in latitude 45° south on the west coast, and cruise off-shore
out of sight. Many guns had been struck down into the holds
to increase stability and reduce rolling in the hard gales shortly
to be expected.

Unknown to Anson, Pizarro's squadron sailed from the
River Plate on the 22nd January, four days after his own
squadron had left St. Catherine's. The chances of an engagement were therefore high.

The weather deteriorated almost as soon as Anson put to
sea, and on the third day the whole squadron was encompassed
by a violent squall with the wind increasing to storm force from
the east. Visibility rapidly diminished to a few yards, and ships
were soon out of sight of one another. Guns were fired from
Centurion, ordering the squadron to bring to. At noon the
storm began to ease, and the fog suddenly dispersed. The *Pearl*
had disappeared altogether. The *Tryal* was seen to be a great
way to leeward, having lost her mainmast on which so much
time had been spent. Anson ordered the *Gloucester* to take her
in tow, and the squadron now resumed course to the southward, to arrive without further incident at St. Julian's in
Patagonia on the 17th February. All being well, the next stop
would be in the South Sea, and hey-ho for fortune. Such a
prospect buoyed the hopes of even the sick. All would be well
eventually. It is clear from the records that the resolution and

preparedness shown by Anson were an inspiration to many who might otherwise have given up hope.

Shortly after arrival a sail was seen to seaward, and Anson ordered the *Gloucester* and the *Severn* to investigate. This was at six in the morning. From the ships at anchor inshore it was later seen that the strange sail was none other than the *Pearl*, and there was general rejoicing at the renewal of strength of the squadron. Although *Severn* was within recall and now gave up the chase, *Gloucester* continued to close the *Pearl*. The latter crowded on sail and stood away, preparing meanwhile for an engagement, with hammocks in nettings and guns run out. As *Gloucester* closed, recognition became mutual, and the two ships returned to harbour. The *Pearl* arrived in harbour at two in the afternoon, and at once bore down upon the *Centurion* to pass exciting news to the Commodore. The first lieutenant, Salt, now in command, informed Anson that Dandy Kidd, the captain, had died during passage on the 31st January. Moreover, three weeks after the *Pearl* had lost sight of the squadron she had sighted a squadron of five warships, fairly close inshore. There was great joy among the ship's company until it was suddenly realised that there were Spanish men-of-war, the leading ship wearing a red broad pennant at the main, similar to that worn by *Centurion*. *Pearl* had crowded on sail, and bore away, followed by all five Spaniards. One of the ships was remarkably like the *Gloucester*, and it was for this reason that the *Pearl* had prepared for action when chased by *Gloucester* on arrival off St. Julian's. The *Pearl* had had a narrow escape from the Spaniards, and had survived by cutting across a shoal too shallow for the bigger Spanish ships who, finding that they were unable to catch *Pearl* before nightfall, gave up the chase and resumed their course southward. The ships were described as two of seventy guns, two of fifty, and one of forty guns. This was the first reliable evidence received by Anson.

St. Julian's Bay was one of the few sheltered anchorages on this coast, and it was essential to stay here until the *Tryal* had been fitted with a new mainmast, for she would be unable to round the Horn in her present sorry condition. With two separate squadrons converging on the Straits le Maire, the chances of meeting increased. Anson was reluctant to stay at St. Julian's any longer than necessary, for fear of being trapped in harbour.

A further change of commanding officers now took place. Anson transferred the Hon. George Murray from the *Wager* to the *Pearl,* to succeed the deceased Dandy Kidd, and transferred Cheap from the *Tryal* to the *Wager.* Cheap had thus in a few weeks enjoyed rapid promotion from lieutenant of the small sloop *Tryal* to taking command of the 28 gun sixth-rate *Wager* with a ship's company of 160 men. In view of subsequent events it is worth reflecting on the fact that Anson, a shrewd judge of men, must have had confidence in Cheap. It is certain that Cheap had in marked degree those qualities of determination, loyalty, and fortitude that the Commodore valued. He was also an able navigator and seaman. He was a big man and feared nobody. Inflexible in his ways, he was unrelenting in his wrath. Not a man doubted his ability as a commander. Where he failed was in his understanding of his officers and men, nearly all of whom he treated harshly, lacking confidence in any of them. Cheap had little control of his temper, and was easily moved to furious fits of rage. Discipline in those times was maintained not by an appeal to commonsense, but by the continual instillation of fear and by the frequent award of the most brutal punishment. The sentence for conviction of desertion or mutiny was hanging at the yard-arm. Few captains had the leadership and compassion which were so evident in Anson, though many officers who served with him in this expedition were greatly influenced by his character, and later reached high rank in the Navy. Such were Peircy Brett,

Keppel, Saunders, de Saumarez, Hyde Parker, and the Hon. John Byron, a midshipman in the *Wager*.

The little *Tryal* was now fitted with a spare main top-mast from the *Wager*. The result was a success, for the masts in shortened form were more suitable for withstanding the tempests of Cape Horn. To lose a mast in those waters would practically doom a ship to destruction. Anson, ever ready for a surprise encounter, ordered that those guns that had been removed to the hold should now be brought up and mounted. To make room for these, the gun decks were cleared, and provisions transferred to the store ship *Anna*, it being decided that she must continue with the squadron.

Talk reached the *Wager* of the remark made by her former captain, Dandy Kidd. A few days before his death in the *Pearl*, he was heard to refer to the appalling condition of the *Wager* and to a curse which would spell her doom. Notwithstanding cheerfulness and enthusiasm, he had said, events would prove to be very different from those expected, and in place of great fortune their expedition would end in absolute ruin. This spread despondency. The ill omens of contrary winds and sudden storms were recalled. Reflections on the increasing toll of scurvy and the treacherous attitude of the Portuguese governor at St. Catherine's caused many to lose hope.

But on Friday the 27th February the squadron weighed and proceeded from St. Julian's. In little more than a week, on the 7th March towards noon they entered the Straits le Maire. The day was bright with sunshine, and a strong following wind and a favourable current hurried the squadron through the Straits at eleven knots. Here at last was the junction between the Atlantic and the Pacific Oceans, and it was generally felt that there was nothing now to separate them from their goal of treasure but the open sea. Their greatest difficulties were past. They had found the entrance to the Straits without mishap.

We can picture the squadron with the *Tryal* and *Pearl* in the

van, on an ultramarine sea flecked with huge white horses. In
the centre were the *Severn, Centurion,* and *Gloucester. Wager*
and the little *Anna* brought up the rear. To starboard was the
barren and desolate land of Tierra del Fuego; to port, the
ragged snow-covered precipices and rocks of Staten Island.
They had reached the southern latitude of 55° and soon would
be rounding the Horn to proceed westward for the wealthy
coasts of Chile and Peru.

Momentarily forgotten on this brilliant day was Dandy
Kidd's forecast, and ignored was the rapidly growing list of the
dead. The chaplain of the *Centurion* refers to this joyous day
of sunshine in winter: . . . " We passed those memorable
streights, ignorant of the dreadful calamities which were then
impending, and just ready to break upon us; ignorant that the
time drew near when the squadron would be separated never
to unite again, and that the day of our passage was the last
chearful day that the greatest part of us would ever live to
enjoy."

CHAPTER 2

WAGER BACKGROUND

ANSON'S SHIPS were classified 4th, 5th or 6th rate, according to the number of guns. The *Centurion, Gloucester,* and *Severn* were all 4th rate and could be expected to fight in the line of battle with powerful three-deckers that carried 100 guns. The *Wager* was a small ship, a 6th rate of only 28 guns, and her main function in this expedition was to carry portable guns and ammunition for landing purposes, and much of the equipment needed for an assault on enemy bases, as well as merchandise for trade and exchange. Cheap was well aware of this, and must have been particularly reminded by Anson of the difficulties and shortcomings which would follow *Wager*'s separation from the squadron. Cheap was determined therefore to make the next rendezvous at all costs, but having little confidence in his officers, revealed little of his intentions, and positively refused to countenance or discuss any of their suggestions.

Cheap's next in command was the lieutenant, Robert Baynes, the only other commissioned officer in *Wager*. He seems to have been a spiritless and ineffectual officer, lacking both leadership and confidence, although happy to enjoy the benefits of his rank without accepting the responsibility. The remaining officers were the warrant officers, the life blood of the ship, and the midshipmen. Normally the warrant officers were the solid corps of professional seamen; officers by virtue of training, experience, and ability. They were also men who possessed a basic education, but lacking the polish and background of family influence, seldom had opportunities of reaching commissioned rank.

Among Cheap's officers there were some to whom he took great exception. Most of them were frightened of him, but John Bulkeley, the gunner, was not. Something of a sea-lawyer, with an agile brain and a ready tongue, he was never backward in presenting his case if he thought it just, even though he knew it would upset Cheap. With his ability, confidence, and fearlessness, Bulkeley was a natural leader, though unable to exercise his powers until misfortune struck the *Wager*.

It is apparent that the master, Thomas Clark, was ineffectual and was particularly disliked by Cheap. We shall hear little of him. The boatswain, John King, however, was a man of violent temper, and we shall later see what a trouble-maker he could be. He very much envied and resented Bulkeley's qualities of leadership and his ability as a seaman, and began to fear him, particularly as Bulkeley kept a private journal in which disparaging and incriminating remarks might well appear.

The carpenter, John Cummins, was less dominant, and no leader as was Bulkeley, but an able man in his particular profession, clear thinking, determined, and practical. Few of the *Wager*'s crew realised how much they owed to this officer.

The purser, Thomas Harvey, was a young man of twenty-five, probably of some means. The surgeon, William Elliot, was also a young man, big and strong. Both he and Harvey would be officers of some education, and would frequently be invited to the captain's table. They were regarded as 'civilian' officers, and took no part in the working of the ship. Another whom

Cheap liked was Hamilton, the lieutenant of marines. We shall hear also of John Jones, the master's mate, who outshone his master at navigation, and of Robert Elliot, the surgeon's mate, who appeared to practise more surgery in the interests of humanity than his namesake the surgeon. It is odd that both should have the same name.

There will be a brief reference to Thomas Maclean, the cook, aged eighty-two, who was to survive so much only to die when safety was in sight. A cook was at one time a ' civilian ' officer, but became down-graded with the passage of years. We shall hear often of the cooper, John Young, who wrote " an affecting narrative of the unfortunate voyage " which is perhaps the best written of the many stories though, as with all of them, giving only one point of view.

Of the four midshipmen who sailed in the *Wager*, classed as petty officers in those days, the Honourable John Byron was destined to fame. Subsequently he rose to the rank of Vice-Admiral, and acquired the nickname ' Foul Weather Jack ', his presence at sea always being associated with storm and tempest. He admired and was loyal to Cheap, and had a very different slant from that of Bulkeley. He was also to become the grand-father of the poet, Lord Byron.

Two other midshipmen in the *Wager*, Alexander Campbell and Isaac Morris, also wrote a story of adventures. The sad case of Cozens, the fourth midshipman, we shall hear of later. Cheap seems to have disliked them all except Byron.

Wager's gun-deck was 123 feet long, with the cannon arranged in rows on each side. These fired balls weighing nine pounds, a small affair compared with the 24-pounders of the 4th rates or the 42-pounders of the great 1st rates. The gun carriages were clumsy and difficult to move. They pointed through square ports cut in the ship's sides. In rough weather these ports would be closed with heavy wooden doors. The great weight of cannon placed a severe strain on the structure of the ship, particularly during excessive rolling. They also reduced stability or the tendency for a ship to return to the upright position in heavy weather. But ships were built of oak, and strengthened with great beams and heavy knees designed to resist punishment. It was not so much the size of a ship as its stability and stoutness which would contribute to safety. These factors could easily be neutralized, the first by top weight or badly stowed armament and equipment, the second by neglect and decay.

The men lived below when not on watch, and here they kept their chests, mess-tables, crockery, and private effects. Little light or air penetrated when the ship was secured for rough seas. At night the lower deck was full, with the men sleeping in hammocks slung from the beams. The normal complement on this expedition had been swollen with thirty or more soldiers, but most of these being invalids or pensioners from army hospitals, had died when scurvy made its evil appearance: the oldest went first. Their departure was little regretted, since it eased the crowding. Some of their effects could be purloined. Their deaths could often be concealed for days during which their provisions were consumed, though the purser would soon put a stop to this, in order to feather his own nest by keeping the dead men on his books for some time after their death. A purser had to pay a large sum for his office in which peculation was regarded almost as legitimate practice.

The ship was a little world, self-sufficient, in which many members were not seamen at all, but skilled craftsmen and their mates. Among the professional seamen were the master and two master's mates, the boatswain and two boatswain's mates, the gunner and two gunner's mates, the four midshipmen, the quartermaster and quartermaster's mate, and the main body of lower-deck seamen, referred to as such because they lived on the lower deck. Among the craftsmen and non-seamen were the carpenter, purser, surgeon, cook, steward, sailmaker, cooper, armourer, clerk, corporal of marines, marines, servants, mates, and yeomen.

The gunner of the *Wager*, John Bulkeley, refers specifically, as though it were unusual, to the fact that he had charge of a watch during the whole voyage. The reason is obvious, for Bulkeley was an outstanding warrant officer, perhaps the ablest person in the ship, not excepting Cheap, the captain: the master, Thomas Clark, was on the other hand incompetent.

In action there was a job for everyone, and within limits, the bigger the crew, the greater and faster the fire power. During this century Britain was more often at war than not. But even when not fighting, the ship would provide work for all, not only in day-to-day maintenance and sailing, but in repairs and replacements.

The big jobs in working a ship constituted the spreading and handing of sails, the overhauling of halyards, and the tending of lifts and braces. In rough weather heavy movable objects such as guns had to be secured; and pumps had to be worked continuously. At the best of times there were never too many men, for the ship carried three masts, on each of which were two and sometimes three square sails bent on wooden spars called yards. These had to be set or furled, depending on the moods of wind and weather, and the course required to steer. To shin up the shrouds and lay out on a yard to set or furl was a relatively easy matter for a fit man in good weather. But in rough weather, in heavy seas with the ship lurching and heaving, this could be a hazardous task, made particularly dangerous in the high southern latitudes of Cape Horn and in conditions where frozen hands were common. Many came to such service unwillingly, having been delivered from gaol or caught by the press gang. Those who joined voluntarily, if not hiding from something worse, were lured by the chance of prize money or the enormous daily ration of brandy available.

In the England of those days, theft, bribery, debauchery,

deceit, brutality, and blackmail were common. Protection was provided by the law, but its enforcement was difficult, though the dangling corpses at Tyburn acted as a deterrent. On board His Majesty's ships enforcement was in the hands of the captain, who wielded considerable power, supported by his officers and the possession of arms. Fear was the spur which enforced discipline. Punishment was carried out ceremonially, with an armed guard present and the ship's company assembled to witness. Under such circumstances few captains would be liked by their men, though they might be admired. Bitter grudges would be stirred up, perhaps to be written off or paid back in a moment of thoughtlessness, temporary weakness, unpreparedness, excessive provocation, or a sudden change of circumstances such as the loss of a ship.

Few Englishmen really like to be disciplined. Even in the Hitler war there were cases of prisoners adopting the attitude " we are all equal now " until reminded that pay would continue in accordance with rank and service, subject to good behaviour. But at the time of Anson's expedition pay ceased at once when a ship was lost, and there were many who considered that discipline ceased accordingly. Anson himself put this matter right when later serving on the Board of Admiralty.

But under normal circumstances the captain was king. Subject to orders from higher authority, in this case the Commodore, the captain could order punishment and ration provisions. Cheap was in the unfortunate position of being not only the new captain of the ship, " never as good as the last ", but in any case had had only a few weeks' experience of command.

What sort of clothes should we see at this period? This was eight years before Anson introduced a standard naval uniform for flag officers and captains, an expensive privilege which was slow to spread. Nevertheless the army had worn uniform for centuries, and it had been the custom for ships' officers to wear something comparable as a badge of authority, though without any regulations to make it compulsory or standard. Marines wore their regimental uniform, and boats' crews were usually dressed alike, but on board ship the men wore what they liked. Ships carried stores of clothes for issue on repayment at reasonable prices, and it is for this reason that seamen dressed with some sort of uniformity: buckled shoes and durable stockings, short open jackets, baggy trousers either short or long, a kerchief, and almost invariably a hat.

What were the occupations when off watch? These were few at the best of times, and in heavy weather would be negligible. Below decks would be coldness, humidity, vitiated air, a stench, and evidence of a daily increasing sick list with men confined to hammocks, sometimes for weeks, before they died. Is it surprising that many turned to the soothing remedies of the liberal supplies of wine, brandy, and rum, in an effort to stupefy the senses, and to shorten the seemingly endless misery and desolation and terror and bodily punishment inherent in man's attempts to beat the weather?

CHAPTER 3

ROUND THE HORN

THE JOYOUS sight of the squadron hurrying through the straits with following breeze and favourable current, at eleven knots into the Pacific in brilliant sunshine, was short lived. Even before the ships were clear of the straits the sky suddenly clouded over. The wind headed them in violent squalls. Topsails were handed. Mainsails were reefed. Now they met the full east-flowing current which flows continuously round the Horn. In no time ships were being driven eastward towards a lee shore. The snow-covered precipices of Staten Island loomed nearer.

The sternmost ships of the squadron, *Wager* and *Anna*, were in imminent danger. Driven eastward, each narrowly missed the rocky shore. With relief Anson noted their escape.

Now followed the testing time that was to be spoken of for many, many years to come as a time of almost unbelievable endurance: " the beginning only of sorrows ". Doubts began to arise as to whether it was even possible to double the Horn against the strong current and the constant westerly wind. Even the experienced old salts confessed that they had never before seen such tempestuous weather; and what they had so far regarded as storms were mere gales compared with these winds which raised mountainous waves and filled their minds with continual terror. This was the weather which was to continue with little respite, day after day, week after week, month after month, interspersed with periods of sudden and surprising moderation, during which double-reefed mainsails would be set, to be followed by topsails. And then the wind would return with doubled force and suddenness, whipping the sails from the yards and tearing the stout canvas into shreds. The ships would then lie-to under bare poles, completely at the mercy of the tempestuous waves.

Even in the large ships the motion was severe. In the *Wager* the rolling was incessant. This ship was often gunwales under and laboured so violently that it was difficult to maintain a hold. Hail, snow, and sleet accompanied the storms. Ice encased the rigging. Feet and hands were frost-bitten. A wild jerk would force a man to release his grip. In a fraction of a second he would be dashed to the deck. One dislocated his neck; another fractured his thigh; another his collar-bone. Some were killed. The best seaman was blown overboard and was last seen struggling strongly in the confusion of the seas. The labouring of the ship loosened her upper-works, letting in sea-water through her seams.

Five days after passing through the straits where the *Wager* and *Anna* had narrowly escaped shipwreck, the wind moderated though still from the west. The seas still ran mountains high, but for four days the ships were able to make sail, proceeding generally in a south-south-westerly direction. They were now well south of the latitude of Cape Horn, but making so much easting due to leeway and current that they despaired of ever reaching their objective. And as they proceeded further south so it became colder.

Navigation was at this time rough and ready. The ship's latitude could be deduced reasonably accurately each day at noon, from the altitude of the sun measured with an instrument which was the forerunner of the present-day sextant.

Estimation of the ship's longitude, however, was difficult, as this requires an accurate knowledge of the time at which an observation is taken. Reliable chronometers were a thing of the future.

This problem was particularly applicable in rounding the Horn where, in addition to being without a reliable longitude observation, the reckoning might be sadly out due to east-flowing currents and continuing head winds. It would be extremely hazardous to strike northwards until one was absolutely certain of being well to the west of the terrible coast of Tierra del Fuego, after allowing ample compensation for the easterly drift.

With constant westerly gales, this fact in itself must have made many wonder, at least those still capable of thought, whether it was worth pursuing the venture. A worse factor was the increasing sickness which so reduced the number of available hands for working the ship that it was often difficult to keep pumps going and set or hand the sails. Anson was nevertheless resolute, and constantly urged better station keeping. The *Centurion* could point closer than most, and being a faster sailer was able to wear,* so as to bear down on and urge the stragglers without the squadron losing any ground.

There followed a succession of violent storms, and periods of less fury, during which sails were split, yards were sprung, rigging was damaged. Nothing really serious happened until the 31st March, when the *Gloucester*'s mainyard broke in the slings. The weather was better than it had been for several days. The Commodore immediately ordered all ships to send carpenters to the *Gloucester* to repair the damage as quickly as possible, to avoid delay. John Cummins, the carpenter of the *Wager*, transferred to the *Gloucester*. But before the work in

---

*Wear: to put helm up and pay off so as eventually to bring the wind from the other side without at any time heading into it as is inevitable when tacking; the reverse of to tack.

the *Gloucester* had been completed the weather broke, and as each days passed it worsened. On the 8th April, at three in the morning, the most terrific of storms struck the squadron. Several guns were heard. This indicated that ships were in distress. The worst stricken was the *Wager*, now straggling far to leeward of the other ships, with no more than a stump where her mizzenmast had been, and with her shrouds torn out of her chainplates, so that much of her rigging was useless. Little could be done as her carpenters were still away in the *Gloucester*. Transfer by boat was out of the question.

The next day, the 9th April, the *Anna* broke her forestay and the gammon of her bowsprit. She was now in danger of losing all her masts. All ships of the squadron were still in company: but this was the last day. During the night of the 10th April, both the *Pearl* and the *Severn* suffered such injury to their rigging that they fell away to leeward and were never seen again by the Commodore, though he sent the *Tryal* to leeward in search the following day. In view of a mischievous suggestion that the captains, Murray and Legge, were in collusion and had agreed to desert Anson, it is fair to refer to the log of Lieutenant Innes of the *Severn* for the 10th April, which says:

"The Ships—upper Works and decks wery Leaky, the Seamen never dry in their Hammacks, the rigging wery bad. Severall of the Lower Shrouds broke and stranded and the Seamen mostly sick and those that come up on the Deck are Lame and wery Weak."

The *Pearl*'s log for the 10th April says:

"Strong gales and squally . . . broke two of the Straps of the lower Dead Eyes in the Main Chaines, att 1 a.m. split the foresail, lost sight of the Commodore and all the squadron, att 2 lay too under the Ballenct Mizn, att 5 made sail, att 6

B

saw one of the Squadron, which proved to be the *Severn*."

At this time there were 102 men on the sick list in the *Pearl*. A week later there were 110. Only eight men could be mustered in one watch, and seven in the other. Men were dying every day; some days one or two, some days as many as four.

It is clear from a study of their tracks that both *Severn* and *Pearl* continued to try to beat to westward for seven days after losing touch with the Commodore. On the 17th April rigging and sails were in such a condition that "wee are not Able to beate any longer ". The following day the two captains bore away to leeward in order to save the ships. Their rigging and sails were in a deplorable condition, and the *Pearl* was short of water. Out of a complement already reduced to a half, fewer than one man in every ten was able to crawl out of his hammock for his watch on deck or to man the pumps.

Conditions were little better in the remainder of the squadron. On the 12th April it blew harder than ever and the waves were prodigious. At seven in the morning an enormous sea struck the *Wager*. Bulkeley, the gunner, was on watch and was carried over the wheel. He described it as the largest swell he had ever seen. The cutter was lifted bodily off the crutches and deposited alongside the bridge, badly holed. The longboat filled with water, adding to the top-weight in the ship. King, the boatswain, suggested heaving the cutter over the side, but was restrained by Bulkeley. There was little love lost between these two.

Cheap was very ill in his cabin and unable to come on deck, but gave orders to Bulkeley to save the cutter, drain the longboat, and get the jib-boom and sprit-sail yard in, to reduce the risk of the next big sea carrying away the bowsprit. The carpenter was still on board the *Gloucester*. No boat work had been possible since he transferred from *Wager*.

On the following day, with ships still under reefed mainsails, the Commodore bore down on the *Wager*'s weather quarter to come under her lee and speak with her. He was much concerned at the loss of *Wager*'s mizzen-mast and her slow progress, and enquired if anything could be done by the way of a jury rig. The weather moderated the next day, the 14th April, and the carpenter, Cummins, was able to return to the *Wager*. Cheap asked him about a jury rig but was little mollified at hearing the proposal to fit a forty foot boom to the stump of the mizzen-mast, on which a sail could be hoisted. He seemed much more concerned at laying the responsibility for the lost mast upon the master, Thomas Clark, and tried to get the carpenter to agree that the mast would not have been lost but for Clark's incompetence and negligence. Dissension was already rife in the *Wager*, augmented by sickness, foul weather, and misfortune. Cummins had made a detailed examination of the chains and chain-plates, and given it as his opinion that the mast had gone because the chain-plates were rusted through. To his credit, he listened to the captain in silence, refrained from further comment, and, being a man of action, got straight on with the job.

On the 19th April they had the finest day since passing the straits. The crazy ships *Gloucester*, *Wager* and *Anna*, lagging astern, now set about repairs, while *Centurion* and the little *Tryal* kept ahead. In the *Wager* repairs were made to the rigging, and a new mainsail bent on. For the moment hopes rallied in the breasts of the more stalwart.

Scarcely a week earlier had come a shattering and disappointing realisation concerning the slowness of progress westward. According to the reckoning, the squadron had made a westing of almost 20° of longitude since passing through the Straits le Maire, so that they thought themselves to be at least 300 miles to the westward of the westernmost point of Tierra del Fuego, and therefore able to stand with safety to the northward to the less turbulent waters of the lower latitudes. The

course was north-north-west. Suddenly, between one and two
in the morning, the weather cleared. There, but two miles distant, was land, bright in the moonlight: a lee shore. The wind
was on the port quarter, blowing in squalls from the south-west.
Swiftly the alarm was given. Slowly it spread from ship to
ship. Destruction seemed inevitable. As swiftly as the weather
had cleared, the wind now shifted to west-north-west. Slowly
each ship wore round. The rocky shore which had loomed
persistently nearer in the moonlight now receded. Once more
the stand to southward was resumed.

Many regarded this as a miracle. But for the clearance, the
moonlight, and the shift of wind, shipwreck had been inevitable. On consulting the chart and knowing the latitude, 54°
20° south, it was quickly deduced that this was Cape Noir off
the western end of Tierra del Fuego, at the southern outlet of
the Straits of Magellan. The joy and gratitude following their
miraculous deliverance were short-lived. It became apparent
that the actual westing they had made since passing through
the Straits le Maire was only half the estimate. Again they
would have to stand to the south, to face the westerly blasts
and the hail, sleet, and snow, inching westward day by day,
and perhaps on some days, with the more unfavourable wind,
losing it all, as they were carried helplessly in the current that
never ceased to bear them eastward.

There was great dejection, particularly among the sick. It
was a symptom of scurvy that irresolution and disappointment
prolonged and worsened the effects of the disease. The loss of
the *Severn* and *Pearl* had been a great blow. Apart from the
uncertainty of the fate of ships and crews was the realization
that the squadron had lost more than a third of its fire power.
This, together with the sorry condition of sails and rigging, and
the widespread defects and damage, cast a gloom which would
not be dispelled. It was unlikely that they could put up much
opposition if they should fall in with Pizarro now.

The more stalwart had no such views. Anson's leadership continued to keep ships and men up to the mark. Although his squadron had suffered, Anson realised that Pizarro must also have suffered. Cheap was a dedicated follower of Anson, and was resolved to do his duty in bringing *Wager* to the next rendezvous in spite of the handicap of a jury rig and defective rigging. Considerable work was carried out on this bright sunny day of the 19th April, a cap being fitted to the stump of the mizzen-mast, and the spare studding-sail boom being stepped to it, with reinforcement of rigging where possible.

Between four and six in the first dog watch, the Commodore's light could be seen at a great distance ahead. Bulkeley was officer of the watch. As repairs had been completed he was in great hopes of catching up. At six, Clark, the master, came on watch to relieve the gunner, and to the latter's surprise said he could not see the Commodore's light. On being informed, the captain came on deck, and asked the master if he could not see the *Centurion*'s light, which was apparently visible to many who were on the quarter-deck. Dissension had been growing for some time. There was now an open rift between the captain and the master.

At the end of the last dog watch, at eight, Lieutenant Baynes relieved the master. The light was visible to him, but the wind was freshening and visibility was decreasing. At nine the Commodore's light was no longer visible. At ten the wind had freshened to such an extent that it was necessary to hand the foresail. During this operation, one of *Wager*'s seamen was struck overboard and never seen again. By morning there was no sight of either the *Centurion* or the *Tryal*, and, as the day advanced, both the *Gloucester* and the little *Anna*, the former with a new mainyard, the latter with a new mainsail, outpaced the *Wager* and disappeared over the horizon ahead.

" This was a great Misfortune to us " wrote Campbell,

" we being at that Time in a very bad Condition, having lost our Mizen-mast some Days before. Here I must observe, in Behalf of our Lieutenant, Mr. Beans, who had the Watch that Night, and has had some Reflexions cast on him, for losing sight of the Commodore, that I had the Watch with him that Night, and was most of the Time on the Foretop-sail-yard, in order to take in the Foretop-sail; and I could not see the Commodore: But the Lieutenant did often call to know if I could see Mr. Anson's Lights. The 23d, I narrowly escaped drowning. Going up the Fore-shrouds, I was knock'd down by a Man falling from the Futtock-shrouds; but I lighting between the Sheet Anchor-stock and the Shrouds, was preserved, tho' the other Man was drowned."

The *Wager* was now quite alone.

A rumour spread through the lower deck that provisions would have to be rationed; there would soon be a curtailment of the daily allowance, for they would never catch up with the rest of the squadron.

The gunner seems to have been foremost in apprehending the tone of discontent which was spreading through the ship, begun as soon as Anson's personality was removed from the scene. On the 21st April, Bulkeley was in the stewards' room when a seaman, Joseph King, no relation to the boatswain, arrived to get a pound of bread.

Bulkeley heard the seaman ask the steward if the water ration was to remain as before.

" No, God damn you," replied the steward. " Now that the Commodore has gone, you shall find the difference."

Bulkeley informed the captain that there might be a mutinous disposition arising, which could be inflamed if there was any notion of restricting provision further. Cheap at once ordered him to issue every officer with a brace of pistols, and to ignore the affair he had witnessed.

The *Wager*, now lagging some days astern of the rest of the squadron, continued to make an offing to the southward until, on the 1st May, she was deemed to have made sufficient westing to make it safe to go about on to the port tack. With the wind at south-west, a course was laid to the north-westward.

On this day, the captain, after consultation with the officers, ordered the best bower-anchor to be cut away, as it would be impossible to secure it to the mast on anchoring, owing to the crazy state of the shrouds and chain-plates: in fact the fore-mast would be endangered if they were to do so. The wind veered westward after four days, and course was shaped for the land. Few seemed concerned excepting the gunner. Bulkeley represented to the lieutenant his concern at the ship making for a lee-shore in her disabled condition. Why should she make for the land, if the rendezvous was to be the island of Juan Fernandez, lying 300 miles off shore?

Lieutenant Baynes explained that the captain was determined to make for the first rendezvous which had been named by Anson. This was the island of Socorro, in latitude 45° south, only a few miles off the mainland, and strategically situated for the mounting of an assault on the Spanish port of Valdivia. Such an assault would require all the equipment and stores carried by the *Wager*, and Cheap was determined to be there with Anson. The island of Juan Fernandez had been named only as a second rendezvous for those failing to turn up at Socorro in time.

The lieutenant agreed with Bulkeley that the present course was a dangerous one. He himself had unsuccessfully urged the captain to go straight to Juan Fernandez, and now suggested that the gunner should try to persuade him of the danger in making for a lee-shore.

By this time there were many who were concerned to see masses of rockweed floating past the ship. One of these was

the Honourable John Byron, who suggested to the gunner that
the ship could not now be far from land.

Soon after this, the captain sent for Bulkeley.

" What do you make the longitude?"

" Eighty two thirty," answered the gunner.

" What distance do you reckon yourself off the land?"

The gunner replied that this would put them sixty leagues
from the land, but, with caution, explained that the whole
squadron had already been endangered off Cape Noir through
underestimating the strength of the east-bound current.

" If the same current continues," said Bulkeley, " we can't
be above twenty leagues off the land."

" There's no accounting for currents," said Cheap. " Sometimes they set one way, and sometimes another."

" Very true, sir. But as the ship has been under reefed
courses, with the mizzen-mast gone, she must drive to leeward,
and be nearer the land than expected."

Cheap then asked the gunner if he was aware that the next
rendezvous was the island of Socorro in the latitude of 45°
south, and not the island of Juan Fernandez which he suspected the gunner and others fancied.

" Sir," replied Bulkeley, " the ship is in a very bad condition
to approach a lee-shore. And even if it were possible to bring
the ship to an anchor, we should never purchase the anchor
again."

" I don't intend to come to an anchor," said Cheap. " For
there are no soundings until well within seven leagues of the
land. I shall stand off and on for twenty-four hours; and if I
don't see the Commodore, or any of the squadron in that time,
we shall then make for Juan Fernandez."

Once again the gunner remonstrated. " The ship is a perfect
wreck, sir. Our mizzen-mast gone, with all the standing rigging fore and aft; and all our people down. There are only
twelve fit for duty."

" It does not signify," replied the captain, completely swayed by his sense of duty to Anson. " I am obliged and determined to go for the first rendezvous."

On the 13th May, at eight in the morning, the straps of the forehalyard blocks parted. The yard was got down and the blocks were strapped on. The ship's head had been between north-east and east-north-east. The wind, often at gale force, had varied between south and south-east, but was now freshening and veering westerly. The ship lay to, with reefed mainsail, port tack aboard, and the foreyard down. Under these conditions she was drifting rapidly to the east.

At nine, Cummins, the carpenter, went forward to inspect the chain-plates, and thought he caught a fleeting glimpse of the land, very dimly to the north-north-west. He asked the boatswain's mate, who was with him, if he could see land, and the answer was " No." He then pointed it out to Baynes, the lieutenant, who said it was impossible, for there could be no land to the north-north-west. No action was therefore taken. This may seem incredible until it is realized that the chart in use on board *Wager* was drawn from that published with the account of Sir John Narborough's voyage, and did not follow what Narborough himself had observed. The coastline was as in former Spanish charts. These indicated a coast in a rough direction from north-by-east to south-by-west with very little indentation or projection. It would therefore seem impossible that there could be any land in the direction seen. Land should first appear on the starboard bow.

The chart, however, had omitted the vast promontory, almost an island of 100 miles across, later called Peninsula de Tres Montes, which projects westward from the mainland, and has to its southward the great gulf of Peñas. The *Wager* had already entered the gulf and was slowly becoming embayed. Under mainsail only she was making considerable leeway to the eastward.

At two in the afternoon the gunner was officer of the watch. All the hands that could be mustered from the ship's company in this watch were the midshipman Alexander Campbell, one boatswain's mate, four seamen, and the master's servant, and these were now employed in swaying up the foreyard. Bulkeley felt obliged to help and was on the foreyard himself when, to his astonishment, he saw land on the port beam; high land and hummocks bearing north-west. He immediately came off the foreyard and went below to the captain. Here was a worse predicament than he had foreseen. Not only was there the lee-shore of the continent to the eastward, but it now appeared that they were embayed to the north and north-west. Wind and current were driving them towards the east. From a sailing point of view the ship was almost disabled. From a navigational point of view the ship was perilously close to a lee-shore on the rocky coast of Chile, and probably in a bay of unknown rocks and small islands as well.

The captain immediately ordered the foreyard to be swayed up. All available hands, including officers, were now called. No more than a dozen could be mustered. The foresail was set, and the hands wore ship to starboard. This operation took three hours, but *Wager's* head now pointed south-westward, with the wind on the starboard tack. It was still blowing hard. But in her crazy condition, without topsails, carrying much lee helm necessary to compensate for the missing mizzen, she made considerable leeway. Cheap was energetic in driving his sickly depleted crew. Not a minute could be wasted: not an opportunity missed to trim sheets and braces. As he was rushing forward he missed his hold, lost his footing, and was taken by a great sea to the foot of the quarter-deck ladder. Stunned and disabled, he was carried straight to the surgeon's cabin. His left shoulder was found to be badly dislocated, " soe that the head of the Bone came down below his Armpit ".

Soon afterwards Baynes and Bulkeley were sent for. Cheap,

almost delirious with pain, seemed mortified at his incapacity, and explained that it was quite impossible for him to come on deck. In view of the gravity of the situation he exhorted the lieutenant and the gunner to do their utmost to make an offing. A good look-out was to be kept, and when possible the main-topsail must be set so that the ship would point closer to the wind and make less leeway. They were to work watch and watch. The lieutenant was to have Cummins, the carpenter, working in his watch. Cheap again expressed his contempt and concern for the master. He considered him insufficiently competent to take charge of a watch, and directed Bulkeley to act with him in his watch and see that nothing went amiss.

A terrible night of anxiety followed. There was a gale of wind and torrents of rain, with a heavy overcast of low cloud that made the night very dark. It was impossible even to see the length of the ship. Bulkeley kept the first watch, during which they carried the mainsail, foresail, and mizzen-staysail. He found it quite impossible to set the maintopsail, and informed the captain. Apart from the difficulties of a missing mizzen-mast and broken rigging fore and aft, most of the sails were badly worn. The topsails at the yards could not be loosed without being torn to shreds: no spares were available. The ship was making good a track little better than south, though her head lay to the south-west.

Bulkeley was relieved by Baynes at midnight. Hard winds and rain continued, the wind veering steadily. At four, Bulkeley took over the morning watch. *Wager*'s head was pointing towards the west. But the night was as dark as ever. The old ship lumbered in a heavy sea, still making considerable leeway to the eastward. Course made good was little better than south-south-west.

At half past four the *Wager* struck aft on a sunken rock. It was still dark. The impact was not great and soon she lifted, heaving with a rising sea. The sounding was fourteen fathoms.

Cheap sent word to anchor. But almost immediately *Wager* struck again right aft, broke the tiller head, and heeled over, almost inundated by the sea. In her hold was a ½-ton anchor belonging to the *Centurion*. The violence of this grounding forced one of the anchor flukes through the bottom. Within seconds another mountainous sea struck. *Wager* was again lifted. The mainsail was now clewed up, and Bulkeley ordered steering with the fore sheets, easing or hauling as required. The idea now was to run for the land which could faintly be seen to the southward with the coming dawn.

By this time all those who could stir below were on deck. Men appeared who had not been seen for weeks, terror on their faces, fear forcing their limbs to move. Many poor wretches in the last stage of scurvy died in their hammocks, trapped by the inrush of sea below. Still the gallant *Wager* forged ahead. The man at the helm kept his station, though the wheel was useless. When asked by the officer of the watch if the ship would steer, he was seen to try the wheel, and to reply calmly, as though they were merely at some naval exercise. One of the master's mates, John Jones, an excellent seaman and a good navigator, appeared on deck. For several days he had been sick in his hammock. He did his best to rally the onlookers. Many of them showed signs of panic.

" My friends," he exhorted, " let us not be discouraged. Did you never see a ship amongst the breakers before? Come, lend a hand; here is a sheet, and here is a brace. Lay hold. I don't doubt but we may bring her yet near enough the land to save our lives."

This seemed to stir even the half-dead. How often have brave words of encouragement saved lives, even in the most hopeless moment. In the half light of dawn, great foaming breakers could be seen on rocks surrounding the ship. Some of the sick were petrified with fear. Others were stupefied with the sight of breakers. Many were shot helplessly across the deck by the violent lurches. Some appeared incapable of any action. One of the most highly regarded seamen was with difficulty prevented from hurling himself over the side. Another man, deprived of his reason, flourished a cutlass over his head, and called himself King. When approached, he struck out, and continued to be a menace until he was himself struck down.

Still the little *Wager* ran on, lurching violently in the seas. It was growing lighter; but the weather was still extremely thick. Suddenly she struck again. She now came to a grinding halt, stuck fast in the opening between two massive rocks. With the surge of a rising sea she lifted slightly, only to crash more heavily into her resting place between the rocks. Her sides were bilged: her lower decks began to flood. But the vast rock to windward moderated the violence of the seas.

Day broke, and the weather suddenly cleared to reveal land at no great distance. Bulkeley at once got the barge, the yawl, and the cutter into the water, directing men desperately keen to assist. Many had taken on a new lease of life and were anxious to be the first ashore.

In the words of John Young, the cooper, " . . . the gladsome shore was a chearing view, no small abatement of our calamity. It was a circumstance of mercy towards us, requiring the sincerest acknowledgements, that our vessel was not instantly dashed to pieces . . . Some expressions [of thanksgivings] were uttered; but oaths and execrations greatly prevailed."

Cheap was still disabled, and confined in great pain in the surgeon's cabin. He gave orders through midshipman Byron for the wreck of the foremast and mainmast to be cut away, to reduce the strain on the hulk, and for a boat to be sent inshore to investigate. Bulkeley, the gunner, took charge of these operations. John Snow, one of the master's mates, took the barge ashore, almost overloaded with seamen desperately anxious to leave the wreck and to try something new. His instructions were to return immediately with a report on conditions ashore and information about shelter, water, fruit, and whether the land was inhabited.

An hour passed and there was no sign of the barge. Bitter disappointment was expressed by those on board, especially led by Lieutenant Baynes, who seemed more disgruntled and more angry with Snow than the rest. Cheap now instructed Baynes to take the yawl inshore, make a reconnaissance, and be sure to bring back the barge, even if the mate refused to return. In a short while the yawl returned, but without the lieutenant. The yawl's crew gave a favourable account of what they had seen, but there was widespread anger that Baynes himself had not returned.

Insubordination was already evident. Little was possible at this time to check it or to punish it, and the seed of insurrection was sown. Those officers who were competent, principal among them being Bulkeley, had already exerted themselves to the utmost, and were far too busy to deal with the rabble. The greatest anxiety was shown among the majority to get ashore. Those two in whom the greatest authority rested were far from the scene: the lieutenant was ashore, the captain confined to a sick bed, delirious with pain, mortified by the loss of his ship, and fulminating with frustration.

Persuaded by his officers, and assured that all the men who wished had already got ashore, Cheap allowed himself to be lifted out of his bed, put into a boat, and carried ashore with the army officers, the midshipmen, and all remaining warrant officers excepting four: these were the master, the boatswain, the gunner, and the carpenter who remained on board for the night. Both on board and ashore there was great dissension and lack of authority, with a growing feeling of resentment towards the captain in spite of his condition, for it was generally considered that his obstinacy was to blame for the loss of the ship. Midshipmen Byron and Campbell, together with Elliot the surgeon, Hamilton the lieutenant of marines, and

Harvey the purser, stood loyally by Cheap. Few personal belongings could be rescued. Byron describes how he went below to his chest at the bulkhead of the wardroom, but the ship was open to the sea, grinding violently with each lurch, and he was forced to enter the boat without saving anything.

Scarcely had the captain left than anarchy broke out in the wreck. The boatswain, who had been laid up for weeks, was foremost in getting at the liquor. Relieved at the thought of a miraculous escape from almost certain death, those now left on board lapsed into drunkenness, anxious to make the most of unlimited wine and absence of authority. Night coming on, it blew hard from the north, and great tumbling seas crowded over the hulk, pounding and twisting her in sudden jerks. The more terrible the weather the greater the resort to intoxication. Violent outrage and disorder followed. The wine in the lazarette was broached. Arms chests were broken open. Cabins were plundered. Men who were mad with liquor and insensible of pain, clad themselves in rich apparel and waved swords and pistols, and threatened to murder all who opposed them. Some fell in a drunken stupor, and were swept away by a surge of the sea or drowned where they fell.

" As soon as the Captain got into this Hut," said Campbell, " he order'd me to take the Yaul, and see if the Men on board would come a-shore. Accordingly I went, but found them all in such Confusion as cannot be imagined by any who were not Eye-witnesses of it. Some were singing Psalms, others fighting, others swearing, and some lay drunk on the Deck. Seeing them in this strange Disorder, I spoke not a Word to any Body, but observing some Casks of Ball and Powder on the Quarter Deck, I began to put them into the Boat; whereupon two of the Men came to me, crying out ' Damn ye! you shall not have them, for the Ship is lost and it is ours.' A third came with a Bayonet, swearing he would kill me; adding these Words, ' Damn ye! you have carried a strait Arm all the Voyage, and you shall suffer for it.' And with that he threw the Bayonet at me, but miss'd his Mark, and I immediately got into the Yaul, and returned to the Shore."

But already there were those who were thinking about the future, and the possibility of escaping from this barren shore. And already there was a dangerous division into groups. With the loss of the *Wager*, discipline and loyalty were in danger of being driven completely away.

CHAPTER 4

THE SPANISH SQUADRON

A POWERFUL SPANISH squadron had been fitted out and placed
under the command of Don Pizarro for the purpose of annihi-
lating Anson's squadron. It consisted of the following warships:

Ship	Guns	Men
Asia	66	700
Guipuscoa	74	700
Hermiona	54	500
Esperanza	50	450
St. Estevan	40	350

In addition, this squadron, vastly superior in number of guns
and men, carried a Spanish regiment of foot for the reinforcement of the garrisons in the South Sea.

While at Buenos Ayres, Pizarro received detailed information concerning Anson's squadron at St. Catherine's from the
Portuguese governor, and sailed as soon as possible, intent on
reaching the Pacific Ocean before Anson. It was shortly after
his departure that the *Pearl* had fallen in with the Spanish
squadron, at first mistaking the *Asia*, Pizarro's flagship, for the
Centurion. *Pearl* had had a narrow escape from capture.

In his hurry to get into the South Sea, Pizarro had not waited for the provisions which were to replenish his squadron at Buenos Ayres. Moreover his seamen had been bribed by an advance of pay made because of the excessive hardships to be expected round Cape Horn. By the time the squadron had begun to thrash into the westerlies off the Cape, there was a great shortage of provisions. The Spanish sailors, for all their money, were unable to buy food: except perhaps a rat. A rat would fetch a price of four dollars. Those men still capable of working at the pumps, in spite of hunger and fatigue, received a daily allowance of an ounce and a half of biscuit. Those who were too sick or fatigued to be able to assist received no more than an ounce of wheat.

Pizarro was nevertheless through the Straits le Maire before Anson, and beat south-westwards to round the Horn. Here he arrived at the end of February, and almost immediately the squadron ran into trouble, the *Guipuscoa, Hermiona,* and *Esperanza* being separated from the admiral in the *Asia.* A week later the *Guipuscoa* lost sight of the *Hermiona* and *Esperanza.* On the following day, the 7th March, there blew a storm from the north-west of such force that all ships were driven eastward. After various and fruitless attempts to make a westing, each ship gave up the unequal struggle. This was the storm whose tail-end met Anson's squadron shortly after their emergence from the Straits le Maire, and all but drove the *Wager* and the *Anna* on to the rocky coast of Staten Island. In the subsequent struggle with contrary winds, foul currents, heavy seas, scurvy, exhaustion, and disablement through decay, all the British ships, excepting the *Pearl* and *Severn,* successfully doubled the Horn: a measure of Anson's leadership and the toughness of British seamen. But of Pizarro's squadron not one got round. Pizarro himself arrived safely at Monte- video in the River Plate, with the *Asia,* the following May, followed a few days later by the *Esperanza* and the *Estevan.*

Not more than half the ship's company of the *Asia* survived to reach port: likewise that of the *Estevan*. The *Esperanza* was still more unfortunate. Of the 450 seamen she had brought from Spain, only fifty-eight remained alive. The whole of the regiment of foot had perished but for sixty survivors who returned to the River Plate.

More unfortunate still were the *Hermiona* and the *Guipuscoa*. The former was never heard of again. The crew of the latter, having reached the limit of endurance, of fatigue, hunger, and misfortune, compelled their captain to run the ship ashore on the coast of Brazil, from which 400 men got safely ashore.

Thus the threat from Pizarro was temporarily out of the way, though we shall hear of him again. Anson however had no knowledge of the fact that there was no opposition to him in the South Sea. Nor did he know of the fate of the *Pearl* and *Severn*, forced to drop out of the expedition through shortage of hands; or of the *Gloucester*, *Tryal*, and *Anna*, who were to join him at Juan Fernandez in the Pacific after great hardships, their ships' companies terribly diminished by daily deaths due to scurvy. But first the little *Anna* would narrowly miss disaster off the coast of Chile, not far from the *Wager*'s final resting place.

Nor could the Commodore know of the disaster to the *Wager* herself, now a total wreck. He would nevermore see the guns and equipment she carried for assaults on Spanish bases, or the various spares for the squadron, such as anchors and spars. Lost also was the merchandise with which she had been laden, intended for purposes of barter.

But we must leave Anson now, and return to the *Wager*. Resolute among her survivors was Captain Cheap, though temporarily disabled. He was determined to rejoin Anson at all costs, but was not prepared at this stage to divulge his thoughts or plans to the disorderly rabble who had got ashore.

CHAPTER 5

EVENTS AT WAGER ISLAND

By NIGHTFALL on the day of *Wager*'s grounding, 140 officers and men had got ashore, thankful for an apparently miraculous deliverance from shipwreck. The prospect was however grim. Apart from a few large windswept trees and bushes, the foreshore was rocky and barren. Beyond the foreshore the ground was marshy, and in a short distance ended in seemingly impenetrable woods. The spot the survivors occupied was in a bay surrounded by hilly promontories. The one to the north, which they subsequently called Mount Misery, was extremely steep, the sea surging at its feet. In order to get over it, to reach the next bay where some of the wreckage had been washed up, steps were cut into the rocky face. There was a hut at a short distance from the beach, in which lances and primitive weapons had been left, apparently by Indians. Here the captain took up residence.

Torrents of heavy rain accompanied by a cold wind continued through the night, and men huddled under the shelter of one enormous tree, maintaining a huge fire, not only to provide warmth but to counter possible attacks from wild animals. There was also much concern that they might be attacked at night by Indians. An elderly lieutenant of the land forces died

52

of exposure during the night, though accommodated in some sort of hovel. Of those under the great tree, two men perished of cold and exhaustion.

Early the following day, Friday the 15th May, the *Wager* was bilged amidships by a great sea, and settled further into her rocky cradle. Many of the drunkards had drowned, and corpses floated about in the waterlogged holds. Bulkeley thought the ship was on the point of breaking up. He and Cummins collected as much bread as possible, together with powder and ball, and in the afternoon went ashore with those drunkards who had sobered a little from their debauch of the night before. Many of these men wore finery and rich apparel stolen from officers' cabins during the night. They now presented a comic spectacle, for their working trousers and dirty check shirts could be seen under their fine clothes. Their swaggering received a rude shock. As they stepped ashore they were greeted by Lieutenant Hamilton of the marines and Harvey the purser, both armed with pistols. In a short time and with no attempt to continue their brave show, these dejected actors were forced to strip their fine clothes and give up stolen property, and subject themselves to discipline. They looked more like transported felons than the conquering heroes they had fancied themselves.

Before leaving the wreck, Bulkeley unsuccessfully searched his cabin for his journal. He also looked for other journals, none of which he could find. It was at this juncture that he began his new journal, recording the days' transactions from the time of the wreck. A day or two later he found parts of the master's journal washed up on the beach, evidently destroyed by hand, and had good reason to believe that all journals had been stolen and destroyed. He does not say so, but one can infer that this was the work of John King, the boatswain, who remained on board the *Wager* for a few more days, with a few drunken seamen, unable to resist the lure of free and unlimited

wines and spirits. King was a quarrelsome and rebellious character who was already spreading the seed of sedition. He could
see no reason why there should be any subservience to authority
or submission to orders. It was now a free for all, and the
battle would go to the strongest. The procedure now was to
drink and be merry, and arm yourself to ensure that nobody
interfered. But the more they drank the less merriment they
found, and the more furious the arguments that developed.

The weather was still boisterous. Heavy seas threatened
to break up the wreck. Even the drunkards were afraid. On the
16th, the boatswain, quite alarmed at the prospect of destruction, made signals requesting a boat. But the sea was too rough
for boat-work. King, to show his wrath and impatience, and
presumably to indicate also his contempt for Cheap, trained
one of the quarter-deck four-pounders to bear on the captain's
hut ashore. He fired twice. The balls passed just over Cheap's
hut. An attempt was now made to bring the boatswain ashore,
but it was found impossible to lay a boat alongside the wreck.
King and his companions became mad with rage and set about
smashing everything that came their way. Again they broke
into cabins and chests to resume their looting, and now quarrelled over the spoils, carrying their intemperance to the
greatest excesses. There was evidence of murder by strangula-
tion on some of the corpses later found in the wreck. The
greatest preoccupation of the boatswain and his companions
was the acquisition and possession of arms and ammunition,
the better to support their claim for immunity from the authority of the captain. They repeatedly reassured themselves that
his authority ceased with the loss of the ship.

It was on this day that the gunner and the carpenter got
the men on shore to haul up the cutter, a boat no longer than
thirty-two feet, and invert it so as to rest on tall props. Thus
it served as a shelter from the seemingly incessant rains. For
food the men were subsisting on a few wildfowl, shellfish, and

the carrion crow that preyed on the mangled corpses driven on to the beach by the surf. No vegetables or fruit grew here, but there was a kind of wild celery which proved beneficial to those who were sick of the scurvy.

The 17th May was Whitsunday. Perhaps a few of the *Wager*'s survivors found time privately to offer thanks to the Almighty for their deliverance; sailors, though unwilling to demonstrate it, are generally religious, especially in times of adversity. To a few must have come the thought, what next? Doubtless the majority were still suffering from the shock of shipwreck, and had no thought as yet for the future.

During the following two days the captain ordered Bulkeley to take a party on board to attempt the recovery of provisions. Two casks of flour and some wine were got out of the lazaretto, and by opening up the hold they were able to fish out some beef and pork, using long poles with hooks attached. This grisly procedure was obstructed by the large number of bodies floating in the water. Only the forecastle and the quarter-deck were visible above sea-level. A visit was made to the carpenter's shop to retrieve the tools and nails which would be essential for construction ashore and boat repairs and alterations.

Cheap ordered a store tent to be set up near his hut, and appointed the midshipmen to take turns in keeping watch over the provisions and stores at night. As each boat-load was pulled ashore it was met by either the captain (now partially recovered from his disability), the surgeon, Hamilton the lieutenant of marines, or Harvey the twenty-five year old purser. These four seem to have been closely associated. It was apparent that they intended to maintain authority, for they always appeared on the beach with arms to ensure that there was no embezzlement and to supervise the storage of the provisions in the store tent. Baynes, the lieutenant of the *Wager*, is notable for omission from reports of transactions, and it is evident that Cheap would at this stage have nothing to do with him, having lost all confidence in him when he failed to return from his reconnaissance ashore. Cheap was convinced that the *Wager* could have been hauled off the lee-shore if topsails had been set, and he blamed Baynes for the fact that they had not been set.

For four days after firing the quarter-deck nine-pounder at the captain's hut King remained obstinately on board the wreck. On the 20th May, in sheer desperation he left the ship to be pulled ashore, arrayed in a ridiculous suit of laced clothes. As he stepped ashore he was met by Cheap who hurled epithets at him and struck him to the ground with his cane. For a second or two King lay motionless on the beach, to all appearances dead. On recovering, he saw a cocked pistol in Cheap's hand. With singular submission, in marked contrast to his earlier behaviour, he exposed his breast, convinced that he was to be shot. Cheap now relented, told the boatswain what he thought of him, and turning away left him. There were many observers of this scene, and some regard for the strong and decided manner in which the captain handled it. But already there was resentment at the necessity for a show of arms to maintain authority, and a growing desire for freedom from subservience.

There was still need for speedy work to be done in getting out provisions from the wreck, and much was achieved by scuttling the decks and making holes of access to certain store-rooms. Wherever the men scuttled, dead bodies were found: victims of the inrush of sea when *Wager* was first bilged. Barrels of flour, casks of peas, oatmeal, brandy, and wine were retrieved and taken ashore. Midshipman Byron found such work during the day, combined with watches at night on the provisions tent, most arduous. In spite of Cheap's precautions much theft took place. Byron disturbed one transgressor at night, and at pistol point tied him to a post. No issue of provisions took place until the 25th May, eleven days after the wreck, and it is probable that Cheap felt compelled by that time to begin rationing in an attempt to end depredation of the stock. Rations consisted of half a pound of flour and a small piece of salt pork. Hunger was fairly general, for there were many mouths to be fed, probably of the order of 130, and considerable difficulty in obtaining much of the local food. Cheap would not permit boat work at night for fear of embezzlement. He insisted on boats being drawn up on the beach before nightfall. There was widespread resentment on this account, even from the warrant officers, since the weather was often easier at night, and the sea moderate, with sufficient light from the moon to make salvage operations feasible.

On the 20th May the longboat was got out of the wreck by cutting away the gunwale. Several more bodies were found, and it was evident that many of them were men who had drunk themselves insensible and had been overtaken by the inrush of the sea. While the men were engaged in this operation three canoes of Indians were seen rounding one of the points. The Indians were black-haired and of short stature. In spite of the cold weather they wore no clothes except feathers and a loincloth of animal skin. They seemed to be very curious at the sight of white men, and hesitated in their approach. Some crossed themselves, giving evidence of acquaintance with Spaniards. In due course they were enticed alongside, given some wine and two bales of cloth, and directed to the captain on shore. Cheap gave them each a hat and a soldier's coat, which delighted them, but was unable to extract any intelligence from them. In return they presented some highly edible mussels and two dogs which were quickly slaughtered and roasted. This thought may fill dog-lovers with revulsion, but the degree of hunger can be realized from the fact that only a day or so before, a boy was forcibly restrained from eating the liver which he had picked up from one of the mangled corpses on the beach. Men were dying every day of the combined effects of hunger and exposure to the cold.

Two days later the Indians made a further visit to the captain, this time bringing three sheep and some more mussels.

The first occasion of a visit to the wreck by Baynes the lieutenant was the 27th May, almost two weeks after the grounding of the *Wager*. It is apparent that neither captain, officers, nor crew had any respect for Baynes. The leader coming to the fore was evidently Bulkeley, an officer of ability and confidence who was already beginning to look ahead with a view to an escape of all the survivors. He supervised the cutting down and removal of the wooden awning of the *Wager*; this was then taken ashore to be fitted in due course to the longboat as a deck.

Cheap also had his plans but he kept them very much to himself. He was not a man to discuss or to reveal his intentions; he meant to continue his autocratic rule as though nothing had changed. The fact that he and the three officers living near him were usually armed was much resented by the men. The presence of arms emphasized that doubt might exist about authority. The taut discipline of life in a ship of war, where the captain's word was law, had ended.

The atmosphere prevailing at this time is best described by John Young, the cooper of the *Wager*:

" The ill Humours of several amongst us fermented apace. Discipline was an insupportable Grievance to them. They behaved as if they thought all Authority had perished with the Ship, as if all were now upon a Level, or, as if the Officers carried it as strictly as if all Things were in a right Train; which was certainly a great Indiscretion. They appear'd on the Beach in Arms, narrowly inspecting everyone who return'd from the Wreck, to see they secreted nothing, but deliver'd whatever they brought, to the Purser."

This sense of insubordination and discontent was manifest

in the departure on the 3rd June of ten men, who were quickly termed deserters and are recorded as such in the various journals. This is an interesting point indicating that many, in spite of a growing discontent, instinctively felt that there was a duty for a continuing allegiance, even though it was known that pay ceased with the loss of the ship. Thoughts may have been tempered with the prospect of being denied even the back pay that was due to them, should they deliberately disobey the orders of their erstwhile captain.

Wednesday the 3rd June was a day of hard gales from north-north-west with an abundance of rain. The men were employed in retrieving from the beach things like a hogshead of brandy, bales of cloth, hats, and shoes that had been washed ashore from the wreck. The deserters made straight for the woods. In addition to seven seamen there were three men whose services to the community could be ill spared. These were James Mitchell a carpenter's mate, William Oram also a carpenter's mate, and John Russell the armourer. Nearly all the deserters were factious and desperate men, and there was reason to believe that James Mitchell had committed two murders, the first on the person found strangled on board, and the second on the body of a man discovered among the bushes of Mount Misery, stabbed to death. The seven seamen deserters were Joseph King, John Redwood, Dennis O'Lary, John Davis, James Roach, James Stewart, and William Thomson.

An informer, David Buckley, revealed to the captain that the deserters had been restrained from blowing up his hut the night before. A train of gunpowder, together with half a barrel of explosive, was found already laid. It is apparent that Cheap's life was in danger, for it had been only two weeks or so earlier that he had been fired on by the boatswain.

The deserters had thought they were on the mainland, but now presumed that it was an island on which they had been wrecked. They settled at a spot three miles from the rest, living on seaweed and shellfish, and began to build a canoe to effect their escape to the mainland. Bulkeley paid them a visit with Cummins, five days after their escape, and returned to see them again the following day with the surgeon's mate Robert Elliot. He was wise to be accompanied in visiting such desperadoes, particularly as his mission was to persuade John Russell the armourer, and William Oram the carpenter's mate, to return without revealing the object of his visit to the remainder. These two men were almost indispensable for boat construction. Bulkeley was successful and returned with the men. They were given a pardon by the captain.

A most serious incident had occurred two days earlier which was to have grave consequences. This involved a clash between Cheap and a midshipman, Henry Cozens. The latter was generally well liked by the men but changed character immediately he had had a drink too many and then became violently cantankerous.

It was a Sunday, the 7th June, now a working day like any other day, in view of the race with time to get provisions out of the wreck before it disintegrated. A cask of pork, two barrels of flour, some wine, bales of cloth, carpenter's stores, and a cask of peas had been brought ashore. The beach was steep, and Cozens was making heavy weather of rolling the cask of peas uphill, having over-indulged in drink while on the wreck. He stopped near the captain to complain saucily.

"You're drunk," roared the captain; and Cozens immediately answered back:

"With what should I get drunk, unless it be with water?" He made no attempt to move on.

"You scoundrel," said Cheap. "If you can't do it yourself, get more hands, and roll the cask up."

Cozens bawled out for more hands and stood still helplessly.

" Remember Captain Shelvoke* . . ." he cried out insolently. At this Cheap struck him with his cane, which act provoked a stream of drunken abuse and foul language. It was apparent to onlookers that this normally likeable midshipman had been plied with liquor and egged on by a stronger but doubtful character to challenge Cheap's authority. Nevertheless the fact that he had been struck by a much bigger man in anger aroused sympathies among the onlookers. Cheap had him arrested and confined in the store tent under the care of a marine sentry.

That same evening Cheap went to visit Cozens. The prisoner was still full of abuse, and apparently liquor too, for he immediately asked if he was to be kept there all night. The gunner heard Cozens speak insolently to the captain, telling him that he had come to sea to pay Shelvoke's debts, as if in an attempt at blackmail. Then he added, " Though Shelvoke was a rogue, he was not a fool; and by God, you are both."

At this provocation the captain made as if to strike Cozens again, but the sentry intervened, deploring the act of striking any prisoner. Being a soldier he was exempt from Cheap's authority. Cozens shouted and behaved outrageously, attempting to stave in a cask of brandy. Cheap deemed it wiser to release him rather than confine him, especially as he was uncertain of the attitude of the sentry. Cozens had always seemed harmless in the past. Whoever it was that had put Cozens up to his tricks must have felt that he had won an important point. All this happened on Sunday the 7th June.

Two days later a further incident involving Cozens arose. William Elliot the surgeon, who lodged in the captain's hut, had paid a visit to Bulkeley's tent. Eighteen people lived here, one of whom was Cozens who was again drunk. Cozens provoked Elliot with abusive language, and followed him out as he left the tent, still abusing him. Elliot was a young man and

*Shelvoke was captain of the *Speedwell* lost in the island of Juan Fernandez in 1720, and had had a mutinous crew.

strong. He quickly overpowered Cozens, tied his hands behind him, and left him.

That same evening the captain sent for Bulkeley and Cummins for a consultation. They found him with his usual companions, the purser, surgeon, and Hamilton, and also on this occasion Baynes the lieutenant. Cheap said that he had no reason to suspect them (the gunner and carpenter) of disaffection, in fact they were the only two among the rest that he could trust, but he was concerned about disturbances generally and a growing atmosphere of insubordination manifest by Cozens' insolent behaviour. The gunner assured Cheap that the eighteen men in his tent were all stout fellows and generally well disposed towards the captain. They would never engage in mutiny against him or any other officer acting for the public good and on behalf of His Majesty's service. These were fine words, but as yet Bulkeley had had no occasion to differ strongly with his captain. He comments on the fact that this was the first occasion on which Cheap ever had consultation with his officers, and states that they might have escaped their present unhappy fate had consultation sometimes taken place on board. Cheap was too headstrong and lacking confidence in others to think much about discussion of points. Orders were given that the sentry at the provision tent was to keep a watchful eye at all times. Notwithstanding this, some flour and gunpowder were stolen from the tent that very night.

On the following day, Wednesday the 10th June, during issue of provisions and wine, the boatswain's servant, a Portuguese, was thought to say that one of the men had had his allowance stopped. Cozens was at this moment with the boatswain, a fomenter of trouble and perhaps one of the main culprits behind the scenes. Heavy rain was falling. Although the matter did not concern him, Cozens went straight to Harvey the purser to demand the reason for the stoppage of a man's allowance, perhaps provoked by King.

There had been fierce words between Harvey and Cozens only a few days earlier. Cozens' approach through the rain was so belligerent that Harvey drew his pistol and fired. John Young the cooper was standing by the purser. He jerked the pistol with his elbow just as it went off. The shot missed Cozens. At the sound of the shot alarm quickly spread. Somebody cried, " The dog has arms." Harvey shouted, " Cozens is come to kill us." From the captain's hut nearby, Lieutenant Hamilton rushed out. " Mutiny," he yelled. Cheap jumped out of his hut, carrying a cocked pistol. " Where is the villain?" he shouted. Cozens, incensed with rage, now left the purser and advanced menacingly on the captain. Cheap fired as he came within arm's length. Cozens, hit in the cheek, dropped to the ground, speechless yet conscious, and lay there bleeding profusely.

John Young writes of this fatal day, Wednesday the 10th June. Referring retrospectively to the impulse which made him nudge the purser's pistol:

" It were to be wished his Death had then immediately happened; for it would have been less misery to himself, and attended with far less mischief to others; but it was the will of Providence, that our Commander should be the Instrument of his unlucky Fate, and thereby bring upon his own Head, an almost insupportable load of Vexation."

The captain immediately sent for all hands, for there was much murmuring and discontent. Bulkeley decided to attend without arms, although the captain had instructed officers previously to be armed. He noted that Cheap, Hamilton, Harvey, Elliot, and two of the army officers, Ewers and Fielding, were all armed. He thereupon called the captain's attention to the fact that he and Cummins were unarmed, greatly concerned

to impress upon Cheap that he was loyal. As the accepted leader
in a tent of eighteen of the stoutest fellows, Bulkeley was begining to be regarded with suspicion by the captain.

Cheap dropped his firearm to the ground and said, " I have
sent for you to let you know that I am still your commander
and intend to remain your commander. Let every man now go
to his tent." Every man obeyed. Cheap was still in command.
But the seeds of discontent were growing apace.

The officers walked with Cheap to where Cozens lay on the
ground, his right cheek resting on the palm of his hand. He was
still alive and conscious, although unable to speak. Not a man
had gone to his help, fearful of the wrath of the captain who
made it quite apparent that he was unforgiving and unrelenting. He ordered Cozens to be carried to the sick-tent where the
surgeon's mate Elliot dressed the cheek. In probing the wound
the surgeon's mate discovered a ball about three inches below
the right eye. The surgeon refused to attend Cozens, and left
all treatment to his mate. It is clear that he was under orders
from Cheap, though some felt that the atmosphere was now so
tense that if Cozens were to die of treatment as his patient it
might be ascribed as revenge on his part.

On the following day the surgeon's mate asked Dr. Oakley
the army surgeon if he would assist in the removal of the ball.
Until he asked permission of the captain, Oakley was agreeable
to help. In the afternoon the surgeon's mate performed the
operation without assistance, dressed the wound, and was hope-
ful of recovery. Cheap was adamant in refusing any further
help for Cozens. Three days after the wounding, Cozens
appeared to be recovering and asked to be returned to
Bulkeley's tent where he had originally lived. Bulkeley and
Cummins together waited on the captain, and requested permission to transfer Cozens. This was refused vehemently by
Cheap saying " No. I am so far from it, that, if he lives, I
will carry him a Prisoner to the Commodore, and hang

1. Anson, probably about 1740

2. Press Gang with victim.   *J. Gillray*

3. The Spur to Ser-
vice; but the Navy
Agent was seldom
prompt in payment.
'Prize money due ten
years ago to be paid
two years hence' says
the notice.

him." Cozens continued to languish in the sick-tent which
was no more than a canvas covering thrown over some
bushes.

The men were exasperated at Cheap's inhumanity and rav-
ings, particularly as Cozens had never been seen with any firearm or weapon, and in his sober moments had been much
liked. To allow him to linger unattended and in pain was considered inhuman and most reprehensible, and it seemed to
many that Cheap was enjoying his revenge in a sadistic manner. Better to have dispatched Cozens at once. Cheap, though
notoriously quick-tempered, was reported to have a generous
nature. It was apparent that he was behaving with unshakable
resolution regardless of personal feelings, in an attempt to show
the men that there was no relaxation of his determination to
maintain authority. Unwittingly he was playing into their
hands. Cozens was the scapegoat, innocent of mutiny: King
more likely the scapegallows, who was to go scot-free.

Bulkeley writes for Wednesday the 24th June:

" . . . departed this Life Mr. Henry Cozens, Midshipman,
after languishing fourteen Days with the Wound he had
receiv'd in his Cheek: We bury'd him in as decent a Manner as Time, Place, and Circumstances would allow. There
have died sundry Ways since the Ship first struck, forty-
five Men; seven have deserted from us, and still continue
away; remain and now victual'd one hundred Men."

The cooper wrote:

" . . . it was said that though the deceas'd was a con-
ceited busy Fellow, that was not a sufficient Reason for
Killing him: That he had never appear'd in Arms; and
to shoot a Man thro' the Head, on a mere Surmise, without
any Inquisition or Process of Law at all, was something

C

worse than Manslaughter, and what the Captain's Commission could not bear him out in . . ."

Midshipman Byron, a great admirer of Cheap, merely wrote:

"This event, however, contributed to lessen him in the regard of the people."

Certainly this was the turning point.

CHAPTER 6

DEADLOCK

THE SHOOTING of Cozens and the inhuman behaviour of the captain produced two immediate results. The first was a growing hatred of Cheap: the second a distant respect for his obvious intention to maintain authority at all costs.

The need for discipline in the matter of provisions soon became evident. Although a boat was sent off to the wreck with a number of hands almost every day to salvage food and wine to add to the store ashore, and in spite of the smallness of the rations that were allowed, it was realized that provision could not last more than a month or two. Rations were still being supplemented by fish or fowl when available, but these were so difficult to get, and the weather was so cold and exacting, that men often preferred, out of working hours, to remain in the shelter of their tents rather than expose themselves to a mission that might prove fruitless and exhausting.

In spite of a sentry being posted at the store tent, provisions disappeared. During the night of the 10th July half a barrel of flour was taken away. On the 1st August some brandy was removed. Ten days later the purser spotted a man crawling from under the tent. He had secreted about his person flour sufficient for one day's ration for all the survivors. Some salt beef was found under his coat, and three more pieces of beef were found hidden in bushes nearby. Both the sentry Thomas Smith and thief Rowland Crusset were marines living in the same mess. When it was realized that theft had been going on for some time with the connivance of trusted marine sentries, the seamen were enraged and rushed with arms to Bulkeley's tent. They wanted to lynch the marines and have the provisions transferred to the gunner's tent.

Bulkeley realized at once that an ugly situation had arisen and spoke to the group who were agitating for revenge. He could be very righteous when exigency required it. He agreed that punishment should be given but it could be given only after a proper trial. Violence was tantamount to mutiny, and must be checked. Reluctantly the group withdrew, satisfied that justice would be carried out.

At this moment the gunner and carpenter were sent for and on appearing before Cheap heard the details of the thieving. The captain explained that he had no jurisdiction over marines and would hand them over to Captain Pemberton, the senior soldier, whose title was Commander of His Majesty's Land Forces. "For robbing the store tent," said Cheap, "the prisoners deserve death." All agreed that the theft was a terrible crime and the prisoners should die.

Captain Pemberton sent for Bulkeley and Cummins. He had little regard for either Cheap or Baynes, and said as much, implying that he considered both Bulkeley and Cummins to have the confidence of the remainder. He said that he would go as far as Martial Law allowed in the matter of punishment, but on consulting the Articles of War found that the maximum punishment possible was 600 lashes.*

Although Pemberton had lost his respect for Cheap, the ship's officers, certainly the gunner and carpenter, still had a

---

*More than a century later in 1866 an Act of Parliament limited flogging to forty-eight lashes for a single offence.

regard for naval discipline and knew the penalties for ignoring
or disputing the authority of their captain who maintained that
while the hulk of the *Wager* remained, and with it the stores
and provisions belonging to His Majesty, he was still in command. Their main complaint in the past had been the captain's
lack of consultation with his officers. It now seemed that Cheap
was aware of this, for he was constantly sending for them to
discuss problems. The subversive work of the boatswain was
well understood. He, as well as the master and the lieutenant,
counted for little in the day's transactions and general administration. Bulkeley writes for Monday the 15th June:

"Turn'd the Boatswain out of our Tent for breeding
Quarrels; his turbulent Tongue was so well known to the
Captain, that he express'd himself pleas'd at our turning
him out, and said he was surpriz'd we ever admitted him
among us."

Cheap deplored the fact that the marines who had filched
provisions should escape capital punishment. In the event both
Smith and Crusset received 400 lashes spread over two succes-
sive days; the remaining 200 lashes were abated. This infuri-
ated Cheap. It can well be understood when we read an extract
from Bulkeley's transactions for Wednesday the 12th August,
the day following the theft.

"Hard gales from S.W. to W. with heavy Showers of
Hail and rain. Serv'd out Provisions To-day, a Piece of Beef
for four Men; some Time past we have had but a Quarter of
a Pound of Flour per Man per Day, and three Pieces of
Beef; we live chiefly on Mussles, Limpits, and Clams, with
Saragraza and Thromba; . . . this last we boil, the Saragraza
we fry in Tallow: Even those Shell-Fish and Weeds we get
with great Difficulty: for the Wind, the Rain, and Coldness

of the Climate in this season, are so extremely severe, that
a Man will pause some Time whether he shall stay in his
Tent and starve, or go out in Quest of Food."

Two days later they found a "new Way of managing the
Slaugh; we fry it in thin Batter with Tallow, and use it as
Bread "; and after a further two days, presumably due to lack
of vitamins, "The People generally complain of a Malady in
their Eyes; they are in great Pain, and can scarce see to walk
about ".

On hearing of the mitigation of punishment of the two
marines the sailors were in an uproar. Bulkeley suggested sending the thieves to join the deserters. Cheap, still recognizing the
authority of Pemberton to deal with their disposal, decided
that the two culprits should in future have no rations at all
from the common stock and must fend for themselves.

Further visits had been made by Indians arriving in canoes.
On the 25th June it appeared as if they had come to settle with
the *Wager* survivors, for they arrived in five canoes laden with
seal, shellfish, and four sheep, and brought their wives and
children. There were fifty altogether in the Indian party.
Canoes were hauled ashore, and four wigwams were erected
with a covering of seal skins and the bark of trees. The sight of
women must have had a devastating effect on men who had
seen none for six months. Nevertheless the Indians seemed at
first friendly. In spite of the cold they wore no clothing except
a woollen scarf about neck or waist. They were intensely inter-
ested and amused to see their reflections in a looking-glass, and
could hardly be prevailed upon to return the object of their
interest, frequently peering behind. The males were indulgent
and did little more than provide wood for fires which they
always kept alight, leaving the women to act as slaves and go
off in canoes to dive for sea eggs. All were of small stature, flat
nosed, and with deeply sunken eyes. These people were most

concerned in the presence of death, and behaved with solemnity and gravity at burial services.

After two weeks the Indians departed as suddenly as they came. They tried to explain that they must go to look for seal but the obvious reason was the constant attempts made by the sailors to seduce the Indian women. With them went a constant though slender supply of food, for the women had given them sea eggs derived from deep diving in five or six fathoms of water. In this occupation they remained submerged for several minutes.

Boat trips to the wreck continued but increasing difficulty was experienced in finding food. The upper works had parted from the lower deck on the 15th July, and instead of retrieving casks of beef or pork the men found hatchets or bales of cloth. Some food had been washed ashore. Bulkeley says: "We took up along Shore, Abundance of Cheque Shirts in Dozens, also Caps, Bales of Cloth, and Pieces of Beef and Pork." But it is obvious that there was not much of the latter, and what could be seen was difficult to retrieve. "John Anderson, a seaman," says Bulkeley, "walking round the rocks, and reaching after a Piece of Beef, slipping his Footing, was drown'd."

All this time the slow task of lengthening and refitting the longboat had proceeded, though with no clear plan as to her ultimate destination or purpose. She had been got out of the wreck on the 20th May and hauled up on the shore. Owing to a misleading chart there could be no certainty as to the position of the wreck of the *Wager*. By sextant the Latitude was established as between 47° and 48° south. In the distance eastward could be seen the Cordilleras of the mainland, but the vast stretches of water in the immediate vicinity of the wreck in the form of creeks and lagoons left an impression of being separated from the mainland. Exploration was out of the question, not only owing to the difficulty of the terrain and the great breakers everywhere along the rugged coast, but because every man had to be fully employed in the grim struggle for existence. "Nor were we assisted," says Byron, "by any observation from Mount Misery, our prospect that way being intercepted by still higher hills and lofty woods."

The capable Cummins, whose industry and ability all commended, set to work on the task of lengthening the longboat, first laying blocks into which the boat could cradle. On the 18th June, after sawing the boat in two, he extended her overall length and keel by practically twelve feet. This would make her nearly fifty feet long, with a beam of nine feet, and accommodation for eighty men fairly tightly packed. She was to be schooner rigged. Much work would be required in shaping knees and planks, and then in constructing a deck and seaworthy hull of sufficient strength to withstand heavy seas. The men generally regarded this as a worthy project. There were still no plans however and although it was obvious that the completion of the longboat would take some months, there was a vague feeling that in due course there would be some prospect of getting away in her from this dismal spot called Wager Island.

Realizing now that their stay would be longer than at first expected, the men improved their shelters. The idea of building spread. "Indeed," writes John Young, "we found the Carpenter's Ability of great use to us at Land, as well as on the Ocean; for by his Assistance, soon after coming ashore, we had erected several Conveniences for our Habitation . . . One of our Houses . . . was a superb Structure, with distinct apartments for almost twenty Persons . . . richly covered, externally as well as internally, with several hundred yards of English Broad-Cloth."

The desire for privacy, to avoid a quarrelsome atmosphere, is apparent. "For my own part," says Byron, "seeing it was the fashion, and liking none of their parties, I built a little hut just big enough for myself and a poor Indian dog I found in the woods, who could shift for himself along shore, at low water, by getting limpets. This creature grew so fond of me and faithful, that he would suffer nobody to come near the hut without biting them."

This was too much for some of the hungry cut-throats. Byron describes how one day when at home in his hut he was visited by a party of men who said they were starving and wanted his dog. "They took him away by force and killed him," says Byron; "upon which, thinking that I had at least as good a right to a share as the rest, I sat down with them, and partook of the repast." Three weeks later he was glad to make a meal of the paws and skin which had been thrown aside.

The pressing calls of hunger drove men to desperation. But one, Richard Phipps, a boatswain's mate, used his wits and built himself a craft from half a water barrel lashed to two logs. With this he went looking for wildfowl, and had a lucky escape one day when his craft capsized. He managed to scramble to a rock where he remained for two days before being discovered by a boat party which had also been sent wildfowling. Byron himself had a narrow escape when away in a roughly built punt, looking for food. A sudden squall drove the punt free after the occupants had landed on a high rock ten miles from the camp. It is certain that they would have been lost but for the presence of mind and bravery of one man who plunged into the icy sea and swam to recover the drifting punt. In situations such as this they occasionally shot geese with plumage of bright colours. Though they often penetrated the thick woods they found very few birds. The woods were unpopular as it was rumoured that they were inhabited by wild beasts.

Near the end of July, with the longboat construction proceeding slowly but still far from completion, there began to take shape certain views on the future which hitherto had scarcely been contemplated. With the survival of crown property such as the longboat and the three other *Wager* boats,

and the salvaged stores and provisions, there was manifestly
some evidence of the need for the authority which Cheap continued to wield, though much resentment from the harder cases
among the ship's company at its enforcement. These men not
only spread disaffection, but quarrelled with one another. They
insisted among themselves that their present misfortunes were
due to the captain's obstinacy and that he was a murderer.
Bulkeley daily grew in stature and righteousness. He complained that his life had been threatened and then posed as a
long-suffering champion of an almost lost cause. Cheap himself
had been able to justify his autocracy in view of threats to his
life. Bulkeley's thoughts and enterprise are best revealed in his
own journal for Thursday the 30th July.

"Wind still at N.W. and rainy Weather. This Day
departed this Life Nathaniel Robinson, the last private Man
of the Invalids: there are now only two left, viz. the Captain
[Pemberton] and Surgeon [Oakley]. Being at the Honourable Mr. Byron's Tent, I found him looking in Sir John
Narborough's Voyage to these Seas; this Book I desired the
Loan of, he told me it was Captain Cheap's, and did not
doubt but he would lend it me; this Favour I requested of
the Captain, and it was presently granted. Carefully perus-
ing this Book, I conceived an Opinion that our going through
the Streights of Magellan for the Coast of Brazil, would be
the only way to prevent our throwing ourselves into the
Hands of a cruel, barbarous, and insulting Enemy: Our
Long-Boat, when finished, can be fit for no Enterprize, but
the Preservation of Life: As we cannot act offensively, we
ought to have regard to our Safety and Liberty. This Evening Proposals were offered to the Officers concerning our
going through the Streights of Magellan; which at this Time
they seem to approve of."

The very fact of writing this so meticulously with reasons for his opinion that they should journey southward seems to indicate that Bulkeley had given thought to the matter for some time, and moreover that he was aware of the captain's wish to join Anson somewhere to the northward. It is certain however that the Spaniards on this coast had a reputation for barbarous treatment of prisoners, and there was therefore sense in Bulkeley's scheme. The chances of escaping capture without the full resources of a man-of-war could not be high.

The north-westerly increased to gale force and continued with rain and hail for three days, during which the daily work of salvage, boat construction, and seeking for food continued. Bulkeley had sounded the officers on his scheme. He now sounded the men and found most of them anxious to get away. He remarks on the 2nd August, " The People are now very quarrelsome and discontented "; and on the next day, " Fine Weather (which is a Prodigy in this Place). The People fall into Disputes concerning the Boat, where we are going to proceed with her, when she is built and ready for going off."

The far-sighted Bulkeley, being well aware of the mercurial quality of seamen in distress, and keen himself on the written word, prepared a paper for signature by those who declared support for his scheme. He understood the sheep-like behaviour of the masses. He also needed to show the captain, rather than tell him, what support there was for the scheme, and wished to indicate that the whole thing was the result of mature consideration and careful assessment by the navigators. This would obviously be the best way to tackle the obstinate character who was never prepared to discuss an idea: present him with a ready-made, well supported plan. Some there might be who were in doubt; this would give them an opportunity of making up their minds.

As soon as the paper was drawn up men flocked to sign it with great enthusiasm and joy, as though this was a ticket for immediate passage to England without further worry or toil or hardship. With the exception of Cheap and Baynes, and those officers who had closely associated themselves with Cheap, all the officers signed the paper at once: these included all three of the midshipmen. Bulkeley says that it was signed by all the seamen in general, except the captain's steward, Peter Plastow, nevertheless there are many names missing. The paper was also signed by Captain Pemberton, commanding His Majesty's land forces, and by the lieutenants of marines, Fielding and Ewers. Cheap's close associates, Hamilton the lieutenant of marines, Elliot the surgeon, and Harvey the purser, refused to sign.

Bulkeley, together with the master, carpenter, and boatswain, took his paper to the captain at midday on Tuesday the 4th August when the rations were being served from the storehouse, and read it to Cheap. It ran as follows.

"We whose Names are under-mentioned, do, upon mature Consideration, as we have met with so happy a Deliverance, think it the best, surest, and most safe Way, for the Preservation of the Body of the People on the Spot, to proceed through the Streights of Magellan for England. Dated at a desolate Island on the Coast of Patagonia, in the Latitude of 47 Deg. oo Min. South, and West Longitude from the Meridian of London 81 Deg. 40 Min. in the South-Seas, this 2d Day of August 1741.

John Bulkeley,	Gunner
John Cummins,	Carpenter
Thomas Clark,	Master
John King,	Boatswain
John Jones,	Master's Mate
John Snow,	ditto
Robert Elliot,	Surgeon's Mate
The Hon. John Byron,	Midshipman

Alexander Campbell,	Midshipman
Isaac Morris,	Midshipman
Thomas Maclean,	Cook
John Mooring,	Boatswain's Mate
Richard Phipps,	ditto
John Young,	Cooper
Richard Noble,	Quarter-Master
William Rose,	ditto
William Hervey,	Quarter-Gunner
David Buckley,	ditto

Seamen

John Bosman	John Petman	William Oram
William Moore	William Callicutt	Moses Lewis
Samuel Stook	George Smith	Nicholas Griselham
Henry Stevens	Peter Deleroy	Samuel Cooper
John Montgomery	James MacCawle	Benjamin Smith
John Hayes	John George	John Duck
John Hart	John Shoreham	James Butler
James Roach	Richard East	
Job Barns	William Lane	

" We whose Names are under-mentioned; have had sufficient reasons, from the above-mention'd People, to consent
to go this Way, Sign'd by

" Capt. Robert Pemberton, Commander of his Majesty's
Land-Forces.

" William Fielding,

" Robert Ewers,   Lieutenants."

Having listened to the contents of the paper read by the gunner, the captain with no visible emotion calmly said he would
consider the matter and give them an answer. With this he dismissed the four officers. To a deputation on the following day,

consisting of the same officers minus the boatswain, but with the addition of the master's mate and the midshipmen, Cheap gave much the same answer, saying that he required time to come to a decision. Bulkeley made it clear that their primary interest was self-preservation which they regarded as a duty above any other interest or obligation, thus implying that they would follow their scheme even if the captain failed to concur. It was a clear ultimatum: do as we propose or we disobey you.

The next day was Thursday the 6th August, and Bulkeley was determined to clinch the matter of departure. He records hard gales again, this time from west-south-west, and the usual rain. At noon, he and Cummins went to see Captain Pemberton, presumably to look for further encouragement, after which they visited Baynes. While they were with Baynes the latter was sent for by Cheap, and an hour later Bulkeley and Cummins were sent for.

" Gentleman," said Cheap, somewhat pathetically, " I have considered the contents of your paper, so far as it regards the preservation of the people on the spot. It has given me a great deal of uneasiness and lack of sleep, because I think you have not weighed the affair rightly.

" Do you know?" Cheap continued. " The Straits of Magellan are more than 160 leagues south-west from us, and the wind against us. Then there is the same distance to run on the other side of the straits to the first port, with the wind always against us, and with no water to be had."

Bulkeley boldly assured the captain that they were not more than ninety leagues from the straits, and Cummins said that he had estimated that the longboat could carry a month's water allowing a quart daily for each man. Cummins added that it had been agreed among themselves that they would insist upon putting ashore for water whenever the weather permitted, and would suffer no obstruction.

Bulkeley pointed out the impracticability of ever reaching

the island of Juan Fernandez, a hundred leagues out in the ocean, in a small boat. In any case the Commodore and the rest of the squadron might also have shared their own fate. Here Cheap interrupted to say that the rendezvous had been Valdivia, on the coast in 40° south latitude, a Spanish base with little or no force. He expected to find Anson there.

There followed an altercation between Cheap and Cummins the latter in a very reproachful mood. The lieutenant Baynes was silent. The captain had suggested that if they went north-ward it would be possible to capture one of the trading vessels working from Chile.

" How can we take a vessel?" said Cummins. " Our enemies know as well as we do of our squadron and will be well armed and ready."

" What are our small arms for?" asked Cheap, determined to have his way. Cummins then pointed out that the planks of the longboat were no more than three quarters of an inch thick, so that one shot below the water-line would be fatal.

Cheap continued by saying that they might just as likely meet an enemy in the straits if they were to go southward. Bulkeley said there would only be Indians there. " Those we can master at our pleasure."

The captain seemed for a while to countenance the gunner's plan. " When we come to St. Julian's," he said, " we shall be sure of salt in plenty for our provisions, without which our fowls will not keep above two or three days. Besides, when we come to the River Plate, we may meet with a prize, they not being acquainted with any English vessel like ours, with schooner sails; by which means we may run up river, and take a larger vessel."

Still thinking aloud, the captain continued, " But what business have we at the Rio Grande? We must go to the Rio Janeiro."

" We shall be oblig'd to stop at every place along shore for supplies," said Bulkeley. "And at St. Catherine's the Governor will certify us as the people who were in the squadron."

"That's true," said Cheap, "and I can get bills of credit in any port of Brazil. Besides, our people may separate, some to other ships. With less hands and fewer mouths to feed we could go to Barbados."

"We might venture to England with twelve hands," said Cummins.

"Certainly with thirty," said Cheap.

During all this discussion Baynes had spoken not a word. The carpenter who was in belligerent mood asked him why.

"I'll give my opinion later," replied Baynes. He was not very bright but may have realized that Cheap was temporizing. He was terrified of Cheap, and probably thought it best to hedge for as long as possible.

"I knew nothing of your being acquainted with the scheme, Mr. Baynes," said the captain, "until Mr. Bulkeley told me yesterday. At the same time, I expect you will be the first to sign the paper."

Bulkeley, naturally thinking Cheap referred to the paper that had been read to him, responded with some warmth, indicating that although Baynes had agreed to the scheme, though at first refusing, he had later declined because there was no room left for his signature at the top of the list.

"I don't mean your paper," said Cheap darkly, and Bulkeley at once said that no other paper would be agreed if it was contrary to theirs. The atmosphere had become explosive again.

Cummins attacked. "Sir, 'tis all owing to you that we are here. If you had consulted your officers we might have avoided this misfortune. Considering the condition the ship was in, she was not fit to come in with the land, all our men being sick, and not above three seamen in a watch. Suppose the mast had gone by the board, as was every moment expected."

"Gentlemen," said Cheap, "you do not know my orders.

There never were any so strict given to a commander before. Had I but two men living besides myself, I must and was obliged to go to the island of Socorro in 45° south. I had to go there at all costs."

Bulkeley suggested that something must have been left to the discretion of commanders so as not to endanger His Majesty's ships. The captain then said he was agreeable to taking his chance with the rest, in whatever was deemed to be the best for the general interest, but urged further consideration until the longboat was ready.

" You have known, sir, from the time you first heard the proposal, that the people are uneasy, and the work will be at a standstill until the matter is settled. The sooner you resolve," said Bulkeley, " the better."

" I intend to have a consultation among my officers," said Cheap with an air of finality, as if to dismiss his visitors. " Have you any more objections to make?"

" Yes," replied Bulkeley audaciously. " One thing more, sir; which is that when you leave here, you do not come to an anchor, or weigh, or alter course without consulting your officers."

These words angered Cheap, but quickly controlling himself he said, " I was your commander, gentlemen, until the ship parted, or as long as any stores or provisions could be recovered, and I know not why I should be deprived of my commission now."

" We have always obeyed you," said Bulkeley, " and will continue to support your authority as long as it is for the common welfare." Such words made it clear that obedience from now on was conditional. In fact there was to be no obedience unless orders sounded reasonable. Whether reasonable or not was a matter for discussion. If under discussion there would be wide differences of opinion, and there was no certainty as to whose opinion mattered in the future or what course should be

followed. The rot had already set in. Whether or not there
was reason in Bulkeley's plan, it was at present the choice of
the masses. It was evident that Cheap was not in favour of it,
not only because he could see flaws, but because it savoured of
desertion of the idea implicit in the order to " annoy the
Spaniards in the South Sea." Many of the rabble thought that
Anson's ships must have perished or failed, as in fact had happened to the Spanish squadron. But Cheap was of sterner
stuff; raised in a firmer mould: and obviously under the spell
of resolution and determination which the quiet Anson im-
parted to all who served with him.

Cheap acknowledged that he had been well served, and that
the gunner and carpenter were the officers on whom he had
hitherto depended. He relied on a continuance of their support. They promised this " with our lives " but added the
clause " within reason ", and the meeting broke up.

Bulkeley writes, " After this Consultation the Captain seldom
came out of his Tent, which occasion'd great Disturbance
among the People."

John Young was more penetrating. " These Disputes and
Civilities," he says, " were equally insignificant; the contending
Parties were neither reciprocally convinc'd nor reconciled."

CHAPTER 7

MUTINY

THE CARDS were now on the table. Cheap was still nominally in command. But continuation of command would be conditional on doing what the masses wished.

On the day following the long consultation of the 6th, when the captain had seemed on the point of agreement, the navigators worked out the distances and courses for the passage southward in accordance with Sir John Narborough's book. From this it appeared that the journey to Brazil through the Straits of Magellan was quite feasible. This news greatly encouraged the mob, and there were great mutterings and murmurings against the captain. The men were certain that he would oppose the plan. This led to a further long consultation on Saturday afternoon the 8th August at the request of Bulkeley. When confronted Cheap produced the same sort of arguments about water and contrary winds. The gunner and carpenter gave the same reasonable replies. The lieutenant then intervened. Bulkeley complains, " This was the only Time the Lieutenant ever spoke in Publick on the Affair; he always allow'd when absent from the Captain, that going through the Streights was the best Way; but in the Captain's Presence he sided with him, and was for going to the Northward." Baynes made two objections in the presence of the captain but had to agree with Bulkeley and Cummins that they were pointless.

No agreement was reached at this meeting, but on the day following, Bulkeley and Cummins again called on the captain, this time with the master and the boatswain. Cheap found the quartette unanimous in opinion that they should travel through the Straits of Magellan. He therefore agreed that if the wind did not " set in against them " at the equinox on the 21st September he would agree to go that way.

Work proceeded on the longboat which was now heeled over for hull planking.

Three nights after the meeting at which the lieutenant behaved so ineffectually he made a surprising proposal which is recorded by Bulkeley. It is worth reproducing here, not only as a reflection on the practice of religion at sea in those times, but as an instance of the general mistrust which was spreading through the camp at Wager Island. In 1626 a sum of four-pence a month had been extracted from the pay of each sea-man, ostensibly to augment the naval chaplain's small stipend of fourteen shillings a month and to induce more preachers to go to sea. This had had little effect. There were few parsons at sea. Nevertheless the " parson's groat " was rigidly deducted from the seaman's pay and found its way into various pockets.

Bulkeley writes:

" At Night, Lieutenant Baynes surpriz'd us with a new Kind of Proposal we little dreamt of, which was, to have a proper Place of Devotion to perform Divine Service in every Sabbath-Day: For this Sacred Office our Tent was judg'd the most commodious Place. The Duty of publick Prayer had been entirely neglected on board, though every Seaman pays Fourpence per Month towards the Support of a Minister; yet Devotion, in so solemn a Manner, is so rarely perform'd that I know but one Instance of it during the many Years I have belong'd to the Navy. We believe religion

to have the least Share in this Proposal of the Lieutenant.
If our Tent should be turn'd into a House of Prayer, and
this Project takes, we may, perhaps, in the Midst of our
Devotion, be surpriz'd, and our Arms taken from us, in order
to frustrate our Designs, and prevent our return to England
through the Streights of Magellan, or any other Way."

The gunner was a shrewd man and sensible of the critical
position in which he now found himself as the leader of a fac-
tion opposing the captain's wishes. So far he had behaved dis-
creetly but a continuation of a deadlock would almost certainly
stimulate rash action on one side or the other. The captain
was not without followers. Referring to a later incident, John
Young writes:

" What help'd to ingratiate Bulkeley very much with the
Crew, and gave him an extraordinary Ascendance over 'em,
was, a Notion he industriously spread, of going in Danger of
his Life, on account of his being looked on as a most strenu-
ous Promoter of that Project they fancied to be so entirely
for their Advantage; and the Quarter-Master (one Noble)
ministred him a fine Opportunity for such an Insinuation, by
threatening to Shoot him, professedly, for his Forwardness
in that Affair."

This explosive attitude is readily understood, for not only
was there a general uneasiness at the lack of an agreed plan
for getting away, and a feeling that the little authority still
remaining was uninspired and contrary to the general interest,
but an increasing shortage of food that drove hungry men to
desperate remedy and thoughtless action. Whereas the mixture
of seasoned hands and the thugs and inebriates pressed into
service at Portsmouth could be brought together peaceably
under the strict discipline of ship routine, anything was now

possible. Patience was non-existent and tempers were short. Retribution might be avoided.

The carpenter, whose prime occupation was the completion of the longboat, saw one morning a seaman cutting up an anchor stock for firewood. This had been shaped and designed as a post for particular use in the boat. At the sight of this Cummins was unable to contain himself. Although there was a general wish for advancing the work, as it would speed the day of departure, Cummins had found little effectual help and a widespread indifference towards the actual construction of the schooner. This act temporarily turned his brain. In no time he was raving and delirious. This caused general apprehension, for he was the only man who could direct and complete the work of conversion. All possible methods were applied to restore Cummins to normal, and by the following morning he was sufficiently recovered to tackle the work as usual.

The store tent was again robbed on Sunday the 23rd August, this time of brandy sufficient to supply half a pint a day to all the men for twelve days. Bulkeley and Cummins went with the lieutenant to consult Cheap who recommended an immediate enquiry and the severest punishment on the offenders. One of the marine sentries was found drunk at his post, and the following day, after a rigid examination, the boatswain named marines Smith and Butler as the thieves. Trial and punishment rested again with Pemberton.

It was now discovered that considerable drunkenness was attributable to reasons other than direct theft, and information reached Bulkeley that some men were being supplied with great quantities of liquor, in spite of the nominal ration of half a pint a day. He was also told that the purser held daily conversation with an increasing number of "rebels" (against Bulkeley's scheme), suborning them with bribes of rum and brandy. The gunner was immediately full of righteous indignation concering these "rebels", and aware now that the cap-

tain continued his opposition to the scheme for returning to
England through the Straits of Magellan. It was apparent that
he had no intention of returning to England, and by the per-
suasive effects of strong drink was daily buying adherents
to his own proposal to go northward. The cooper describes it
nicely.

"The Gunner and Carpenter were mightily alarm'd at
this, supposing the Captain had spirited up a Party against
their Scheme, which they regarded as a kind of Subornation
of Treason, against his Sovereign, the People."

The "People" were certainly put out and disturbances
increased, accompanied oddly enough by four great earth-
quakes, three of which were frightening with violent shocks
and trembling of the earth. The lack of rigidity of huts and
tents enabled them to survive with little damage. Hard gales of
wind continued, with heavy showers of rain.

Indignant at the prospect of his plan failing because of
growing opposition, Bulkeley went to the lieutenant to see what
should be done. Baynes was pleased to be consulted, as this
added to his small stock of prestige. He suggested that another
paper should be drawn up declaring the general determination
of the ship's company to go through the Straits of Magellan.
This should be taken to the captain for agreement and signature, in order to put an end to the growing disturbances and
conflict of opinion. Thinking probably of his own neck the
lieutenant added that each officer should have a copy of the
paper so as to justify his action when they arrived in
England.

Bulkeley thereupon drew up the following paper:

"Whereas upon a General Consultation, it has been
agreed to go from this Place through the Streights of Magel-

lan, for the Coast of Brazil, in our Way for England: We do, notwithstanding, find the People separating into Parties, which must consequently end in the Destruction of the whole Body; and as also there have been great robberies committed on the Stores, and every Thing is now at a Stand; therefore, to prevent all future Frauds and Animosities, we are unanimously agreed to proceed as above-mentioned."

This paper was presented to the lieutenant with the request that he would obtain the captain's signature. Baynes seemed overcome with his own importance and now made the most astounding proposition.

" I cannot suppose the Captain will refuse the signing of it; but if he is so self-willed, the best step we can take, is to put him under arrest for the killing of Mr. Cozens. In this case I will, with your approbation, assume command. Then our affairs will be concluded to the satisfaction of the whole company, without being any longer liable to the obstruction they now meet from the captain's perverseness and chicanery."

These were strong words and can be regarded as nothing short of intended mutiny. The captain was to be presented with an ultimatum. The intention to arrest him on the charge of killing was conditional only on his refusal to sign the paper, and was not otherwise applicable. It could only therefore be regarded as a flimsy pretext for the lieutenant to get his own way and his own command. It was also agreed that the purser should be sent off the island for stirring up the " rebels "; presumably for inciting rebellion against the mutineers. The charge by these righteous officials was that the purser had acted " contrary to his Duty, in Contempt of the Articles of War, the Laws of his Country, and the known rules of the Navy ", these were brave words. Furthermore it was resolved that anyone stirring up further trouble, presumably opposition to the proposal to journey southward, should be disarmed. It is odd to compare this attitude with the fact that the boatswain had got off scot free after firing a gun at the captain.

Both the gunner and the carpenter received the lieutenant's advice with approbation, though it is surprising that two such strong characters should be so gullible in the presence of this weakling. They must have been relieved to find that their scheme was backed by higher authority, however vacillatory. But the gunner had the lieutenant's measure. " By this Day's Proceedings," wrote Bulkeley, " we thought the Lieutenant a Gentleman of resolution; but the Words and Actions of People do not always concur." Proof of the last sentence soon followed.

A great consultation took place in the captain's hut on Friday the 28th August. The lieutenant was already with the captain when the master, boatswain, gunner, carpenter, Mr. Jones the master's mate, and Mr. Campbell, midshipman, all arrived as deputies sent by the men. Not only were they all armed, but the men who had sent them were likewise armed. As soon as the officers were seated a short discussion took place as to the punishment appropriate for marines Smith and Butler who had robbed the store tent. They were sentenced to be banished to the mainland or some other island. Bulkeley then raised the matter of disaffection among the men, and the necessity for coming quickly to a decision, expecting the lieutenant to confront Cheap with the new paper calling for the captain's signature. Baynes made no move. He remained silent.

" Gentlemen," said Cheap, " this is no time for men to raise disputes and foment disturbances about the way home, when we are in no condition to go at all. This can only aggravate our present misfortunes. It is quite indifferent to me whether we go northward or southward, as I have no plan except for the welfare of all. Whichever way you go I will take my Fate with you."

All now looked at the lieutenant who had sponsored this meeting. He sat silent, as if unconcerned about this or any other proposal. Bulkeley thereupon took out his own copy of the paper and in a dramatic fashion read it out. On conclusion he asked Cheap to sign. This threw the captain into a towering rage. Now speechless, he refused to countenance any further proposal. Bulkeley tried to change the subject, suggesting that they would need to carry provisions to last at least ten weeks. Cheap would not answer. The gunner then commented on the obvious effects of liquor on some of the crew and suggested that it should be buried. The captain, still in a passion, refused to take any notice of the assembly and indicated that the conference was over.

On leaving the captain, all the officers, with the exception of Baynes, proceeded to Pemberton's tent to see what should be done next. Pemberton was seated in stately fashion outside his tent, surrounded by the men. Above his tent flew a flag. The officers informed him of the failure of their mission to the captain, and asked Pemberton if he would accept their allegiance and direct them concerning the next move. Pemberton, not being a naval officer, suggested that if the captain should persist in his refusal to sign, thereby declining to take part in the journey to the southward which the majority favoured, he should be deposed and the command given to the lieutenant in accordance with Baynes' own proposal. Pemberton said he would stand by them. This immediately raised acclamation from officers and men alike: there were cheers, and cries of " For England."

Cheap, hearing the noise, was now concerned and sent for the officers to ask what the shouting was about. On being told that it was proposed to take the command from him and transfer it to the lieutenant, since he had no regard for the safety of provisions, Cheap kept quite cool, raised himself to his full height, turned directly to the lieutenant, and in an authoritative voice said, " Who is he that will deprive me of my command?" Then brusquely to Baynes, " Is it you, sir?"

Baynes looked terrified, completely intimidated by the captain's appearance, and replied at once, " No, sir."

The other officers, leaving Baynes in the captain's hut to protest his innocence, returned to Pemberton. They had not been there a quarter of an hour before Cheap sent again for them. Back they went, and with them several of the men. The officers were armed with pistols, already cocked, and the men had charged muskets. The atmosphere was tense.

Bulkeley was the first to be called in. On entering he saw the captain seated on a chest, with a cocked pistol on his right thigh. Remembering Cozen's fate he immediately withdrew, and asked Mr. Jones the master's mate to inform the captain that he did not think it proper to appear before a cocked pistol.

Cheap threw his pistol aside and appeared at the front of his hut. This was recognized as a brave act by the armed mob facing him. He addressed the throng in a steady voice.

" What are your grievances?" he asked. " In the name of God I am willing to put them right, and to go southward with you if that is your resolve."

There was a roar of response the gist of which was to demand that a reserve of provisions for the sea journey should be set aside and the remainder shared out. Cheap expressed surprise at the groundless charge that the stores had been neglected, in view of the measures he had taken for their security. He also warned the men of the futility of dividing out the provisions now. Many of them would be unable to refrain from eating to-day and starving to-morrow.

Cheap's words fell on deaf ears. The mob were now beyond control. The men had seen the officers defy the captain: they would now defy the officers. What was the difference? They had nothing to lose. Perhaps they were egged on by the boatswain. By persuasion they were gradually restrained from carrying out fully their demands, but only after being promised a pint of brandy per day, which by calculation could last only a further three weeks.

"Had their demand been fully gratified," said the cooper, "the most pernicious Consequences might have ensued; they would have rioted in spirituous Liquor, and, when intoxicated, have broke out into the most shocking Disorders, which must probably have issued in Murders at that Time, and Famine afterwards"; similar in fact to the drunken orgies and brutalities that took place on board the wreck for some days after the grounding, under the leadership of the boatswain.

Bulkeley, now finding the captain somewhat mollified in temper, informed him that he was not the leader in this affair.

"How can I think otherwise?" answered Cheap.

"Sir, the paper I read you was your lieutenant's. There sits the gentleman, let him disown it if he can."

Cheap looked at Baynes with disgust and remarked, "Mr. Bulkeley has honestly clear'd himself." The breach was temporarily healed; a glass of wine was drunk, and an invitation issued to Bulkeley and Cummins to sup with Cheap that night.

During supper the gunner raised the matter of the cocked pistol. "Had I advanced, one of us must have dropped," he said.

"Bulkeley," answered the captain, "I do assure you, the pistol was not designed for you, but for another, for I knew everything beforehand."

This remarkable day of the 28th August ended apparently in temporary tranquillity. "We talk'd of indifferent Things," writes Bulkeley, "and spent the Evening in a very affable Manner."

But the cooper writes, "The Temper of the People seem'd for the present to be somewhat quieted, but the pacific Disposition was soon expell'd, by the turbulent Passions that were become habitual in them. Vexatious Incidents succeeded one another daily and gradually paved the Way, for that *Coup d'Eclat* which soon followed."

Five more Indian canoes arrived on the 29th August with fifty Indians: men, women, and children. They were not so generous as the previous visitors and refused to part with anything. Perhaps they sensed the mutinous spirit and explosive atmosphere. They launched their canoes the next morning and went off.

On the 1st September the carpenter was shot in the thigh by the captain's cook Thomas Maclean with large pewter slugs, but little injury resulted owing to the distance between them. Nobody knew if this were accidental or by design. The cook whose age was eighty-two was given the benefit of the doubt but nevertheless disarmed.

News arrived on the following day that three of the deserters, James Mitchell, Joseph King, and Owen Thomson, had gone to the mainland in a punt which they had made. The other deserters had visited the camp on the previous day to explore the possibilities of their being received back. There was little enthusiasm. Living was now very hard, seaweed being the only possible supplement to the meagre ration of flour, and very rarely shellfish.

The store tent was again robbed on the 6th September. Five of the marines who were suspected, dreading the punishment, did not wait to be charged, and fled to join the deserters.

On the 8th September William Harvey quarter-gunner, presented a paper signed by himself and six others: David Buckley, quarter-gunner; Richard Noble, quarter master; William Moor, cook; William Rose, quarter master, John Hayes, seaman, and John Bosman, seaman, to which was added on the following day the name of Peter Plastow the captain's steward who had been a great favourite of Cheap. This read as follows:

"To acquaint you, the Gentlemen, Officers, and Seamen of the Ship *Wager*, that, for the Easement of the Boat now building, we do agree to go in the Yawl, after she is fitted up, with allowing us our Share of Provisions, and other Conveniences, to go in her to the Southward, through the Streights of Magellan, for the Coast of Brazil."

This paper is of interest because of its apparent recognition of a vestige of authority and control, in spite of the frequent remarks in Bulkeley's transactions and John Young's narrative concerning "uneasiness", "no discipline", "scarce any work", "everything at a stand", "murmurings", "villains", "turbulent passions" and "treason."

On the 24th September the captain sent the gunner away with the barge to make a survey of the coast to the southward; with Bulkeley went ten men, Mr. Jones the mate, Byron the midshipman, and Harvey the purser, the latter because of his artistic ability. On the first evening they found a good harbour, killed a "fine large Bitch, big with Puppies", and supped heartily. On each succeeding night they were successful in finding a bay or harbour as a refuge from breaking seas, and fed well on wildfowl. On returning on the 28th to Wager Island in a strong gale, they found the longboat almost finished, ready to be caulked and have her bottom paid with tallow and soap. But Byron writes, "The old cabal, during our absence, had been frequently revived; the debate of which generally ended in riot and drunkenness. This cabal was chiefly held in a large tent . . . from whence were dispatched Committees to the captain, with the resolutions they had taken with regard to their departure; but oftener for liquor."

The captain had again suffered a change of heart. The lieutenant acquainted the officers that the captain said he was now resolved to maintain his authority to the full extent and to govern in accordance with the rules of the Navy. There was no reference to future plans. To show their contempt and independence the men dug up the brandy casks that they had recently buried for safety, and issued half a pint for every man. They had already consumed that which had not been buried. The gunner and carpenter swore they would never go near the captain again. It was apparent to them that Cheap had no intention of going to the southward. It also seemed that he hoped to obstruct them in their own plans. Apart from his close associates, particularly lieutenant Hamilton of the marines, the captain was now without any support whatsoever. He had changed his mind once too often.

Bulkeley examined the powder situation on Thursday the 8th October, and finding that there were a number of half barrels of powder in excess of what would be needed in the longboat, proposed to the lieutenant that the surplus should be emptied into the sea and the empty half barrels used as water casks. As he had resolved not to consult the captain again, he requested Baynes to inform Cheap. The latter was by now unapproachable so the lieutenant, who was always afraid of him even at the best of times, said he would send Thomas Clark the master. Clark returned from his mission completely subdued, having been expressly forbidden by Cheap to start a single grain of powder or destroy any crown property without his order.

This was the last straw. Since no dependable agreement could be obtained from Cheap, the mutineers would have to take the law into their own hands as proposed by Baynes. Pemberton presided over a meeting on the beach that afternoon and harangued the seamen about the obstinacy of the captain and his undependability. Cheap would be arrested and confined for the murder of Cozens, and taken to England for trial. Pemberton assured the assembly that this would be done, not out of spite, but as a duty in the failure or omission of which he himself would be called to account on returning to

England: perhaps every man present, too, being deemed accessories to the bloody fact.

There was immediate and unanimous agreement with this mutinous motion. To ensure success without opposition, surprise must be achieved, and Lieutenant Hamilton must be arrested at the same moment. Baynes, Bulkeley, Cummins, and Jones seem to have been most forward in planning the arrest which was to be carried out by armed seamen the next morning.

Cheap had not the least suspicion of this conspiracy, obviously reassured by the frequent protestations of loyalty on the part of the gunner and carpenter whom he regarded as virtually in control. Not a word of the planned insurrection leaked out, which indicates that his erratic behaviour had made him friendless.

Early in the morning of the 9th October, armed sailors entered Cheap's hut, tied the captain's hands, and removed arms and possessions. Lieutenant Hamilton was arrested at the same time, in his tent, though apparently for no other reason than that he was a close associate of the captain.

Cheap, completely surprised, realized that it would be folly to resist, but in a loud voice asked what they meant by such unparalleled insolence. "Where are my officers?" he shouted.

At this, the master, gunner, carpenter, and boatswain went in.

"Gentlemen," said Cheap belligerently, "are you sensible of what you are doing, or of the consequences you must incur for such villainy?"

"Yes, sir," was the reply. "We have done nothing that is not the result of sober consideration. We are to take you prisoner to England, there to be tried for the murder of Mr. Cozens. This is at the instance of Captain Pemberton."

"What has Pemberton to do with me?" asked Cheap. "Is he

4. Model of the *Centurion*, 60 guns, 400 men: Anson's flagship in his voyage to the South Sea.

5. An Eighteenth Century Sloop of about the same size and fire power as the *Wager*.

Etching by R. Pollard, T. Mitchell.

6. Making the most of the last few hours. Farewell and embarkation at Portsmouth Point: late 18th century.

7. Ships in a gale, under courses only, all topsails furled.

your commander, or am I? Here are my Instructions." He took out of his pocket a copy of his Instructions.

Cheap was taken out of the hut, his hands tied behind him. He continued to upbraid the officers with vehemence. For nearly half an hour the altercation continued, Cheap warning his warders of the penalties they would certainly suffer for their treacherous actions. They for their part told him that he had shown no consideration for their escape from this desolate place or for their welfare, and appeared to aim at their destruction rather than their preservation.

The boatswain made full use of this opportunity to pour foul language on the captain for having struck him when drunk, and for making him look so silly. He provoked the captain to the utmost with taunts, and would certainly have received another thrashing had Cheap's hands been free. " Then it was your time," explained King, " but now, God damn you, it is mine."

" You are a scoundrel," said Cheap, " for using a gentleman so when he is a prisoner."

Turning to the seamen he said, " Very well, gentlemen, you have caught me napping: I do not see any of you in liquor. You are a parcel of brave fellows." Then he added bitterly, " But my officers are scoundrels." Perhaps he had particular memory of the gunner's frequent assurances of loyalty.

Turning to the gunner he asked, " Where is my lieutenant? Did he not head you?"

Baynes was then called, and on arrival was questioned by Cheap. " What is all this about, Mr. Baynes?"

" Sir, it is Captain Pemberton's orders," replied Baynes.

" Captain Pemberton has no authority to do this. It is you who will answer for it. If I do not live to see England, I hope some of my friends will." He further declared that he never intended to go to the southward, and would not go off with them in the longboat, for he had too much honour to turn his

D

back on his enemies. He would rather be shot by the mutineers. This declaration surprised many, especially as he had given his word to go southward. He spoke already as if he were a dying man. He was not at this moment keen to return to England, as he knew that he would have to undergo a severe court-martial for the loss of H.M.S. *Wager*. There would be a weight of evidence pointing to the fact that he had hazarded the safety of his ship by approaching a lee shore.

Cheap asked if he could remain in his own hut, but this request was refused and his things were transferred to the purser's tent, which was next to Hamilton's: both could then be guarded by one guard. This consisted of six men and an officer. As he was moved off Cheap said cynically:

" Gentlemen, you must excuse my not pulling my hat off, my hands are confined." And then to the lieutenant, " Well, *Captain* Baynes! You will doubtless be called to account for this hereafter."

Such words must have terrified Baynes. Perhaps he could already see the noose dangling round his neck. He had tried so hard to make it seem that others were responsible for the mutiny he himself had engendered. After hearing the captain's words the gunner and carpenter must also have been concerned. Perhaps the prospect of the captain not returning to England to give evidence momentarily relieved them of some anxiety.

The thoughts expressed by the cooper are of interest.

" The Gunner and Carpenter," wrote John Young, " certainly deviated from their Duty: They should not have hearkened to such a Motion of the Lieutenant's, without opposing and expressing a due Abhorrence of it; whereas they received it rather with Approbation. These two Men were all along, as I have already observed, the principal Agitators in the Project of going homeward through the Streights. I am inclin'd to think they were influenc'd by honest Motives; and I own they might very justifiably endeavour to engage the Captain to act as the common Interest required; and in default of his doing so they might have left him, and taken their own Course; but to lay violent Hands on him, was in my Opinion, altogether indefensible, it was undeniably an illegal mutinous Procedure."

That it was mutiny was undeniable. But who was really to blame? It was the weak-minded lieutenant who first thought of arresting the captain should he be obstinate in signing the paper, and it was he who proposed that the killing of Cozens should be a good enough reason for doing so. Nevertheless he had not the courage to come into the open on this point or to oppose the captain in person.

The cooper, "who was an Eye Witness of all the Affair," blames the gunner and carpenter as leaders of the mutiny, more particularly so as they declared their loyalty and support, and Cheap responded expressing a confidence in their reliability.

"The Captain," he says, "had entertained a great Jealousy of the Influence they both had over the People, knowing them to be active Spirits, and fond of being considered as Persons of Consequence; but they had of late so abounded in Professions of Duty and Attachment to him, that they gradually effaced those disadvantageous Impressions, and insensibly instilled a Confidence in their Fidelity, notwithstanding their appearing so often at the Head of his Officers; nor could he ever conceive, that any thing would have induced them to go to those Lengths against him."

Those lengths were certainly mutiny. But the damage had been done, and the gunner and carpenter were now committed. By now they realized their folly. But it was too late to retract.

CHAPTER 8

DEPARTURE OF THE *SPEEDWELL*

AT NOON on Tuesday the 13th October 1741, five weary months
after the loss of the *Wager,* the *Speedwell* got under sail to
leave Wager Island. In company were the cutter and the
barge. On the previous day the longboat had been launched
and christened *Speedwell* with all due ceremony and joy, and
hopes were high of getting back to England. Few appreciated
the perils that lay before them or the hardships and misfortunes
which must follow. The combined crews totalled eighty-one;
fifty-nine were in the *Speedwell,* twelve in the cutter, and ten
in the barge.

In tones reminiscent of Henry V on the eve of Agincourt,
John Young wrote, " You may now fancy us embark'd, enter-
ing on our important Voyage, all of us stock'd with eager
Desires, feeble Hopes, and gloomy Apprehensions. Danger
hastily pursued and overtook us. We were not out of Wager
Bay, as we called the Place of our Embarkation, when the
Speedwell split her Topsail, and was at the Brink of perishing
on the Rocks."

Events had moved swiftly since the arrest of Cheap and
Hamilton four days earlier. This had provided Bulkeley with
the opportunity to confirm and go ahead with his plan to journey southward. Vacillation had ended. Cheap continued to

denounce the proposal, deploring a scheme that would "lead so many brave fellows to face ten thousand difficulties."

"By going northward there is the island of Chiloe" (in 43° S no more than 200 miles distant) persisted Cheap, "where we need not fear taking prizes, and may have a chance to see the commodore." Cheap's plan may have sounded reasonable, but by this time Anson had already left the second rendezvous at Juan Fernandez with his three remaining ships and their sadly depleted crews. He had taken some handsome prizes while operating off Valparaiso in latitude 33° south. It is most unlikely therefore that Cheap would ever have caught up with the Commodore even had he himself taken a prize. His valour and persistence were matched by his stupidity.

Bulkeley was equally persistent, and one must admire his moral courage in the face of such authoritative opposition, for he alone was the sponsor of the southward plan which would take them to the stormy high latitudes in the vicinity of Cape Horn. It is also interesting to see his reference to the supreme penalty which must have hung like a continuing shadow over all his thoughts. Cheap frequently reminded the mutineers of the hanging that must greet their arrival in England.

"Sir," responded Bulkeley, "You have said that we shall be called to our account in England: I must tell you, for my part, had I been guilty of any crime, and was sure of being hanged for it in England, I would make my choice to go there, sooner than to the northward. There is a chance in going northward of a worse fate, namely a Spanish prison." Prospect of work in the Spanish mines for life was a great deterrent.

The captain had virtually resigned his command and submitted to the authority of the "People". The latter now elevated the lieutenant to the supreme appointment of commander, but with restrictions. It was considered provident to draw up a constitution with four articles in which one detects the hand of Bulkeley the sea lawyer.

"Whereas Captain David Cheap, or Commander in H.M.S. *Wager*, never consulted any of his Officers for the Safety and Preservation of the said Ship, and H.M. Subjects thereto belonging; but several Times since the unhappy Loss of the said Ship, he has been solicited in the most dutiful Manner, promising him at the same Time to support his Command with our Lives, desiring no more than to go off Heart in Hand from this Place to the Southward, which he gave his Word and Honour to do; and being almost ready for sailing, did apply to him, some few Days past, to draw up some proper Articles, in order to suppress Mutiny, and other material Things, which were thought necessary to be agreed to before we went off; but he, in the most scornful Manner, hath rejected every Thing propos'd for the Publick Good; and as he is now a Prisoner, and the Command given to the Lieutenant, upon his Approbation of the following Articles.

"*First*, As we have no Conveniency for dressing* Provisions on Board the Vessel for a third Part of the Number to be carried off the Spot, therefore this Day serv'd out to every Man and Boy twelve Days Provision, for them to dress before we go off; and also it is agreed, that whoever is guilty of defrauding another of any Part of his Allowance, on sufficient Proof thereof, the Person found guilty (without any respect of Person) shall be put on Shore at the first convenient Place, and left there.

"*Secondly*, In regard to the Boats going off with us, we think proper to allow one Week's Provision for each Man appointed to go in them, in order to prevent Separation from each other, which would be of the worst Consequence of any Thing that can happen to us: to prevent which we do agree, that when under-way they shall not separate, but always keep within Musket-shot, and on no Pretence or Excuse whatso-

*Cooking.

ever go beyond that reach. The Officer, or any other Person, that shall attempt a Separation, or exceed the above mention'd Bounds, shall, on Proof, be put on shore and left behind.

" *Thirdly,* It is agreed in order to suppress Mutiny, and prevent Broils and Quarrels on Board the Vessel, that no Man shall threaten the Life of another, or offer Violence in any Shape: the Offender, without any respect of Station or Quality, being found guilty, shall be put on Shore and left behind.

" *Fourthly,* We do agree, whatever Fowl, Fish, or Necessaries of Life, we shall happen to meet with in our Passage, the same shall be divided among the whole: and if Captain David Cheap shall be put on Board a Prisoner, it shall not be in the Lieutenant's Power to release him.

" The aforesaid Articles were agreed to, and sign'd by the undermentioned:

> Robert Beans, Lieutenant
> Thomas Clark, Master
> John King, Boatswain
> John Bulkeley, Gunner
> John Cummins, Carpenter
> Thomas Harvey, Purser
> Robert Elliot, Surgeon's Mate
> John Jones, Master's Mate
> John Snow, Master's Mate
> The Hon. John Byron, Midshipman
> Alexander Campbell, Midshipman
> Isaac Morris, Midshipman
> Thomas Maclean, Cook
> Richard Phipps, Boatswain's Mate
> John Mooring,   do.
> Matthew Langley, Gunner's Mate
> Guy Broadwater, Coxswain

Samuel Stook, Seaman
Joseph Clinch,   do.
Joseph Duck,   do.
Peter Plastow, Captain's Steward
John Pitman, Butcher
David Buckley, Quarter Gunner
Richard Noble, Quarter Master
William Moore, Captain's Cook
George Smith, Seaman
Benjamin Smith,   do.
William Oram, Carpenter's Mate
John Hart, Joiner
John Bosman, Seaman
William Harvey, Quarter Gunner
Richard East, Seaman
Samuel Cooper, do.
Job Barns,   do.
James Butler,   do.
William Rose, Quarter Master
John Shoreham, Seaman
John Hayes,   do.
Henry Stevens,   do.
William Callicutt, do.
John Russell, Armourer
James MacCawle, Seaman
William Lane,   do.
James Roach,   do.
John George,   do.
John Young, Cooper
Moses Lewis, Gunner's Mate
Nicholas Griselham, Seaman.

These forty-eight signatures include, besides those of Bulkeley and Cummins, those of the three midshipmen who wrote narratives, and that of John Young the cooper. These were probably the officers, petty officers, and principal men. The land officers, marines, junior rates, servants, and boys did not sign.

Pemberton having brought about the arrest of Cheap and Hamilton now withdraws from the picture. Doubtless he was given a comfortable berth in view of his rank as a soldier. Byron on the other hand had to doss down with the seamen.

Cheap made it clear that he would not go off with the long-boat party: he said he would rather be shot. Bulkeley consulted the " People " about this point, indicating certain advantages. There was not one dissentient voice. In fact the men were so relieved at the prospect of leaving the captain behind that with great condescension one or two suggested that the barge and yawl should be left for the captain's use, together with his share of provisions. Hamilton and William Elliot the surgeon volunteered to remain with Cheap, but not a man otherwise: their act of humanity was ascribed by the cooper to an apprehension of dangers and distresses rather than to friendship.

On the morning of *Speedwell*'s departure the barge took Mr. Snow, one of the master's mates, on a visit to the deserters. Cheap had accepted the offer of the yawl, but declined the barge on the grounds that it would be required as a tender to the *Speedwell* for inshore work and surveys. This was regarded by the " People " as a most generous gesture. It would ease a little the overcrowding in the schooner and the cutter. Cheap had requested that the deserters be offered a passage with him to the northward in the yawl; they were to be provided with a half-share of provisions if they agreed to go with Cheap. They readily accepted. There must have been much relief on the part of Bulkeley that they would no longer be his responsibility.

On the morning of departure Bulkeley arranged for the following items to be set aside for the captain's party.

Provisions for the captain, surgeon, and Hamilton:

    Six Pieces of Beef, Six Pieces of Pork, Flour 90 lbs.

Provisions for eight deserters:

    Eight Pieces of Beef, Eight Pieces of Pork, Flour one cwt.

Stores and Ammunition:

    6 Hand grenades

    5 Half barrels of powder

    2 Kegs of musket balls

    Hamilton's pistols and gun

    1 Pair of pistols for the captain

    12 musket flints

    6 pistol flints

    Sundry carpenter's tools

    $\frac{1}{2}$ pint of sweet oil

    2 swords of the captain

    5 muskets

    12 pistol balls

    1 Bible

    1 Azimuth compass

    1 Quadrant

    1 Gunter's scale.

Bulkeley writes at length of his taking leave of the captain at the departure of the *Speedwell*. This reads more like a Gilbert and Sullivan opera than a parting between an arrested commander and the chief mutineer. It resembles the meeting between the major general and the pirate king in the " Pirates of Penzance ".

Cheap spoke to Bulkeley in the " most tender and affectionate manner; and as a Token of his Friendship and regard for me, desir'd me to accept of a Suit of his best Wearing Apparel. He gave me his Hand with a great deal of cheerfulness, wishing me well and safe to England."

We may be justified in relying more on the cooper's version, which reads:

" Just as we were going off, Bulkeley would run to take a final Adieu of that Gentleman [Cheap], and give him a friendly Embrace. He return'd seemingly much affected with the tender Reception he had found, and the melting Farewell at parting. Some of the Circumstances we fancied were of his own Invention, as they were quite unsuitable with the gallant Spirit of that haughty Officer, whose Genius and Disposition were formed to command, but never could descend to cringe or wheedle. To hear Bulkeley's moving Account, you would have thought he was painting the last Seperation of David and Jonathan."

As the *Speedwell* got under way the mutineers gave three cheers for the three lonely figures left on shore. These were returned.

The gunner and many others were unquestionably relieved to be leaving Cheap behind, more especially as they never expected to see him again. Bulkeley's account of the departure scene includes a eulogy which reads like an obituary: " This was the last Time I ever saw the unfortunate Captain Cheap. He was a Gentleman possess'd of many Virtues; he was an excellent Seaman himself, and lov'd a Seaman; as for personal Bravery, no Man had a larger Share of it; even when a Prisoner he preserv'd the Dignity of a Commander; no Misfortunes could dispirit or deject him, and Fear was a Weakness he was entirely a Stranger to; the loss of the Ship was the Loss of him; he knew how to govern while he was a Commander on Board, but when Things were brought to Confusion and Disorder, he thought to establish his Command ashore by his Courage, and to suppress the least Insult on his Authority on the first Occasion. An instance of this was seen on the Boatswain's first appearing ashore; shooting Mr. Cozens, and treating him in the Manner he did after his Confinement, was highly resented by the People, who soon got the Power in their own Hand, the Officers only had the Name, and they were compell'd, for the Preservation of their Lives, to comply sometimes with their most unreasonable Demands; and it is a Miracle, amidst the Wildness and Distraction of the People, that there was no more Blood shed." Cheap himself had said that he must " die by inches in a voyage ". Bulkeley little realized that perhaps the real danger might lie in the weak and incompetent officer who had become his new commander.

But this was not quite the end of the first act. That must be left for a week later.

As soon as the schooner split her topsail the barge came to her assistance. Her own oars were got out and she was pulled clear of the rocks. The boats then bore away for a large sandy bay, where at four the schooner anchored in ten fathoms; the barge and cutter proceeded inshore. The shore was desolate but there were many who preferred this to a night in cramped quarters on board. The following afternoon the boats again got under way to make trial trips, returning once more to their ten fathom anchorage in the place they called Cheap's Bay. The schooner appeared to sail well, though very crowded with her fifty-nine occupants.

Now that Cheap had been left behind, it was considered necessary to put the fact in writing and to have signatures from all those concerned, excepting of course those who had been marooned. They doubtless would have refused signature. This memorial, which was by no means the last, ran as follows:

" These are to certify the Right Honourable the Lords Commissioners for Executing the Office of Lord High Admiral of Great-Britain, That we, whose Names are mention'd, do beg Leave to acquaint your Lordships, that Captain David Cheap, our late Commander in H.M.S. *Wager,* having publickly declar'd that he never will go off this Spot, at his own Request desires to be left behind, but Captain Pemberton, of H.M. Land Forces, having confined him a Prisoner for the Death of Mr. Henry Cozens, Midshipman, with Lieutenant Hamilton for breaking his Confinement, did insist on delivering them up on the Beach to the Charge of Lieutenant Beans; but he, with his Officers, and People, consulting the ill Consequences that might attend carrying two Prisoners off in so small a Vessel, and for so long and tedious a Passage as we are likely to have, and that they might have opportunities of acting such Things in secret as may prove destructive to the whole Body; and also in Regard to the Chief Article of Life, as the greatest Part of the People must be oblig'd, at every Place we stop, to go on Shore in Search of Provisions, and there being now no less than eighty-one Souls in this small Vessel, which we hope to be deliver'd in; we therefore, to prevent any Difficulties to be added to the unforeseen we have to encounter with, think proper to agree, and in order to prevent Murder, to comply with Captain David Cheap's request: The Surgeon also begs Leave to be left with him. Dated on Board the *Speedwell* Schooner in Cheap's Bay, this 14th Day of October, 1741.

> Robert Beans, Lieutenant
> Thomas Clark, Master
> John King, Boatswain
> John Bulkeley, Gunner
> John Cummins, Carpenter
> Robert Elliot, Surgeon's Mate
> John Jones, Master's Mate
> John Snow,   do.
> Captain Pemberton, of H.M. Land Forces
> Vincent Oakley, Surgeon of   do.

This must have been the result of second thoughts. The act of compelling the captain to remain behind would have been incriminating. The memorial however stated, untruly, that the captain had declared that he would never leave the spot, as if to imply that he was afraid of justice. This was incriminating evidence against Cheap, though unsubstantiated. The captain had declared repeatedly that he would go northward to join Anson. His last request before the departure of the mutineers was that the deserters on the other side of the island should be offered a chance of joining him for his journey northward.

But Bulkeley's party were not to have it all their own way. On the following day there was a slight twist in the act before the curtain dropped for the interval.

It was Thursday the 15th October, with an unusual predawn stillness in Cheap's Bay. The *Speedwell* was at anchor some distance offshore. The cutter and barge were inshore. A signal was made by firing five muskets for the boats to come offshore preparatory to making sail. At daylight the three vessels got under sail, the wind now freshening from the west. As soon as they had left Cheap's Bay they ran into heavy seas and a great swell, and were obliged to put into a small bay in which a lee was provided by a large ledge of rocks. It was now realized that there would be repeated needs for repairing sails. It was therefore decided to send the barge with nine hands back to Cheap's Bay, which they had left at daylight, to bring off a supply of canvas that had been left behind.

It is not known if volunteers were called for. The canvas party consisted of two midshipmen John Byron and Alexander Campbell, two quarter gunners William Harvey and David Buckley, two quartermasters William Rose and Richard Noble, one seaman John Bosman, the captain's steward Peter Plastow, and a marine Rowland Crusset. Five of these had been signatories to the petition to journey in the yawl before it was bequeathed to Cheap, "for the easement of the boat now building ". It is certain that they were friends and probably disliked some of the " intolerable Inconveniences " and thugs in the *Speedwell*. Perhaps they were the normal crew of the barge for this week, with Campbell in command. Be that as it may, it is clear that Byron made a special request to be also one of the party to fetch the canvas. It transpired that all in the barge wished to rejoin Cheap.

"Being now out at Sea," says Campbell, " I had an Opportunity of speaking to the People that were with me in the Barge, and represented to them what a Shame it was to leave their Captain in such a Situation; and added, ' That if they did get Home, which they could not reasonably hope to do the Way they were going, they would be hanged for Mutiny. But if, on the other Hand, we should go back to the Captain, and with him to the Northward, we had a much better Chance.' " It is apparent that some collusion had already taken place.

"I thought this a good opportunity of returning," says Byron, " and therefore made one with those who went upon this business in the barge. We were no sooner clear of the long-boat than all those in the boat with me declared they had the same intention."

The barge returned to Wager Island and the occupants were given a welcome by Cheap. They received a small amount of food as a reward, but were told that they would have to fend for themselves from then on. The following day Byron therefore asked leave to return to the *Speedwell* in an attempt to get their share of provisions. Cheap agreed but warned him that if he went in the barge it would certainly be taken back. Byron said he only wanted to be landed on the main, and would walk the rest of the journey and back to the landing place, returning by barge on completion of his mission.

Byron, accompanied by Campbell and three of the barge's

crew, set out on their journey on Sunday the 18th. Byron describes his walk on the mainland as the most dreadful imaginable, through thick woods and swamps all the way. Bulkeley
describes Byron's visit and makes it clear that there was some
deception, though Byron does not say so, for the return of the
barge was promised as soon as the weather improved, Byron
implying that the barge was still in Cheap's Bay. No provisions
were allowed, and Byron returned from his mission empty-
handed, though he was offered a hat to replace one he had lost.
According to Bulkeley, a seaman John Duck forced a hat on his
head which Byron refused, saying, "John, I thank you; if I
accept of your kindness, you must go bareheaded; and, I think,
I can bear Hardships as well as the best of you, and must use
myself to them."

Bulkeley soon afterwards took eight men ashore and went
overland to Cheap's Bay to look for the barge, and to get the
canvas. They found neither. Bulkeley says it was plain that the
barge's crew never intended to return, though they said they
would, but his biggest surprise was that Byron "should be
influenc'd by Mr. Campbell, a Person whom he always held in
Contempt". But he believed that Byron defected because he
was "oblig'd to lie forward with the Men; as were the Carpenter and myself, when below: It is very certain, that we are so
closely pent up for want of room, that the worst Jail in England is a Palace to our present Situation".

The act is about to close with this first setback to the mutineers, the loss of a tender to the *Speedwell* being of more consequence than the defection of nine men, for it would be vital to
go ashore for water and food.

For victuals they were still doing relatively well, finding sea-
fowl and shellfish in abundance. The cold and boisterous
weather continued.

John Young shows how affronted they all were at the change
of heart. With the fall of the curtain on this act we will read an

extract from his " affecting narrative " which grimly reveals the sort of life that now faced the mutineers.

" The Conduct of these People surpriz'd and vexed us not a little. They had all, except the Captain's Steward, approv'd of going Southward, and were ever as forward as any in urging it, and blaming our Commander for being otherwise disposed: What then could engage them to quit us for a different Course? . . . This depriving us of the Barge gave the utmost Uneasiness: For having nothing to serve as a Tender now but the Cutter, we were in Danger of being presently reduced to starve, should any Accident befal her.

" For several Days, after this Separation, we went on encountering every Thing that was most terrible: The furious Waves frequently threatening to overwhelm us: the Rocks often menacing immediate Destruction: and the Prospect of that horridest Tormentor, Famine, continually before our Eyes. All these impending Evils were still enhanc'd, by the indolent listless Temper of some among us, who were, thro' Fatigue and Despair, become regardless of Life, and could scarcely be mov'd to do any Thing toward even their own Preservation; or, by the Inquietude and Turbulence of others, who were ready to Mutiny, tho' they had hardly Room to breath, if their brutal Demands were not instantly satisfied.

" Add to this, that being so closely pent up, the Steams of our Bodies and filthy wet Apparel infected the Air about us to such a Degree, that it was almost intolerable, and enough to cause a Pestilence."

CHAPTER 9

VOYAGE OF THE *SPEEDWELL*

BULKELEY'S PARTY having realized that they had lost the barge, prepared for their journey southward. They proceeded on Monday the 26th October in fair weather, Bulkeley in charge in the cutter for that week towing the schooner out of the bay. In spite of the presence of Baynes in command conditionally, Bulkeley seems to have assumed virtual command and direction, and found little opposition at first to his proposals. The majority were tired and hungry, and content to let somebody else do the thinking and administration. The surprising thing is that Bulkeley found either the time or the facilities for keeping his journal.

At times in severe weather the cutter was taken in tow by the schooner. In coming to an anchorage the schooner relied upon soundings taken by the cutter proceeding ahead. Slowly, by devious routes across boisterous seas and through rocky channels, they made their way southward.

Some extracts from Bulkeley's journal give a good idea of the sort of existence the crews lived. It should be realized that while anchored inshore there was much to be done in seeking food, but while under way there was little that the crews could do because of the overcrowding. The work of sailing the vessels could be carried out by two or three hands only.

"Saturday, 31st October, This Morning cast loose, and row'd towards the Mouth of the Lagoon, designing to put out to Sea; but the Wind blew so hard, that we were oblig'd to come to an Anchor. This Afternoon, in weighing the Grapenel, in order to go to the Cove, we found it foul among some rocks; all Hands haul'd, took a turn round the Mainmast, and went aft: which weigh'd the Grapenel, but streighten'd one of the Flukes: Here the land is very high and steep on each Side; the Carpenter and Cooper were on the highest of these Hills, and found deep Ponds of Water on the Top of them: The whole Navy of England may lay with Safety in many of these Lagoons; but the Coast is too dangerous for any Ship to fall in with the Land. The People To-day were very much afflicted with the Gripes, and Pains in their Side. We are so closely pent up for want of room, that our Lodging is very uncomfortable; the Stench of the Mens wet Cloaths makes the Air we breathe nauseous to that Degree, that one would think it impossible for a Man to live below.

"Monday, November the 2nd, at five in the Morning, Came to sail with the Wind at S. and S. by E. At Noon the Wind came to the W. and W.N.W. in small Breezes: This Day I had a very good Observation, it being the first since we left Cheap's Island. We found ouselves in the Latitude of 50° oo′ S.

"In the Evening anchored in a fine sandy Bay: Here we also saw Indian Huts but no People; To-day we shot wild Geese in Abundance, and got of Shell-Fish, as Limpets and Mussels."

All went well while they had the cutter. But on the 3rd November the cutter parted from the schooner. This was

blamed on the obstinacy of those in the cutter. The trouble
began when the cutter split her square-sail and refused a tow
by the schooner. The schooner followed her, closing rocks and
breakers in squally weather until it was deemed wiser to keep
further off-shore. In a squall those in the schooner lost sight
of the cutter. When the squall lifted, nothing was to be seen
of the cutter. The prospect now was grim indeed for those in
the schooner. Without a boat in which to go close inshore it
was not possible to get food or water. "We are now in a most
wretched condition," wrote Bulkeley: "People on board are so
regardless of Life, that they really appear quite indifferent
whether they shall live or die: and it is with much Intreaty
that any of them can be prevailed on to come upon Deck, to
assist for their Preservation."

The purser had been doing his week in command of the
cutter with ten men. Bulkeley gives the list as follows:

Name	Quality	Age	Where born
Thomas Harvey	Purser	25	Westminster
John Mooring	Boatswain's Mate	34	Gosport
William Oram	Carpenter's Crew	28	Philadelphia
Richard Phipps	Boatswain's Mate	30	Bristol
Matthew Langley	Gunner's Mate	34	Exeter
John George	Seamen	22	Wandsworth
Nicholas Griselham	do.	31	Ipswich
James Stewart	do.	35	Aberdeen
James Roach	do.	21	Cork
James Butler	do.	32	Dublin
John Allen	do.	18	Gosport

Gales continued all that day and the next; in the absence of
food from shore precious rations of flour and beef had to be
issued. On the Thursday following there was a lull with insufficient wind for sailing. While they were at anchor the
boatswain made a raft from bars and water barrels, intended to
carry three men ashore for food. It was not very effectual. No

sooner had it been launched over the side with the three men than it capsized. Two swam back to the schooner. The boat-swain clutched the raft and with difficulty got ashore, returning to *Speedwell* in the evening.

Burney in his *Voyages and Discoveries* says this was " an idle and helpless crew ". He remarks that there was a carpenter on board, an abundance of wood ashore, and in view of the season no reason not to have found a sheltered harbour and built a small boat. But this was a mutinous crew that had seen theft, violence, and murder, who lived in an atmosphere of suspicion, envy, and jealousy, and felt that they owed allegiance to nobody. The lieutenant, the conditional commander, was a weakling. The gunner, the real leader, was under threat of his life, and himself had performed a miracle in keeping so many together in some sort of discipline and in bringing into execution a possible plan. With the daily diminution of food supplies, few except the far-sighted, would have accepted delay at this stage.

However, on the Friday, to the inexpressible joy of all in the *Speedwell*, the cutter was sighted and that night was made fast astern of the *Speedwell* instead of anchoring inshore. Normally when inshore all but four of the cutter's crew slept ashore. On this night only two remained in the cutter as boat-keepers. The congestion below in the schooner must have been frightful. At eleven it came on to blow and heavy rain fell. One of the boat-keepers then shifted to the schooner. At two the cutter broke loose and was quickly carried away. The rain was so heavy that visibility was reduced to a boat's length. The cooper said that James Stewart the boat-keeper cried out when she broke loose, and they did all they could to recover the boat and save him. It is difficult to imagine what they could have done. The gunner said that the boat-keeper could not hear them, and in a short time, the boat being out of sight, they believed she must be stove in among the rocks, and poor James Stewart lost with her. Of the original eighty-one who sailed from Wager Island, seventy-one remained, and all now had to be accommodated in the *Speedwell*. Worse than that was the absence of a boat for inshore work. But few gave much thought to the calamity. Bulkeley found it necessary to read the riot act.

"The loss of the Cutter," he wrote, "gives the few thinking People aboard a great deal of uneasiness; not above six give themselves the least Concern for the Preservation of their Lives, but are rather the reverse, being ripe for Mutiny and Destruction; this is a great Affliction to the Lieutenant, myself, and the Carpenter; we know not what to do to bring them under any Command; they have troubled us to that Degree, that we are weary of our Lives; therefore this Day we have told the People, that, unless they alter their Conduct, and subject themselves to Command, that we will leave them to themselves, and take our Chance in this desolate Part of the Globe, rather than give ourselves any farther Concern about so many thoughtless Wretches: Divided the People into four Watches, to make more room below. The People have promis'd to be under Government, and seem much easier."

The gunner's hopes were not realized. The following morning the men pressed for their provisions to be issued, and though it was four days before the authorized date they would not listen to reason. There followed an event which savours of chicanery on the gunner's part. He says that several of the "People" now wished to be put ashore with their allowance of provisions, expressing an intention of returning to the northward. They thought there was a chance of finding the cutter, or of making a canoe. The cooper writes similarly and says they would not be dissuaded, but adds that they could not be worse off ashore than they were in the *Speedwell* where "we could scarcely breath for want of Space, and were perishing through Scarcity of Food." The schooner was hauled close inshore and the men put ashore.

To square his yard-arm Bulkeley got these fellows to sign a certificate indicating that this was their own choice. It ran:

" These are to certify the Right Honourable the Lords Commissioners for Executing the Office of Lord High Admiral of Great Britain, etc. That we, whose Names are undermention'd, Since the Misfortune of losing the Cutter, have considered the ill Conveniences and Difficulties to be attended, where so great a Number of People are to be carried off: therefore we have requested, and desired the Officers and Company remaining of the same Vessel to put us on Shore with such Necessaries of Life as can be conveniently spared out of the Vessel. We, of our own free Will and Choice, do indemnify all Persons from ever being call'd to an Account for putting us on Shore, or leaving us behind, contrary to our Inclination. Witness our Hands, on Board the *Speedwell* schooner, in the Latitude 50:40 S. this 8th Day of November, 1741. Which was sign'd by the following People, viz."

Matthew Langley, Gunner's Mate
John Russell, Armourer
George Smith, Cook's Mate
William Callicutt, Washerman
John Williamson, Marine
John McLeod, Boatswain's Servant
John Hart, Joiner
Joseph Turner, Captain's Servant
Richard Phipps, Boatswain's Mate
Harry Mortimer, Marine.

Witness:

John Cummins, Carpenter
John Snow, Master's Mate
Vincent Oakley, Surgeon of the Army.

A glance at the names and rates will show that with the exception of Phipps and Langley who were in the cutter's crew when she lost sight of the *Speedwell*, these were men who were regarded as " idlers " and could well be spared and would put up little opposition. Burney goes so far as to say, " There can be no doubt that these men were picked out as sacrifices to the safety of the rest. The certificate, whether obtained from them, or a forgery, was probably one of Bulkeley's cunning contrivances." It may have been an afterthought, as perhaps was the memorial explaining why Cheap had been left behind. There is certainly a similarity between the two.

The " volunteers " were never heard of again.

There were now sixty in the *Speedwell* which was one more than the original number at Wager Island. Two days later, on the 10th December, they entered the Straits of Magellan and went under foresail, steering south-east with a following breeze. " I never in my Life, in any Part of the World," writes Bulkeley, " have seen such a Sea as runs here; we expected every Wave to swallow us, and the Boat to founder. This Shore is full of small Islands, rocks, and Breakers; we are oblig'd to keep her right before the Sea. At Five broach'd to, at which we all believ'd she would never rise again. We were surrounded with rocks, and so near that a Man might toss a Bisket on them. It blew a Hurricane of Wind, with thick rainy Weather, that we could not see twice the Boat's Length; we pray'd earnestly . . . it was granted us from above . . . After sailing amidst Islands, rocks, and Breakers, for above a League, we got safe into a Good Harbour. We call this Harbour the ' Port of God's Mercy ', esteeming our Preservation this Day to be a Miracle. The most abandon'd among us no longer doubt of an Almighty Being, and have promis'd to reform their Lives."

These are strong and moving words from a mutineer, but Bulkeley, like most seamen, was pious.

During the next five days they were able to get ashore occasionally. They procured a mangy dog from Indians, in exchange for a pair of trousers; also a large tough seal, and some mussels, but these were insufficient to stave off the hunger of sixty. On Sunday the 15th November a traffic in food took place on board, beginning with silver buckles being exchanged for flour. Twelve shillings was paid for a pound of flour, rising to a guinea by nightfall. Many were now in an advanced stage of starvation. The next day George Bateman a boy of sixteen died of starvation, and two days later died Thomas Caple, a boy of twelve, son of a deceased lieutenant, whose guardian was on board with him. The guardian had in trust for the boy twenty guineas, a watch, and a silver cup. In response to entreaty from the starving boy to buy flour, he told him he must keep the money in order to buy clothes in Brazil.

" I shall never live to see the Brazil," uttered the poor boy. " I am starving; starved almost to death. For Christ's sake have compassion on me and give me only the silver cup, to procure me a little food, that I may be relieved from my insupportable torture. A morsel of victuals is of more worth to me than all the apparel in the world."

" But his Tears and Solicitations to that obdurate Man," wrote the cooper, " were in vain: Heaven only heard, and succoured him by putting a Period to his Breath."

Both Bulkeley and John Young describe the scenes of starving men and the inhumanity of those still with some food, so intent on their own preservation as to be void of all compassion for those without.

The passage of the Straits of Magellan caused severe differences of opinion between Bulkeley and the lieutenant. From Cape Pillar at the Pacific end to Cape Virgins at the Atlantic end the Straits are nearly 350 miles in length, varying in width from a mile or two in the narrow parts to thirty miles or so in the wider. There is no obvious straight or direct channel all the way through, for in many parts the channel bifurcates or

trifurcates. Even though the mutineers had Sir John Narborough's instructions it was not always clear which course
should be taken, for the simple reason that the navigators were
not always certain where they were. They were not even certain
of having arrived at Cape Pillar at the entrance to the Straits,
where the width is twenty-five miles, though Bulkeley himself
was convinced. Nor were they certain when continuing along
some channel whether this might lead on correctly or come
eventually to an abrupt halt after days of hard and difficult
sailing, for there are lagoons of vast length that eventually lead
nowhere.

"It is no Wonder we were thus sadly embarrassed," writes
John Young, referring to increasing hunger and the mortifica-
tion of having to retrace steps. "Beside the Gunner and Carpenter there was not an Officer on board that would come on
Deck to make any Observations, or would stay there longer
than his Watch absolutely required. If others had done their
Duty as became them in such a Conjuncture, and been as careful in keeping a Reckoning, as, to their great Commendation, it
must be own'd these two were, we had not been exposed to so
many Vexations as we daily suffered, but should probably have
pass'd through the Streights ere this, and been far advanced
beyond 'em to the Northward."

From the 25th of November to the 5th of December they
returned all the way back to the entrance, just to get a sight of
Cape Pillar, so as to ascertain their exact position and starting
point again.

"About Four of the Clock," says John Young, "Mr.
Bulkeley once more got sight of Cape Pillar, bearing W. by N.
at the Distance of eight Leagues. On this fresh Discovery
(which gave him a double Pleasure, both as it serv'd to ascertain our Situation and direct our Course, and as it afforded him
a Subject of Triumph over all the Company) he call'd on the
Lieutenant, and shewing it to him, ask'd, Whether he still

doubted of that being the Cape? The Gentleman, being now convinc'd, acknowledged his Error, and was heartily asham'd and vexed in reflecting on the many Dangers we had encountered, and the Disgrace arising to himself, by his Ignorance and Pertinacity. Had he believed the Gunner, when he formerly pointed out to him this Landmark, or had our Patience held out but long enough to have carried us a few Miles farther, we had escaped numerous Troubles, and not spent a woful Fortnight in coming back, only to have a second View of Cape Pillar."

However the confirmation now removed doubt and put new life into many. Increasing hope of salvation dulled the pangs of hunger.

Three men died on Monday the 30th November. These were Peter Delroy, barber, Thomas Thorpe and Thomas Woodhead, marines. "They all perished for want of Food," wrote Bulkeley: "Several more are in the same Way, being not able to go ashore for Provisions; and those who are well can't get sufficient for themselves; therefore the Sick are left destitute of all relief ". It was clearly now a case of every man for himself. If he were unable to swim, or too weak, he was practically doomed. There was a grisly annex to this note, referring to a fact which the cooper also described. "There is one thing to be taken Notice of in the Death of these People, that some Hours before they die, they are taken light-headed, and fall a joking and laughing; and in this Humour they expire."

However while in the Straits, now convinced they were on the correct route, they found it easier to get ashore to find food such as shellfish, seal, geese, and two dogs which they acquired from Indians: "equal in Goodness to the best Mutton in England ".

" Those we spied, or traded with," wrote John Young referring to these Indians, " had Women among them; but, as soon as we approached, the Females fled into the Woods, so that we had a very transient and imperfect View of them ". This is hardly surprising considering the ragged, dirty, and skeleton appearance of the *Wager* men, many of whom were half demented by now. " However," continues Young, " from such a Behaviour we may infer, their Reservedness and Virtue are not inferior to those of our most delicate European Ladies ". This was a nice bit of irony from one who was near death's door.

On the 8th December marine John Turner died, and on the following day marine Robert Vicars, both for want of food.

The boatswain swam ashore on the 10th to look for fresh water, which he discovered after half an hour. Otherwise there is little reference to this officer at any time except when he is stirring up trouble. He was a low type always consorting with the trouble-makers among the men. It is a relief therefore to hear of him performing some useful act. The *Speedwell* was in a treacherous spot where there was rocky ground and a big rise and fall with fast tidal streams, but it was essential to fill up with water for the long voyage in the Atlantic which they were shortly to begin. Casks were landed with the men at high water and recovered at the next high water. Twice the schooner grounded during this operation but fortunately received no damage.

" We have several Times very narrowly escap'd being made a Wreck," says Bulkeley, " and some Times have been pre-serv'd when we have seen our Fate before our Eyes, and every Moment expected it, and when all the Conduct and Ability of Men could have avail'd nothing. Any one, who has been a Witness of these Providential Deliverances, and doubts the being of a Supreme Power, disqualifies himself from any Title to all future Mercy, and justly deserves the Wrath of an incens'd Deity." Bulkeley could be so righteous at times that one sometimes wonders if Burney's appellation " cunning " is justified. We shall find him guilty of yet another action that

might savour of treachery or callousness, but without knowing
to what extent he was browbeaten by the rest it is unfair to
judge. He himself is always complaining of their mutinous
behaviour.

The final passage of the Straits after returning to the
entrance at Cape Pillar took only seven days, giving an average
of fifty miles a day to Cape Virgins. But they had prior to that
wasted twenty-five days owing to the stupidity and interference
of Baynes. Now they were faced with the long passage to the
Rio Grande, a journey of 1,500 miles. This proved to be the
most straightforward part of the whole voyage, sailing generally
in a direction north-north-east, cutting across the vast bays
from cape to cape. Winds were variable at first in the high
latitudes and often on-shore, frequently blowing strongly, but
progress was rapid. Bulkeley records a day's run from noon the
14th to noon the 15th December as 104 miles, having arrived
in latitude 49° 10′ south. This gives an average speed of $4\frac{1}{3}$
knots, but it seems likely that he is referring to distance and
speed made good in a N.N.E. direction. The distance run
may have been at least half as much again, from which we
might deduce the *Speedwell* as being capable of 8 knots or
more. In general it was seldom that she made good much more
than fifty miles a day.

On the 16th December they put into Port Desire in about
48° south, having now almost reached, in the Atlantic, the latitude in which the wreck of the *Wager* lay on the Pacific side
of the mainland. Here on Seal Island they killed more seal in
half an hour than they could carry off. " The People eating
greedily of the Seal, were seiz'd with violent Feavers and Pains
in their Heads," says Bulkeley. " The People grow very turbulent and uneasy, requiring Flour to be serv'd out: which in our
present Circumstances, is a most unreasonable request: we
have but one Cask of Flour on Board, and a great Distance to
run into the Brazil, and no other Provision in the Boat but the

Seal we have kill'd here: Nay, they carry their Demands much
higher, insisting that the Marine Officers, and such People as
cannot be assisting in working the Boat, shall have but half the
Allowance of the rest: accordingly they have pitch'd upon
twenty to be serv'd half a Pound of Flour each Man, and themselves a Pound. This Distinction the Half-Pounders complain
of, and the twenty are selected to be starv'd."

The original controller of all provisions and supplies in the
Wager, the purser Thomas Harvey, was himself short of food
now, in spite of his office and in spite of his comparative wealth
as a gentleman ashore. The men regarded him as an " idler ";
one of those selected for diminished rations.

On leaving Port Desire on the 26th December, Bulkeley
took Cape Blanco as a point of departure for the long sea journey of 600 to 700 miles N.N.E. to the next prominent cape.
Two days later, in fair weather and only a moderate gale, the
" People " insisted on a final share-out of the remaining flour.
" To prevent a Mutiny," says John Young, " a final Partition
was this Day made of the remaining Flour, amounting to three
Pound and a half each Man. This was soon devoured; so that
we had nothing henceforth to subsist on, but the Seal we
brought from Port Desire; and that, for want of curing, was a
most nauseous Diet, which extreme Hunger only prevailed
with us to feed on: And yet, truly, it was suitable enough, both
to the Disposition and State of those who were forced to eat
it; for as, in Respect of Temper, they were vile enough to
deserve even worse, so were their external Circumstances as
filthy and loathsome as the putrified Fish; nay, of the two, I
think we stunk the most, beside being overspread with Vermin." These final words are reminiscent of the words of Dandy
Kidd, spoken just before his death in the *Pearl* a year earlier.

Poor Thomas Harvey the purser died on the 6th January
during that long sea journey. He was a young man of twenty-
five who had probably paid a large sum for his appointment in

the hope of making a fortune. His opposite number in the little
Tryal was to have much better luck. This was purser Lawrence
Millechamp, who transferred as a supplementary from the
Tryal to the *Gloucester* and later to the *Centurion*. Though
not permitted a share of the vast prize money which went to
every complemented officer in Anson's flagship, he did very
well and eventually returned to England.*

Thomas Harvey's death was the subject of misplaced wit
by John Bulkeley, who wrote: " He died a Skeleton for want
of Food. This Gentleman probably was the first Purser belonging to his Majesty's Service, that ever perish'd with Hunger ".
Four days later he wrote: " We have nothing to eat but stinking Seal, and not above twenty out of forty-three which are
now alive have even that; and such hath been our Condition
for this Week past: nor are we better off in regard to Water,
there not being above eighty Gallons aboard. Never were
beheld a Parcel of more miserable Objects; there are not above
fifteen of us healthy (if People may be call'd healthy that are
scarce able to crawl). I am reckon'd at present one of the
strongest Men in the Boat, yet can hardly stand on my Legs
ten Minutes together, nor even that short Space of Time without holding: Every Man of us hath had a new Coat of Skin
from Head to Foot: We that are in the best State of Health,
do all we can to encourage the rest."

But the best encouragement of all occurred that same afternoon on Sunday the 10th January. Bulkeley had worked his
reckoning at noon to find that they were only thirteen leagues
from land.

" At Four this Afternoon," he wrote, " we were almost
transported with Joy at the Sight of Land (having seen no
Land for fourteen Days before). We ran in, and at Eight
anchor'd in eight Fathoms; fine Sand about a League from
Shore."

*See the author's *Admiral Lord Anson* (Cassell).

Only another 450 miles to the Rio Grande. But starvation had claimed another victim. " This Day perish'd for want of Food Serjeant Ringall."

At four the next morning they weighed and sailed N.E. by E. about a mile off the shore, along a delightful coast on which they could see horses. In the evening they anchored in $3\frac{1}{2}$ fathoms in a sandy bay where to their dismay there were such breakers that they were forced to lie off.

" We had nothing at all on board to eat," said John Young, " and but a single Cask of Water, which last was barely sufficient for the present allaying our parching Thirst . . . We hoped the Skill and Courage of some of us might avail to convey them through the Breakers to Land, and back again to the Boat with Provisions. But now it was not every Man that had Boldness enough to engage in this perilous Undertaking; so that, at first, there was rather a general backwardness. Lieutenant Ewers and two other inferior Officers seeing this, determin'd to excite an Emulation in the Crew, and bravely set an Example, by first plunging into the briny Element. These three were instantly followed by eleven of the Stalwart Fellows among us, who jump'd overboard after them. Thirteen of these Adventurers to our unspeakable Joy, reach'd the Terra firma; and one of them, a Marine, had the Misfortune to be drowned in the Attempt."

The two " inferior " officers were the boatswain and the carpenter.

Four quartercasks were put over the side, to each of which were lashed four firelocks and ammunition. These were driven ashore by the surf.

Bulkeley called this place Shoalwater Bay, and later Freshwater Bay. He describes how those left on board, of whom only two could swim, watched seals being shot, cut up, and cooked. But the wind blew so hard that it was dangerous to allow the schooner any closer inshore. The lieutenant suggested making a raft with a line by which the seal could be hauled aboard, and one of the swimmers to go ashore with it.

"With much Entreaty," says Bulkeley, "these two Swimmers were prevail'd on to cast Lots; the Lot falling on the weakest of 'em, who was a young Lad about fifteen Years of Age, and scarce able to stand, we would not suffer him to go. While our Brethren were regaling in the fulness of Plenty ashore, we aboard were oblig'd to strip the Hatches of a Seal-skin; we burnt the Hair off the Skin, and for want of any Thing else fell to chewing the Seal-skin."

The following morning was calm. The people ashore shot a horse and a wild dog. The schooner was veered close inshore and a raft was made of hatches lashed to oars. Horse, seal, and three casks of water were swum off and hauled on board by the efforts of those ashore. One more quartercask and two breakers were sent ashore to be filled with water. King, Cummins, and Ewers together with two of the men had arrived on board while the remaining eight were still ashore, when, according to Bulkeley, "a Sea-breeze came in, and blow'd so hard that we were oblig'd to weigh; leaving ashore one Quarter-Cask, two Breakers, and Eight of the People". The order of mention is significant. "The Wind at E.S.E. and a tumbling Sea, came to an Anchor about a league off the Shore; we shar'd the Provisions among the Company; we still see the People ashore, but can't get them off."

During the night they had hard gales from E.S.E. and the sea was so great that it broke off the schooner's rudder head. There is no question that in such a position they were wise to put to sea, but they must be condemned for not returning later to embark the stranded men who had helped to provision and water them. The wind continuing from E.S.E., the schooner got under way. "We sent ashore," says Bulkeley, "in a scuttled Puncheon some wearing Apparel, four Muskets, with Balls, Powder, Flints, Candles, and several Necessities; and

E

also a Letter to acquaint them of our riding it out till they could get off."

There were now only thirty-three left on board the *Speed-well*. Fewer mouths to feed, and more room in which to breathe. It is fairly evident that Bulkeley had no intention of returning. Among the eight left ashore, "our brethren" as Bulkeley referred to them in the routine memorial, was midshipman Isaac Morris. He wrote: "The weather was fair, and we expected that the schooner would have stretched in for the land, the breeze being moderate and withal off-shore; but to our surprise she continued under sail from us. The most probable reason we could give for such inhuman treatment was, that by lessening their number they might be better accommodated with room and provisions, and we could not but look upon it as the greatest act of cruelty."

This does not quite tally with the last part of Bulkeley's memorial, "which Cask we saw them receive, as also the Letter that was in it; they then fell on their Knees, and made Signals wishing us well."

The signatories to the memorial were:

> Robert Beans, Lieutenant
> John King, Boatswain
> John Bulkeley, Gunner
> Thomas Clark, Master
> John Cummins, Carpenter
> Robert Elliot, Surgeon's Mate
> John Jones, Master's Mate
> John Snow,   do.

The master has already slipped down two places from his authorized position: but he was dying and practically a skeleton.

The memorial ran as follows:

"On Board the *Speedwell* Schooner, on the Coast of South America, in Latitude 37° 25′ South, Longitude from the Meridian of London, 65° 00 West, this 14th Day of January, 1741-1742.

"These are to certify the Right Honourable the Lords Commissioners for Executing the Office of Lord High Admiral of Great Britain, etc. That we, whose Names are undermention'd, having nothing left on Board the Vessel but one Quarter-Cask of water, were oblig'd to put into the first Place we could for Subsistence, which was in Freshwater Bay; where we came to Anchor, as near the Shore as we could, without endangering the Vessel, having no Boat aboard, and a large Surf on the Shore; therefore Mr. King the Boatswain, Mr. Cummins the Carpenter, and Lieutenant Ewers, with eleven of the People, jump'd over-board, in order to swim ashore, with three Casks for Water; in which attempt James Greenham was drown'd in the Surf, off the Shore: The Sea-Breeze coming on, prevented the People getting on Board the same Night; therefore, on Wednesday Morning, it being calm, they brought to the Beach the Casks fill'd with Water, with Seal and other Provisions in great Quantities, which we haul'd on Board. The Boatswain, Carpenter, Lieut. Ewers, and two of the People swam off; but the Sea-Breeze coming in, and the Surf rising, the rest were discourag'd from coming off: we haul'd a good Birth off the Shore, where we lay the Remainder of the Day, and all the Night. The Greatness of the Sea broke off our Rudder-Head, and we expected every Minute the Vessel would founder at her Anchor. Thursday Morning we saw no Probability of the People coming aboard, and the Wind coming out of the Sea, and not one Stick of Fire-wood in the Vessel to dress our Victuals, and it being every Man's Opinion that we must put to Sea or perish, we got up a scuttled Cask, and put into it all Manner of Necessaries,

with four small Arms lash'd to the Cask, and a Letter to
acquaint them of our Danger; which Cask we saw them
receive, as also the Letter that was in it; they then fell on
their Knees, and made Signals wishing us well: at which we
got under Sail, and left our Brethren, whose Names are
under-mention'd."

Names	*Where born*
Guy Broadwater	Blackwall
John Duck	London
Samuel Cooper	Ipswich
Benjamin Smith	Southwark
Joseph Clinch	do.
John Allen	Gosport
John Andrews	Manchester
Isaac Morris	Topsham

Bulkeley remarks in his journal that "Those People had a
good Prospect of getting Provisions, and we believe Inhabitants
are not far off: they have all Necessaries for shooting; we hope
to see them again, but at present we leave 'em to the Care of
Providence and the Wide World."

The futility of all attempts at discipline and strict rationing
for these improvident mutineers must have been evident in the
minds of the leaders. This is obvious if we refer to the water
situation after leaving Freshwater Bay. On Monday the 18th
January, being reduced to twenty gallons for thirty-three
people, they went to an allowance of a pint of water per man
per day. The water should then have lasted for five days. But
by the following day at dawn "we had not one Drop of Water
on Board". On this day Bulkeley again made a fair landfall. At
four in the morning he saw breakers right ahead, and land
to the northward. They had arrived in the great estuary off the
River Plate, and were approaching the English Bank. Soon they
altered course to sail along the shore, steering all day E.N.E.

to avoid falling into the hands of Spaniards. At evening they put into a fine sandy bay. The boatswain and several others swam ashore to get water. One of these, whether from weakness or the effects of drinking too much water, was drowned in swimming off to the vessel; but a cask of fresh water was got on board to revive the others.

Bulkeley and Cummins went ashore the next morning and met four men. The omniscient gunner could of course speak Portuguese, and learnt that England was still at war with Spain. He also learnt that these men were Spanish fishermen who sold their catch in Buenos Ayres but lived in Montevideo, "two Days Journey from hence". They told Bulkeley that the Spaniards had two 50-gun ships up the River Plate, and one 60-gun ship cruising off Cape St. Mary. This was one of the points the *Speedwell* would have to pass on her way to the Rio Grande. Six weeks earlier a 70-gun ship had parted from her anchors and driven ashore: every man perished.

There were apparently many Spanish settlers in this Portuguese territory. The gunner and carpenter were invited to go with these men, got up behind them, and rode for about a mile to a place where they were entertained "with good Jurk-Beef, roasted and boil'd, with good white Bread". Thinking of their shipmates, or perhaps, more exactly, realizing what reception they would get, the gunner and carpenter asked for bread to take back. They were offered twenty-six small loaves for which a price of four guineas was demanded, and which because they had been without bread so long, they paid. The rest of this tragi-comic opera is delightfully told by the cooper, who was unable to get ashore. One can imagine the chief character: comfortably fat and reassuringly loquacious.

"To soften this hard Bargain a little," says John Young, "a Spanish Priest, Confessor to the Gang, told the Purchasers, that all his Flock would be hang'd, if it were discover'd they had supply'd us with a Morsel of Provision. At the same Time however this Padre was so kind as to offer, in case he had a Gun and Shot, to go kill 'em as much Wild Fowl as would serve our whole Company. On this the Carpenter sent to the Boat for his Fowling Piece and Ammunition, which he delivered to the Father.

" But we did not enjoy the Effect of his Promise: Mr. Cummins lost his Artillery, and we never had the Game: for the Ecclesiastic not coming back by the Time he appointed, and our People having observ'd one of the Company ride off, soon after the former went out (as he pretended) a Fowling; they fancied there was some Design going forward to betray (and perhaps destroy us all)."

" Went on Board," wrote Bulkeley laconically, perhaps rather ashamed at being taken in by a fat priest, " got our Water in, and made all ready for sailing to the Rio Grande."

The lack of food was to be felt seriously during the following days. Each time they attempted to seek food either the wind was contrary or conditions impossible due to breakers and rocks. On Saturday the 23rd January the master Thomas Clark died, followed in death within a few hours by his son. Both were committed to the deep at a burial service on the Sunday. All on board were now in extreme want, perhaps the most pathetic figure being the eighty-two year old cook Thomas Maclean. Ironically he died of starvation within fifteen miles of the shore that was to lead to safety, and within two days of arrival.

It was now hope and expectation only that sustained the crew of the *Speedwell*, frustrated for days in attempts to get food. " Our Disappointment," says John Young, " in Respect of the Provision we hoped for, was a grievous Vexation; one alleviating Circumstance kept up our Spirits! with a brisk Gale in our Favour we were not many leagues off the Rio Grande, which was our desired Port."

On Wednesday the 27th January Bulkeley wrote, " We have

now nothing but a little Water to support Nature. At Noon had an Observation, Latitude in 32° 40′ South: I reckon myself eighteen Leagues from the Rio Grand, and hope to see it in the Morning."

But the end was near, for at six the next morning they sighted the opening of the Rio Grande, having completed the whole journey of over 2,000 miles from Wager Island in fifteen weeks. Of the eighty-one souls who had embarked in the three boats at Wager Island on the 13th October, only thirty now arrived at the Rio Grande. Of these, few were able to walk, and all were starving. Their appearance was so frightful that they were at first regarded with horror by those who came to see them. The stench of their clothes and person can be imagined, and it is all the more creditable that so much compassion and kindness were shown them by the Portuguese authorities. Certainly theirs was a remarkable feat the success of which could be attributed to the gunner and carpenter alone. Without them it would not have been possible even to begin the journey. The fact that the journey was carried out and completed in the face of all kinds of misfortune was due to Bulkeley alone, for without his navigational ability, drive, enterprise, ruthlessness, and those qualities of leadership and resolution that moderated to some extent the futile mouthings and selfish desires of a stupidly brutal mob and incompetent officers such as Baynes, the party would have been wrecked or left high and dry up a desolate lagoon. " I believe," wrote Bulkeley, " no Mortals have experienc'd more Difficulties and Miseries than we have."

Thirty sickly mutinous English sailors had arrived in Brazil. There was still a long way to go to get to England, and there was a war on. We shall follow their subsequent adventures and misfortunes at a later stage. In the meantime it is worth capturing the atmosphere in which they arrived at the Rio Grande, in the words of the cooper:

"On Thursday, the 28th, about seven in the Morning, through the Mercy of God, we discovered the Mouth of the River Grand. The opening of this spacious Stream appeared to our wearied, hungry, and thirsty Souls as the very Gate of Heaven. There is a dangerous Bar at the Entrance, and several Sholes to be carefully passed over, or avoided, in going up it. Mr. Bulkeley undertook to carry us in, and to pilot us to the Town. This he did very judiciously and safely in a few Hours. We dropt Anchor abreast of it, on the East-shore, in less than two Fathom Water. Never did any Creatures come there with more joyful Hearts, or more miserable meagre Countenances. There immediately came a Boat along Side of us, out of which we were boarded by two Men. These were not Custom-House Spies, or Searchers, but of the Military Order. They were vested with Authority to carry some of us ashore, that we might certify the Governor who we were, whence we came, our Business, and the like. We were become such a frightful Crew of Starvelings, that they could not but look on us with a Mixture of Horror and Compassion. Our Gunner, Carpenter, Lieutenant, and Captain P. . . . n went with them. As soon as these landed, they were received with all the Tokens of Friendship imaginable, by every Rank, from the Commander of the Garrison to the lowest of the Vulgar. They were conducted to the best House in the Place, which was the Surgeon's, and there entertain'd with much Affection and Generosity. In the Afternoon, the Governor, who had been Aboard, came to Town. His Behaviour was very humane and courteous; but, however, he was equally strict in examining the Lieutenant, and then Mr. Bulkeley, about a Number of Circumstances. He inquired of the latter (who had been represented to him as our Pilot) if there was any Chart of the Coast on board our Vessel, and being answer'd in the Negative, he was greatly surpriz'd at our venturing on it without one; but profess'd he was mightily pleas'd that we had so happily succeeded. He wonder'd at our hitting the Bar as exactly as if we had frequented the Port; and did not in the Begining forbear insinuating, that we could hardly be such absolute Strangers to the Place as we pretended. But when Bulkeley had set before him the Means whereby he was enabled, with the Blessing of God, to effect all this, and had briefly related our Case, which the other three confirm'd, he not only was satisfied of our being no Impostors, and considered us as real Objects of Pity, but he embraced those four as Friends, rejoycing, as I have already hinted, in the miraculous Preservation and Deliverance, as he deemed it, of us all. He assured the Lieutenant and the rest, that nothing should be wanting which the Country afforded for our Relief and Refreshment. He took those Gentlemen to his own Habitation; and tho' a Quantity of Beef and brown Bread had been sent on board to us, immediately after their going ashore, before he came to Town, yet he now order'd us a further Supply; and gave Directions, that both Officers and People should be plenteously furnish'd with all Conveniences, and that the Sick should be carried to the Hospital, and taken Care of. He was pleased also to give these Persons some Intelligence that was exceedingly grateful to every one of us; and this was of the *Severn* and *Pearl,* two of our unfortunate Squadron, who had undergone many grievous Disasters, tho' not quite so ruinous as those we had suffered. These Ships were now, as he said, at Rio Janeiro, in a distress'd Condition, waiting for an Opportunity of returning to England, whither they had sent for some Hands to work them Home, the Crews that came out with them being so diminished by Death, that there were not Men enough by far left to navigate them. They had parted from the rest of the Squadron off Cape Noir, and put back, as we now first understood, to the Brazils. The former was a new

Vessel; and that Circumstance was thought to contribute to
its Unhealthiness: Before her departure from St. Catherine's
she had thrown more of her People overboard than any other
Ship in Company; so that the Commodore was forced to
recruit her there with a good many fresh Hands; and after
that, so many on board her died, that there was a Necessity
of refurnishing her a second Time, at Sea; notwithstanding
all which, she was reduced to that wretched State I have
mentioned, and had hardly any Men left in her. And tho' the
Pearl was somewhat less sickly than the *Severn,* yet the
Mortality on board her was so destructive, that she was well
nigh depopulated.—But we'll return to our own Affairs.

"After the Governor had thus caress'd and treated our
principal Officers, as I have said, and provided in the friend-
liest Manner for the immediate Support of us all, he desired
our *Speedwell* might be brought as close to the Shore as
could be. This was presently done; and all the Inhabitants of
the Place, Men, Women, and Children, flock'd in Droves to
see this little Ark, in which such a disproportionate Number
of Souls had been so wonderfully sav'd from the devouring
Waters. As soon as she was moor'd, the Governor, the Commander of the Garison, and the Commissary honoured us
with a Visit. When they had surveyed the Vessel, and were
inform'd how many first embark'd therein, at our setting
out, they were utterly amazed, it almost surpassing, as they
said, all Belief. They could not frame any Idea of the Manner in which she was steer'd; they were very curious to be
inform'd what Expedient we had made Use of for this
Purpose; and indeed there did not appear any Place at the
Helm, where a Person might sit to do this Office with Safety.
Bulkeley explain'd to them the Manner however in which it
was perform'd, and they applauded it as an excellent Contrivance. At taking Leave, the Governor renewed his Professions of Concern for our Welfare. He said, our Distress and

Miseries rendered us more welcome in his Eye, than if we had brought the richest Cargoe or Treasures; that nothing in his Power should be omitted for our Relief and Consolation; that the making known our Wants and Desires would be a Pleasure to him, that so he might miss no Occasion of supplying the one, and gratifying the other; and that he would certainly take the first Opportunity of a Ship for sending us to Rio Janeiro, in order for our Passage to England, where, for our own and our Families Sake, he earnestly wished us."

But we must now return to Cheap at Wager Island for whom Bulkeley had already in his mind written an obituary.

CHAPTER 10

FROM BAD TO WORSE

CHEAP WAS overjoyed at the return of the barge, and gave the men food and clothes. Campbell received " three Shirts and two white Waistcoats ". Cheap could play at being captain again; he was in a position to enforce his will on a party that consisted of deserters and mutineers, all of whom had now decided to remain loyal.

At the return of the deserters and mutineers with the barge, the party grew to twenty. With the barge and the yawl available Cheap considered an attempt should be made to pull to the island of Chiloe. The boats must be refitted, and a stock of provisions laid aside for the passage.

For a day or two after their return in the barge, Byron's party had a morsel of food served to them, and Cheap took a hand in the cooking of flour and seaweed fried in tallow. He did little else. After the first two days no more provisions were served: it was now every man for himself.

Three men broke into the store tent to steal flour. They were discovered by the traces of flour scattered about their own tent. Cheap rightly took a severe view of this theft. He ordered the three culprits, Plastow, Ridwood, and Cresswick, to be tied up until they confessed their crime; this they soon did. Almost immediately Plastow escaped and fled into the woods. The other two were severely whipped; after which Cresswick escaped. The following morning Ridwood was taken to a barren island and left there. A boat was sent for Ridwood three days later, but by this time he had died of exhaustion and exposure.

Cheap's party so recently augmented to twenty had already been reduced to seventeen, but with the return of the two escaped prisoners rose again to nineteen.

The weather continued wet and stormy all through October and November of 1741, but with the approach of the summer solstice there was some improvement. A further stroke of luck was the recovery of three casks of salt beef from the wreck which by now had almost completely broken up. The beef greatly restored the party to health and strength. In mid-December it was decided to launch the barge and the yawl, and to travel along the coast northward for about 300 miles to the island of Chiloe.

The boats they had were very small for such a stormy passage as could be expected on this coast, and, although fitted with sails as well as oars, they would cover much of the journey by sustained pulling: exhausting work at the best of times, and particularly so in these conditions without adequate food or water. The barge was a largish narrow boat, a little more than thirty feet in length with a beam of seven feet. The yawl was more squat, well under thirty feet in length with a beam of five or six feet.

Cheap, Elliot, and Byron were in the barge with nine men pulling. Hamilton and Campbell were in the yawl with five men pulling. The midshipmen steered.

In less than two hours the wind freshened and veered to westward, and they met huge seas. Each boat could see the other only when on the crest of great waves. Waves swept over the gunwales, washing provisions from side to side on the bottom boards. Each boat was gradually filling. It seemed impossible to survive in such a sea. The wind was now bearing them on-shore. In desperation they grasped everything within reach and threw it overboard: provisions, stores, ropes, canvas, and grapnels. All the precious items so carefully saved in the last few months were now lost. Night was coming on and the boats were being borne fast towards the surf breaking on great rocks. Suddenly a narrow passage was seen in the half light, and the coxswains steered for this. The two boats brought up in a harbour where the sea was as smooth as a millpond.

"Here we secured the boats," said Byron, "and ascended a rock. It rained excessively hard all the first part of the night, and was extremely cold; and though we had not a dry thread about us, and no wood could be found for firing, we were oblig'd to pass the night in that uncomfortable situation, without any covering, shivering in our wet cloaths. The frost coming on with the morning, it was impossible for any of us to get a moment's sleep; and having flung overboard our provisions the day before, there being no prospect of finding anything to eat on this coast, in the morning we pulled out of the cove." As soon as they pulled out of the cove they again met huge seas. They pulled all day in heavy rain against contrary winds, and at night put in to a swampy shore among some small islands. The barge's mainsail provided some covering from the rain, and a fire was lit. It speaks well for their waterproofing arrangements that they could endure so much sea water and rain, and yet have substance left suitable for firing, and ammunition dry enough for shooting. They were confined in this place for three days. Campbell speaks of finding two of the marines lying in a wet swamp, almost dead of exposure and hunger. He beat them into life to spur them in the search of shellfish. Hunger was satisfied on the day that the surgeon got a goose. He and Hamilton appear to have been good shots, and were indefatigable in their search for food.

The passage was carried out without a chart. In any case no

chart existed at this time which showed even the rough outline
of the great peninsula of Tres Montes, let alone the channels
and indentations among the hundreds of islands. The only way
to find out whether an opening was a channel or a lagoon was
to enter it and see. Frequently they sailed up a lagoon only to
have to turn back.

"Perceiving a large opening," says Byron, "between very
high land and a low point, we steered for it: and when got that
length, found a large bay, down which we rowed, flattering ourselves there might be a passage that way; but towards night we
came to the bottom of the bay, and finding no outlet, we were
obliged to return the same way we came, having met with
nothing the whole day to alleviate our hunger."

Many a night they spent in the boats lying on their oars, unable to get ashore through the surf, and yet required to keep
the boat from being driven ashore by the breakers: all the
occupants cold and wet, and almost starving. Thus they spent
Christmas night.

When ashore waiting for the weather and wind to moderate,
they were frequently able to get seal and shellfish.

They were well on the way towards rounding what was
regarded as a north-west cape beyond which they expected to
find a smoother passage, when catastrophe overtook them.
Bad weather and a fierce tidal race had forced them to return
to a bay where they knew they could get food. All were ashore
except two boatkeepers in each boat lying at makeshift anchors.
One of these was Byron in the barge. During the night the
wind suddenly blew very hard, shifting from north to south,
and raising a great tumbling sea.

"Being extremely fatigued," says Byron, "we in the boats
went to sleep: notwithstanding, however, I was at last
awakened by the uncommon motion of the boat, and the roar-
ing of the breakers every where about us. At the same time I
heard a shrieking, like to that of persons in distress; I looked

out, and saw the yawl canted bottom upwards by a sea, and soon afterwards disappeared. One of our men, whose name was William Rose, a quartermaster, was drowned; the other was thrown ashore by the surf, with his head buried in the sand; but by the immediate assistance of the people on shore," (Campbell, though Byron does not say so), "was saved. As for us in the barge, we expected the same fate every moment . . . we used our utmost efforts to pull her without the breakers some way, but then let go our kellick again. Here we lay all the next day, in a great sea, not knowing what would be our fate."

To make it worse they were cold, wet, and hungry, and could see their shipmates eating seal on shore.

The loss of the yawl was a catastrophe, for it was impracticable to carry eighteen men in the barge in rough seas. A murderous decision was now taken, the four most helpless and sickly being selected to be left behind. These were Corporal Crosslet, and Hereford, Smith, and Hales, four helpless marines who were by now so worn out and spiritless that they put up no opposition to the arrangement. Death to them was preferable to returning to the misery and discomfort of a boat passage in heavy seas and endless rain. They were put ashore with arms, ammunition, a frying pan, and a few necessities. What made the matter so hopeless was that there were few shellfish in this place, which was afterwards called Marine Bay. Spiritless and weak these marines may have been, but their behaviour at parting is to their eternal credit.

"This dismal affair concluded," says Campbell, "the rest of us went in the barge to try the aforesaid Cape again. As the boat departed, these poor fellows standing on the beach gave us a farewell salute with three cheers, and cried ' God bless the King '. Our hearts melted with compassion, but there was no helping their misfortune."

The fourteen occupants of the barge were resolved to get to westward and round the headland in spite of continuing adverse winds, for they felt that once round the cape, conditions would improve. Psychologically they would feel that the worst of the journey was over, whatever dangers might lie ahead. A sense of desperation was overtaking them all. Conditions of life were miserably painful, and there was always the possibility of sudden disaster at hand. Many began to lose the will to survive. Death would be preferable. As they pulled to the westward, heading across the bay for the next headland, the wind freshened and the sea rose. Slowly they opened a bay round the headland to the north. But now, in spite of additional effort and exhausting labour, it became obvious that they were making no headway. The grim despair and hopelessness of it all is best depicted in Byron's words.

" We rowed along shore to the westward, in order to make one more attempt to double the cape: when abreast of the first head-land there ran such a sea, that we expected, every instant, the boat would go down. But as the preservation of life had now, in a great measure, lost its actuating principle upon us, we still kept pushing through it, till we opened a bay to the northward. In all my life, I never saw so dreadful a sea as drove in here; it began to break at more than half a mile from the shore. Perceiving now that it was impossible for any boat to get round, the men lay upon their oars till the boat was very near the breakers, the mountainous swell that then ran, heaving her in at a great rate. I thought it was their intention to put an end to their lives and misery at once; but nobody spoke for some time. At last, captain Cheap told them, they must either perish immediately, or pull stoutly for it to get off the shore; but they might do as they pleased."

The men were exhausted and resigned to their fate. Cheap's words rallied the men, who now pulled with a will to clear the

breakers. It was then decided to return round the headland and give up any attempt to get to the northward. It was
dark before they arrived at Marine Bay where they intended to
look for seal and take off the marooned marines. They were
compelled therefore to lie on their oars all night, keeping the
boat off the surf until daylight. There was then no sign of the
marines, except for a musket and ammunition which had been
left on the beach. In view of the continuing north wind it had
been agreed that the marines should be taken off, if still alive,
and the barge should return to Wager Island, for almost all on
board were now resigned to failure. The marines were never
heard of again.

After an absence of two months Cheap arrived at Wager
Island. It was then mid-January 1742. One man died on passage. There were thirteen left.

"We had now lost all Hopes," says Campbell, "of ever
re-visiting our Native Country, all we expected being to die
at Wager Island, looking on that Place, which we had been so
much used to, as a kind of Home." Campbell says he ate the
liver of a seal, which threw him into a fever and occasioned
all his skin to come off from head to foot.

The first thing done by the party was to secure the barge,
though they had by now given up hope of going very far with
it. On examining the huts which they had left two months
earlier, they found one nailed up; this contained pieces of iron-
work taken from the wreck. They concluded that the place
must have been visited by Indians who had commerce with the
Spaniards to the north, since Indians had no use themselves
for such items as were here stored.

Campbell refers to disagreements which had arisen between
Cheap and Hamilton, as a result of which the captain and surgeon messed together, leaving Hamilton and the two midshipmen to form another mess. Much of the disagreement resulted
from a belief that some of the food which was found was not

equally shared, or perhaps was not shared to the advantage of the captain. Cheap insisted on continuing what he considered to be a captain's privileges, which to the men appeared to be priority in food and exemption from work. He had little regard for the sufferings of others, and certainly failed in one of the prime qualities of leadership, which is consideration for the welfare of those led.

An occasional windfall helped to mitigate the general hunger, and on the 22nd February Hamilton found several pieces of beef on the shore as he returned from a shooting expedition. Campbell borrowed the captain's frying-pan, and when returning it left half of the fat they had used, as a present. This was not well received. Cheap disliked Campbell who complains in his narrative, " Most of the Hardships I suffered in following the Fortunes of Captain Cheap were the consequence of my voluntary Attachment to that Gentleman."

Most of the time hunger continued. Grisly solutions came to mind. " Wild sellery was all we could procure," says Byron, " which raked our stomachs instead of assuaging our hunger. That dreadful and last resource of men, in not much worse circumstances than ours, of consigning one man to death for the support of the rest, began to be mentioned in whispers."

Byron refers to a superstition among the men. They attributed all their recent misfortune and disasters to the fact that the corpse of one of their messmates who had been murdered, had not been committed to a proper burial. The most ghastly noises and supernatural apparitions on a moonlight night had added to their fears, and it was thought proper to inter the body. Perhaps many of them remembered the curse on the *Wager* men, referred to by Dandy Kidd on his death-bed in the *Pearl*.

" That common people in general are addicted to superstitious conceits," wrote Byron, " is an observation founded on experience; and the reason is evident: but I cannot allow that common seamen are more so than others of the lower class. In the most enlightened ages of antiquity, we find it to have been the popular opinion, that the spirits of the dead were not at rest till their bodies were interred; and that they did not cease to haunt and trouble those who had neglected this duty to the departed. This is still believed by the vulgar, in most countries; and in our men, this persuasion was much heightened by the melancholy condition they were reduced to; and was farther confirmed by an occurrence which happened some little time before we went upon our last expedition. One night we were alarmed with a strange cry, which resembled that of a man drowning. Many of us ran out of our huts towards the place from whence the noise proceeded, which was not far off shore; where we could perceive, but not distinctly (for it was then moonlight), an appearance like that of a man swimming half out of water. The noise that this creature uttered was so unlike that of any animal they had heard before, that it made a great impression upon the men; and they frequently recalled this apparition at the time of their distresses, with reflexions on the neglect of the office they were now fulfilling."

Fifteen days after their return to Wager Island they were visited by a party of their old Indian friends who arrived in two canoes. The Indians were astonished to see them here again. The surgeon, who could speak a little Spanish, was able to make the chief, called Martin, understand that they wanted to get to the sort of Spanish settlement near to which some of the tribes lived in the neighbourhood of the island of Chiloe. Gone were Cheap's ideas of capturing a prize and re-joining Anson. He would now be happy to throw himself on the mercy of the Spaniards who at least should feed them even if they were imprisoned. It was agreed that Martin in his canoe would accompany and guide the barge. He was to receive the barge as a reward on arrival at their destination.

Just prior to their departure on the 6th March 1742, a

marine who had stolen a coat fled into the woods to escape
punishment. There were therefore only thirteen in Cheap's
party when they embarked in the barge to pull once again for
the north: this time escorted by Martin. They had a favourable
wind and made good progress. On the third day they reached
a lagoon where Martin's wife and two children lived. Here they
stayed two days to obtain a collection of shellfish, and then
proceeded up a river against a strong stream, with the Chief
and his family in the barge. John Bosman, who had been one
of the strongest of seamen, fell off the thwart. He complained of
exhaustion and begged for food. It is necessary to give Byron's
account of the incident as evidence of the captain's attitude to
suffering and the growing realization of his fiendish disposition. The men were particularly indignant at his behaviour,
and talked of deserting him.

" I had hitherto steered the boat; but one of our men
sinking under the fatigue, expired soon after, which obliged
me to take the oar in his room, and row against this heart-
breaking stream. Whilst I was thus employed, one of our
men whose name was John Bosman, though hitherto the
stoutest man among us, fell from his seat under the thwarts,
complaining that his strength was quite exhausted for want
of food, and that he should die very shortly. As he lay in this
condition, he would every now and then break out in the
most pathetic wishes for some little sustenance; that two or
three mouthfuls might be the means of saving his life. The
captain, at this time, had a large piece of boiled seal by him,
and was the only one that was provided with any thing like a
meal; but we were become so hardened against the impressions of others sufferings by our own; so familiarized to
scenes of this, and every other kind of misery; that the poor
man's dying entreaties were vain. I sat next to him when he
dropped, and having a few dried shell-fish (about five or six)

in my pocket, from time to time, put one in his mouth, which served only to prolong his pains; from which, however, soon after my little supply failed, he was released by death. For, this, and another man I mentioned a little before to have expired under the like circumstances, when we returned from this unsuccessful enterprize, we made a grave in the sands.

" It would have redounded greatly to the tenderness and humanity of captain Cheap, if at this time he had remitted somewhat of that attention he shewed to self-preservation; which is hardly allowable but where the consequence of relieving others must be immediately and manifestly fatal to ourselves; but I would venture to affirm, that in these last affecting exigencies, as well as some others, a sparing perhaps adequate to the emergency, might have been admitted consistently with a due regard to his own necessities. The captain had better opportunities of recruiting his stock than any of us; for his rank was considered by the Indian as a reason for supplying him when he would not find a bit for us. Upon the evening of the day in which these disasters happened, the captain producing a large piece of boiled seal, suffered no one to partake with him but the surgeon, who was the only man in favour at this time. We did not expect, indeed, any relief from him in our present condition; for we had a few small mussels and herbs to eat; but the men could not help expressing the greatest indignation at his neglect of the deceased; saying that he deserved to be deserted by the rest for his savage behaviour."

Another seaman had died in like circumstances, leaving now only eleven in Cheap's party.

It was realized that it would be impossible to continue to pull a heavy barge up stream, in spite of Martin's solicitations. Byron suggests that it may have been a short cut for canoes, but thinks it more probable that Martin was keen to secure his reward of the barge without having to go too far. In any case Martin now found it necessary to go off in his canoe with his family to get seal, a trip which would take three or four days. He left his young Indian servant behind to show the seamen the best places for shellfish at a neighbouring island. They had by now withdrawn from the river attempt, and having returned to the coast buried the two dead men.

Elliot the surgeon was too ill to search for food. The other four officers were away along the coast looking for shellfish. The six men returned from their hunt in a body, with the young Indian servant helping them. They had not been very successful, so Elliot suggested that they should try to get a sea-gull for him. They jumped at the idea. In no time all six were in the barge, together with the young Indian. They shoved off and pulled away from the shore. Desertion could not have been easier.

Now there were five: Cheap, Hamilton, Elliot, Byron, and Campbell. They had lost the barge, and with it almost all their few possessions. If life had seemed desperate before this event, what must it have seemed now? Not only had they lost the means, but they had lost the bargaining power. Moreover, they were on a desolate island. This then was the end. Byron summed it up: "And now all the difficulties we had hitherto endured, seemed light in comparison of what we expected to suffer from this treachery of our men, who, with the boat, had taken away every thing that might be the means of preserving our lives. The little cloaths we had saved from the wreck, our muskets and ammunition, were gone, except a little powder, which must be preserved for kindling fires, and one gun, which I had, and was now become useless for want of ammunition."

CHAPTER 11

FOR ENGLAND AND AN UNKNOWN FATE

THE THIRTY mutineers in the *Speedwell*, with one exception, now lived on the fat of the land at the Rio Grande, and recuperated. The exception was William Oram, an early deserter at Wager Island, who had been persuaded by Bulkeley to return. He was already far gone, dying in hospital.

"We live on the best the Country can produce," wrote Bulkeley, "and have Plenty of every Thing. This Afternoon the Governor, Commandant, and Commissary, came on Board, to see over little *Speedwell*; they were surpriz'd that thirty souls could be stow'd in so small a Vessel; but that she could contain the Number which first embark'd with us, was to them amazing, and beyond all Belief."

The governor told them that they should have everything that the country could afford, and that they must make known their wants. He promised to send them on to Rio Janeiro at the first opportunity. Bulkeley asked the garrison commandant for a house, complaining that the *Speedwell* was rather damp in rainy weather. He was immediately granted one close to the commandant's, and given the key. He took with him the carpenter, the master's mates Jones and Snow, the army surgeon Oakley, and John Young the cooper. There was no bedding, but they had become used to lying hard, and were at least dry and warm. "We heartily wish that all the Persons who surviv'd the Loss of the Ship were in so good a Situation as ourselves," wrote Bulkeley smugly, perhaps wondering particularly about Cheap's situation at that moment.

Baynes and Pemberton were invited to stay with the governor.

But happiness was to be short lived. Very soon it became known that the town was in a state of insurrection. The prosperity and congeniality were but superficial. Matters came to a head when a brigadier arrived from the island of St. Catherine's, 350 miles away, ostensibly bringing arrears of pay for the garrison, but in reality little more than futile promises. The soldiers demanded redress, and the brigadier was only allowed to return to St. Catherine's on the understanding that pay, clothing, and food would be sent to the Rio Grande immediately. It became apparent that the " officers " of the garrison were private soldiers who had dismissed the regular officers and assumed their role and uniforms. The governor had been permitted to remain when he assured them all that he sympathized with their demands and would see that they were granted. The commandant and commissary had also been permitted to remain. This, however, did nothing to help the food supplies which now appeared to have been reduced to a six weeks' stock for a garrison of a thousand. The *Speedwell* men found that provisions were drastically cut: " Our Allowance is now so small," wrote Bulkeley, " that it will hardly support Nature."

The gunner could not be expected to remain inactive. He journeyed two miles from the port to see the lieutenant at the governor's house, complaining that that worthy had not come near them since they landed, and pointing out the necessity not only for food immediately but for passage for all of them to Rio Janeiro, so that they could join the *Pearl* and *Severn*, and help to swell their tragically depleted crews.

Baynes assured him that he was doing his best but that they

would all have to wait until a ship came in. The gunner also visited the commissary, and was able to extract a promise for a ration of bread.

It was more than two weeks later, on the 17th February, that three seamen arrived with a story that they had been marooned ashore from a small ship bringing stores to the Rio Grande from Rio Janeiro. Adverse weather had driven their ship eastward, and they believed she was now at St. Catherine's. The governor detained these men as possible spies. The next day he sent a pilot and two seamen to journey to St. Catherine's Island to investigate, and, if the ship was there, to bring her round. Bulkeley at once took the opportunity of sending a letter, hoping that it would be sent on from St. Catherine's to Rio Janeiro, which was almost a thousand miles from Rio Grande.

The letter was addressed to the Honourable Captain Murray, H.M.S. *Pearl* at Rio Janeiro, and listed all the thirty survivors. Respects were also paid to the Honourable Captain Legge of the *Severn*. It is of interest that the boatswain appears tenth on the list, and by now was treated rather as one of the seamen with whom he shared accommodation. His sense of importance was growing however, now that he was ashore. The letter ran:

"Honourable Sir,

"I take it as a Duty incumbent on me to acquaint you, that his Majesty's Ship the *Wager* was wreck'd on a desolate Island on the Coast of Patagonia, in the Latitude of 47:00 S. and W. Longitude from the Meridian of London 81:30, on the 14th of May, 1741. After lengthening the Long-boat, and fitting her in the best Manner we could, launch'd her on the 13th of October, and embark'd and sail'd on the 14th, with the Barge and Cutter, to the Number of eighty-one Souls in all. Capt. Cheap—, at his own request, tarried behind, with Lieutenant Hamilton, and Mr. Elliot the Surgeon. After a long and fatiguing Passage, coming through the Streights of Magellan, we arrived here the 28th of January, 1741-2; bringing into this Port alive to the Number of thirty, viz.:

> Robert Beans, Lieutenant
> John Bulkeley, Gunner
> John Cummins, Carpenter
> Robert Elliot, Surgeon's Mate
> John Jones, Master's Mate
> John Snow, ditto
> John Mooring, Boatswain's Mate
> John Young, Cooper
> William Oram, Carpenter's Crew
> John King, Boatswain
> Nicholas Griselham, Seaman
> Samuel Stook, ditto
> James MacCawle, ditto
> William Lane, ditto
> John Montgomery, ditto
> John George, Seaman
> Richard East, ditto
> James Butler, ditto
> Job Barnes, ditto
> John Pitman, ditto
> John Shoreham, ditto
> Thomas Edmunds, ditto
> Richard Powell, ditto
> Diego Findall (the Portugueze Boy)
>
> Capt. Robert Pemberton, of his Majesty's
>   Land Forces
> Lieutenants Ewers and Fielding, ditto
> Vincent Oakley, Surgeon of ditto
> And two Marines

"All which are living at present, and waiting an Opportunity of a Passage in a Portugueze Vessel, our own not being in a Condition to proceed any farther, having no Sails, and being so bad in all other respects, that the Governor will not suffer us to hazard our Lives in her; but hath promis'd to dispatch us in the very first Vessel that arrives in this Port; where we, with Impatience, are oblig'd to tarry. We humbly pay our Duty to Capt. Leg, praying the representations of this to him. From

Most Honourable Sir,
Yours, &c."

Three days after being incarcerated, the three seamen spies broke out of prison with five other prisoners and attempted to escape with a large boat, their destination being the River Plate with a following wind. They were pursued and captured, and popped into the guardhouse.

The dispatch of the men to St. Catherine's had given Bulkeley an idea. He now called on the lieutenant to demand horses and a pass for himself, the carpenter, and Jones, all of whom were willing to attempt the overland journey to St. Catherine's. There they would be certain to pick up a passage to the British ships at Rio Janeiro.

"It is our duty," said Bulkeley, "to hasten to their assistance. You ought," he continued to the lieutenant, "to have dispatched a special messenger by land, the very day after our arrival, without regard to expense. We might before now have been assured of a vessel."

Baynes listened with unexpected calmness, and provided the usual excuse that he had thought of this but had been assured that it was impracticable.

"How then did the brigadier come from St. Catherine's?" asked Bulkeley. "And how do people travel weekly? It must

be admitted that it is dangerous and exhausting but not to be
compared with what we have undergone. We lie here at the
expense of the King, and may miss not only the chance of
returning in our own ships, but perhaps of missing a passage in
the Spanish Fleet that is due to leave Rio Janeiro before the
winter. If we delay longer we may be forced to winter here."

Baynes had been ready enough to listen to Bulkeley criticiz-
ing Cheap, but very much resented his present importuning.
He promised to ask the governor at dinner for the necessary
horses and guides, and would let Bulkeley know the result
that afternoon. Bulkeley waited in vain for information, and
wrote an angry letter as follows, which he sent to the lieutenant
the next morning.

" Sir,
   " I am sorry you should give me the Liberty of telling
you, you have not discharg'd your Promise, by letting us
know the Governor's Answer to what we requested: Which
was, at our Expence and Charge, to go to the Assistance of
his Majesty's Ships at Rio Janeiro; since which Time I am
to inform you that we are in want of Provision, having none
of any kind allow'd us Yesterday, and but one small Fish
per Man for two Days before. The Meaning of which I
believe is owing to you, by the endeavouring, through the
Persuasions of the Persons you confide in, to blacken us, and
in so vile a Manner, that you seem unacquainted with the
ill Consequence, which may attend the touching a Man's
Character. We know, and are fully convinced, from what has
been done already, that nothing will be allow'd or granted us
but by your Means: Mr. Cummins and myself ask no
Favour from you, but to use your Endeavours to get us Dis-
patches to the Ships at Rio Janeiro, where every Man must
give Account of his Actions, and Justice take Place. If I am
not mistaken, you told me that what we were supply'd with

here, was a Bounty flowing from the generous Spirit of the
Governor, and the Gentlemen of the Place. If this be the
Case, we ought to be very thankful indeed. I am surprized,
Sir, you don't see the Grievances of the Inhabitants here,
and hear the Soldiers Murmurings for want of their Arrears.
If they should revolt at this Juncture, we shall stand a very
bad Chance. I must acquaint you, Sir, the Vessel we came
in, is not so much out of repair, but that, if you can get
Canvas out of the Store for Sails, we can make 'em, and get
ready for sailing in ten Days Time. And if the Vessel
expected here with Supplies comes in a shorter Time, our
Vessel will be ready fix'd for the Use of the Governor; and
if one Vessel should not be large enough to carry us all off,
we can go in Company. I imagine you know of the Stores
being robb'd, and the Disturbance among the Soldiers, which
must occasion Uneasiness enough, without repeating Grievances, where relief is not to be had. I beg, Sir, you'll get us
dispatch'd with all Expedition to his Majesty's Service, that
we may not lose the Opportunity of joining the two Ships
and the Flota.

SIR, Yours."

This worked like a charm. Baynes mounted his horse less
than an hour after reading the letter, and rode to Bulkeley's
house, a place he had not yet condescended to visit. He took
the gunner and the carpenter before the commandant who
promised fresh beef and fish, but informed them that no bread
was to be had.

William Oram had died that morning, and many of his shipmates were to attend the funeral. The cooper wrote of the
lieutenant's visit, " He was receiv'd by us all coolly enough. We
did not testify any respectful sense of his Condescension in this
Visit, but rather gave him to understand, that his absenting
from us so long was highly disgusting. Most of us were assem-

bled at the Hospital, to take from thence the Corpse of Brother Oram for its interment."

Although the food situation was now easier, the absence of any news of a ship arriving determined Bulkeley to see the governor. The lieutenant encouraged the idea of going overland and presented the intrepid trio, Bulkeley, Cummins, and Jones before the governor. They were joined by Pemberton who, in response to the governor's enumeration of the difficulties, said that he had a duty to join the remnants of a company of soldiers under his command on board the *Severn*. Permission was now granted and arrangements were to be made. The governor concluded by saying that he had a great regard for an Englishman, and they should not want for anything that he could provide.

While Bulkeley was negotiating for guides he received a message from the governor who had just received the agreeable news that four vessels were on their way to the Rio Grande. The overland journey was therefore cancelled. It was just as well, for ten days later on the 19th March, the four vessels arrived from Rio Janeiro and brought information that the *Severn* and the *Pearl* had sailed for Barbados.

With the four ships had arrived the brigadier, bringing money, provisions, and a pardon from the King of Portugal for the rebels. At a forenoon parade of all the soldiers the amnesty was read out and was received with acclamation. But only a third of the money for arrears of pay was available: the remainder was on passage. Acclamation now changed to derision, and there were cries of " All or none." There was much shouting. The brigadier was told that many of them would desert to the King of Spain, who was certain to pay full wages. The rebels also called on their commandant to see that justice was done. The commandant knew his soldiers, but was also aware of his tricky position. He declared that he was ready to give his own life for these brave fellows, but since the King had offered his

pardon, it was his duty to accept it as a common soldier. Hereupon he clapped a gun to his shoulder and slipped into the
ranks. The brigadier immediately ran to him and embraced
him. He assured the erstwhile commandant that a report would
be made and his gallant action would turn out to his honour
and advantage. The idea quickly caught on and the erstwhile
officers followed the commandant's example, returning to the
ranks from which they had emerged during the rebellion. Com-
mands were now restored to the proper officers, and there
followed " Tranquility, good Discipline, and Order."

It is interesting to read the comment of another rebel, that
of the cooper of the *Wager*, who witnessed the scene. He was
a great philosopher was John Young, and, presumably with
many of his *Speedwell* shipmates, often wondered what fate at
the hand of justice might await them should they ever reach
England.

The cooper wrote:

" The rest of the mock Officers thought it was now in
vain to persist. There was no Resource, no Hope of Refuge,
if they continued in their Rebellion. Their Submission, if it
was not voluntary, would be forced; and a severe Punishment would certainly revenge the Refusal of unmerited
Favour. On these Considerations they presently followed
the Commandant's Example. They degraded themselves,
without farther Delay, into private Men; they divested themselves of those usurped Plumes, which they would otherwise
be stripped of with Violence, and quietly reverted to their
proper Subordination.

" Thus the Government recovered the right Channel,
from whence it had been diverted by the Exorbitances of
those to whom the Administration of it was primarily committed. Few Seditions spring from other Causes: Rebellions
are, for the most Part, extorted. There are a thousand

8. H.M.S. *Resolution* in a gale, with courses and mizzen set, topsails furled, and lower gunports closed. In the winds of hurricane force met by Anson's ships round the Horn, ships would have to lie to under bare poles. The resulting damage, loss, wear, and tear can be imagined, particularly to rigging and spars.

9. Loss of the *Wager* 1741

10. Model of the *Tartar*, slightly smaller than the *Wager*, showing longboat.

Offences against the People, which ought to be resisted, for one committed, groundlessly against the Prince; a thousand Encroachments on the Subjects Property, for one on the Prerogative of the Sovereign." . . . "I was led to such Reflections as these, on beholding that ridiculous Scene I have been describing: A Parcel of half-paid, half-fed, half-naked Creatures admitted to Mercy, after audaciously endeavouring to do themselves Justice, on the Authors of their Wrongs; receiving their forfeited Lives, forsooth, from those, whose Crimes against these very Culprits sufficiently merited the Gallows."

On applying for leave to go in the first ship, Bulkeley was told by the lieutenant that he expected to go in her himself. There might even be room for all the officers. The men must wait for the second ship, otherwise there would be over-crowding.

This news incensed Bulkeley, particularly as Baynes would be the only one to continue on half pay. He pointed out that it was the lieutenant's duty as a paid officer to remain behind and look after the men. Nevertheless if Baynes would give him written assurance that he also would continue to be paid from the day of the shipwreck, he would stay behind. Otherwise he knew of no duty which could stop him from making his best endeavour to get to England as soon as possible.

Bulkeley was determined to waste no further words on Baynes, and abruptly left him. Together with Cummins, Jones, Snow, Oakley, and King he went to the governor. Baynes arrived at the same time, and with an ingratiating bow to the governor remarked that Mr. Bulkeley was very angry and did not realize that the governor would not allow the whole party to leave at once. The gunner was about to speak when the governor interrupted. " Those who intended and applied to go by land," he said, with rough justice, " shall be the first to go, and

F

may embark when you will. But," he added, " since the ship
does not belong to the King, you will have to pay for passage
and food. As to that which you have received from us, you are
welcome." This was final, and it left matters very much in the
air, for although one or two had a gold watch which would
realize a substantial sum, the majority had nothing. A suggestion that the schooner should be sold was agreed to by Baynes;
but he later changed his mind on the grounds that she would
not fetch enough money. The whole matter was settled the
next morning, when it was admitted by the lieutenant himself
that the brigadier and the governor had both reproved him for
his readiness to leave his men. He, the marine officers, and the
surgeon's mate, were to remain behind with ten men and two
marines. Bulkeley, Cummins, King, the two mates, Oakley, the
cooper, and six men were to embark in the brigantine *Saint
Catharine* and sail for Rio Janeiro.

According to both Bulkeley and John Young all was now
happiness; for a while. They sailed on Sunday the 28th March,
with adequate salt beef and flour. We read of charmingly pleasant country, fine commodious harbours, abundance of fish,
melons, water, and " the best Milk I ever tasted ". On Monday
the 12th April 1742, " they happily arrived and dropped
Anchor before the great Town, or City rather, of Rio Janeiro."

It must have seemed now that they were nearly home. Days
of fruitless search, starvation, and exhaustion were almost forgotten. It might be thought that the memories of those times,
and the amazing survival of those now assembled at this step-
ping-stone for England, would bring them closer together
spiritually: but we forget the tough, evil characters who had
lain low when there was work to be done and difficult problems
to tackle.

Things began well. They called on the governor who at once
ordered an English-speaking Dutch surgeon to act as their
consul. The officers were to be housed and given a daily subsis-

tence allowance, and on the first day were wined and dined at public expense. Items of domestic utensils and furniture were provided by the consul. " In this Situation," says the cooper " even Mr. Bulkeley, who was so generally discontented, seem'd to be vastly pleased ". But Bulkeley remarks ominously that " this was the first Time of the Boatswain's eating with the rest of the Officers since we left Cheap Island ". Trouble was not far away; in spite of the governor's warning that there must be no disturbance or quarrelling.

The governor had promised an average daily subsistence allowance of eight vintins each; this to be recovered in due course from the British government. He directed that ten vintins were to be paid to each officer, and six to each man, on the principle that the men could work for a living whereas the officers could not.

On the following morning the consul went with officers and men to the Treasury, and asked Dr. Oakley, who ranked as a lieutenant in the Army, to sign for the total amount of subsistence allowance to be drawn. The boatswain, who regarded himself as the senior officer, was enraged at being ignored in this matter and left the company in no doubt of his indignation and anger. The consul was inclined to ignore such behaviour, for he was well aware of the feuds that existed.

Oakley, having signed for the money, and very much aware of the boatswain's wrath, declined the consul's invitation to distribute it, whereupon the consul said he would pay it himself, and announced the governor's directive.

Wrote the cooper:

" The poor Surgeon tho' he had Courage enough to face a wounded Soldier, and could, without trembling, trapan a broken Scull, or perform an Amputation, had not Intrepidity sufficient for encountering the Boatswain's Fury. Hereupon he prayed to be excused the Office; telling the Consul, the

Boatswain was a quarrelsome Fellow, and would, if he undertook it, not only insult and fall out with him, but make the whole Place uneasy, and thereby greatly prejudice all our Affairs. The Consul stared at this Account; told the Boatswain he was sorry to hear such a Character of him, from a Gentleman that wou'd not, he supposed, belye him; and that if the Case was such, to render them all as easy as he could, he would even make the Division of their Allowance himself; And so accordingly he did."

The boatswain argued that the men should receive the same allowance as the officers, and in order to avoid any further turmoil all the officers agreed. The consul gave the boatswain a piece of his mind, and said that payment should be as the governor ordered, whereupon the boatswain at once raised objection against the cooper, saying that he was no officer. He, the cooper, had now got among the officers, all of whom were pirates, especially Bulkeley, but there was no reason for his having an exceptional allowance. The consul said he believed the cooper to be a good, quiet man who would make no objection to receiving a man's allowance. To remove any doubt he would pay the difference himself. The cooper makes no reference to this specific point, other than to refer to the boatswain's scurrilous talk. It is obvious that he was an intelligent observer and a man of education. Perhaps the cooper was somewhat like the cook who in the eighteenth century gradually became relegated from the position of warrant officer and head of his own department in a ship, to non officer status.

As a result of this outburst the gunner asked the consul to arrange for separate accommodation so as to avoid further quarrels. The matter was settled by King saying that he would prefer to live with the men. This left the front room of the house in the entire possession of the gunner, the carpenter, and the cooper. All was now tranquillity: for a while.

The next morning this trio locked the two doors of their room and walked some miles into the country. On returning in the evening they found that the door of their room had been forced and that Bulkeley's sword and scabbard had been smashed as if to deny them any protection. Almost at once two men entered and set about the gunner and the cooper. One of these was Richard East, a *Wager* man, the other was an Irish acquaintance of King's who lived in the town, probably a deserter from the Navy. Cummins rushed out for the guards, soon returning with them to find that the gunner had over-powered East; the cooper's assailant had fled at the sight of the guards.

Bulkeley asked that East should be sent to gaol for assault, but was compelled in accordance with local laws to be detained with his prisoner at the governor's house. The governor sent for him in a few minutes and ordered that he should be released. East was to be detained.

On arrival at his house Bulkeley found a further quarrel developing. The boatswain, with two accomplices who were deserters from the *Pearl* and *Severn*, was violently chastizing the cooper. They now turned their attentions to Bulkeley with violent abuse. They were so belligerent that both the gunner and the cooper thought they were going to be murdered. As soon as their assailants had gone, they left the house, and for safety's sake remained away from it until the next morning when they could persuade the consul to visit it with them. The consul admonished them severely but realizing the menace of the boatswain and his accomplices, agreed to find the officers a house in the country. " He observ'd," wrote John Young, " how scandalous it was, for so small a Number of Men, of the same Nation, Comrades a long Time, Companions in a Series of Misfortunes, and in a foreign Land, at the Courtesy of Strangers, to be at mortal Enmity amongst themselves; thereby adding greatly to their Calamities, and exposing one another to

the Hatred and Contempt of those, to whom it was their chief
Interest to be acceptable. The Boatswain, at whose Behaviour
this Reproof was mainly levelled, was so far from being mended
thereby, that it served only to renew and increase his Rage;
which he let fly at every one about him. In short, his Incorrigi-
bility was so evident, and the Dread of him so great, that it was
resolved to separate from him at any Rate, and get rid of him,
if possible. With this View, Bulkeley, Cummins, the Cooper,
the Surgeon, with two or three more, determined on quitting
those Lodgings in which the Government had placed them, and
taking some Apartment, distant from the Town, at their own
Expence. Accordingly, finding one to their Mind, about a
League off, they hired it, by the Month. They took Possession
that very Evening, and were mighty forward in congratulating
themselves on their imagined Security, at a Retirement so
remote from their Disturber."

Here in the country, two miles from the City, they thought
themselves safe. But the following evening they received a visit
from the two deserter friends of King, in company with an
Irish clerk who lived in the town. They referred to the boatswain as the commander; he had sent them and demanded to
see Bulkeley's journal. The cooper remarks that Bulkeley was
"not used to receive Proposals of this Nature with extraordinary Patience". But on this occasion the gunner was dis-
creet. He gave his visitors each a glass of punch, and said that
his journal was available for anybody who could read. He
added, however, that he could not part with it for any of it to
be copied. Secretly he was afraid of its being destroyed, and
with it the testimony which might save him from swinging at
the yardarm, but he did not of course comment on that fact.
He remembered that journals had been destroyed in the *Wager*
at the time of the shipwreck when the boatswain was the only
officer to stay with the wreck.

He was much relieved when his visitors left. He comments

that "ruffians are to be hired at a small Expence; and there is no Place in the World where People will commit Murder at so cheap a rate."

Between nine and ten that night the three ruffians returned. One of them knocked loudly at the door and demanded entrance. Bulkeley refused entrance, saying that this was no hour of the day for a call or to transact business. They then threatened and said that if they were not admitted they would return with a gang who would prize them all out before daylight. They then left.

As soon as the ruffians had gone, the terrified occupants left the house, got over the back wall, and fled into the country. Early the next morning they called on the consul and asked for protection. He readily understood that the gunner, carpenter, and cooper were all in mortal peril from the mad designs of the boatswain, placed them under protection in a house in the town and undertook to get them on board a Portuguese ship where they could work their passage. The ship was bound for Bahia, and, in due course, Lisbon, and he would arrange for the governor to give them a pass. They remained for almost a month, always in great apprehension that the boatswain would do them some evil if not murder them.

On the 20th May, to their great joy they were permitted to embark in the *Saint Tubes* of twenty-eight guns, bound for Bahia. Their troubles were by no means over. In the morning the captain came on board and expressed annoyance that they should not have waited on him ashore. There was worse than this in store for them. There happened to be a Spanish nobleman on board who resented the presence of Englishmen. He told the captain imperiously that they should not travel in the same ship with him. They must immediately be sent back ashore. Having come so near to the end of their troubles in Rio Janeiro, the trio were now disconsolate with visions of contempt from their shipmates left ashore, added to their own

bitter disappointment at not starting for home after their long
wait. The captain told the Spaniard that he was master in his
own ship, and would carry whom he liked, without being
directed in the matter by anybody. This seemed to have an
immediate effect on the gentleman, who not only removed his
objection but on the following morning entered into conversation with the survivors. He was immediately impressed with the
relation of their misfortune, and said that though their respective kings were enemies at war, they themselves were in a
neutral ship, and he would do them all the service he could.
He extolled the bravery of Admiral Vernon at the capture of
Porto Bello, and applauded the humanity of the English in
their treatment of prisoners, and the boldness and magnificence
of the British Fleet. To his praise he added generosity and
kindness, insisting that the survivors should eat from the
provisions of his own table and drink of his wines.

The thousand mile journey to Bahia therefore passed in joy
and comfort. They were now far removed from the threats of
John King. Daily they were getting nearer home.

Unfortunately for our three survivors, the viceroy at Bahia
was pro-French and anti-English. He was shown the pass from
the governor of Rio Janeiro and told of the generous treatment
and subsistence they had received there. This moved him not
at all. He refused help in any form. He said that if they wished
to get to Lisbon, as indicated on the pass, they could go in the
ship in which they had arrived, for that was the first destined
for that port. In vain did they plead for help, and in vain did
their friendly captain support their pleas, offering at the same
time to maintain them, if only the viceroy would arrange for his
ultimate reimbursement from the consul general at Lisbon.

The gunner, carpenter, and cooper were now stranded in
Bahia, 12° south of the equator, on the coast of Brazil. It was
an expensive and unfriendly city. Their total assets were a little
money that Bulkeley had saved besides his gold watch, and the

willing help of the captain. For four months they stayed here
without any assistance from viceroy or inhabitants; they worked
in order to avoid starvation.

Perhaps the worst of all for them, certainly the most ironical,
was the news that after they had left Rio Janeiro, a British
warship in company with three storeships had arrived with
men and stores for the *Severn* and *Pearl*, previously departed,
and that the remaining ten of the party, King, Oakley, Jones,
Snow, Stook, Shoreham, Pitman, Barns, East, and Powell, had
been taken off from Rio Janeiro to proceed for Barbados.

The captain of the *Saint Tubes* continued his support in
return for a bill on the consul general at Lisbon, which was
drawn up by an English merchant at Bahia. One wonders at
there being no financial help or sympathy from this quarter: it
may have been due to the anti-British attitude which prevailed
in Bahia; but it is more likely that these three could not be
trusted or befriended even by their own countrymen.

On the 11th September 1742, they embarked in the *Saint
Tubes* with their friendly captain, and proceeded for Lisbon.
The passage took over two months during which they encountered stormy weather many times. The behaviour of both crew
and passengers is well described by Bulkeley, in particular an
episode on their approach to Lisbon with a lee shore. " At Four
o'Clock it blew a very hard Gale, and right on the Shore;
the Ship lay to under a Foresail with her Head to the Southward; at Six it blew a Storm, the Foresail splitting, oblig'd
us to keep her before the Wind, which was running her right
on the Shore. The Ship was now given over for lost, the People
all fell to Prayers, and cry'd out to their Saints for Deliverance,
offering all they had in the World for their Lives; and yet at
the same time neglected all Means to save themselves; they left
off pumping the Ship, though she was exceeding leaky. This
Sort of Proceeding in time of Extremity is a thing unknown to
our *English* Seamen; in those Emergencies all Hands are

employ'd for the Preservation of the Ship and People, and, if
any of them fall upon their Knees, 'tis after the Danger is over.
The Carpenter and myself could by no Means relish this
Behaviour, we begg'd the People for God's sake to go to the
Pumps, telling them we had a Chance of saving our Lives,
while we kept the Ship above Water, that we ought not to
suffer the Ship to sink, while we could keep her free. The
Captain and Officers hearing us pressing them so earnestly, left
off Prayers, and intreated the Men to keep the Pumps going,
accordingly we went to pumping, and preserv'd ourselves and
the Ship."

On arrival at Lisbon Bulkeley learnt that Baynes had arrived
in Lisbon before him, and had given a very bad impression
concerning the activities of the gunner and carpenter. He had
left for England in a packet boat. Bulkeley already knew some
of the British residents in Lisbon, and took great delight in
showing them his journal, pointing out that the lieutenant had
kept none. Throughout their stay here the trio were treated
with courtesy and kindness. On the 20th December they embarked in H.M.S. *Stirling Castle* bound for England.

Bulkeley comments on their happiness and the joy of experi-
encing the difference between a British and a foreign ship,
" particularly in regard to Cleanliness, Accommodation, Diet,
and Discipline ". Imagine his consternation on arrival at Spithead, on New Year's Day 1743, within sight of his home at
Portsmouth, after an absence of more than two years, in instant
readiness to join his family ashore, only to learn from the
captain that the three of them were to be detained on board
pending a decision by the Lords of the Admiralty.

Their feelings are best conveyed in John Young's conclusion
to his " Affecting Narrative."

" You will imagine the Joy we felt on sight of our dear
Country, where we look'd for the congratulatory Caresses of

our affectionate Relations and Friends. We thought of nothing now but landing, and going directly to our respective Homes, to receive the Embraces of our Wives and Children. But we had hardly cast Anchor, when the Captain damp'd all the pleasing Emotion of our Souls, by acquainting us, that, in Effect, we were Prisoners: For he told us (which we had not the least Suspicion of, though we knew he sent off a Boat with Expresses) that he had written concerning us to the Admiralty, and that we must remain where we were, till he had an Answer from their Lordships. The Grief we expressed at this Disappointment was proportionate to the Hope we had conceived, That our Sorrows were come to a Period, and that domestic Comforts would extinguish the Memory of past Afflictions. But there was no Remedy beside Patience. We continued in this Confinement, as we now thought it, a Fortnight, which seemed as a Year to us, at the End of which the Lords of the Admiralty were pleased to order us our Liberty. Their Message was to us almost as joyful as a Reprieve or Pardon is to a condemn'd Malefactor. It was no sooner made known to us than we pour'd out Thanksgiving to God, and Blessings on our Benefactors; and immediately, after taking a respectful Leave of the Officers, and Ship's Company, we went ashore to our several Habitations. When we had reposed ourselves there a few Days, we repaired to London, to petition the L—ds of the Ad—y for our Wages, and farther Employment. But, unhappily for us, our Enemies had Influence enough to defeat our Hopes, and protract our Misfortunes. However, what has befallen us thereupon (being without the Period of the Expedition I undertook to give you an account of) shall not be any part of this Relation."

What was to befall them was yet unknown. The lieutenant had already sent in a narrative. Their Lordships thereupon

ordered an enquiry into the whole affair, but later decided that
no examination should take place until the return of either
Commodore Anson or Captain Cheap.

Bulkeley concluded his journal hopefully. " It was also
resolved, that not a Person of us should receive any Wages, or
be employ'd in his Majesty's Service, till every Thing relating
to the *Wager* was more plain and conspicuous. There was no
Favour shown in this Case to one more than another; so that
every body seem'd easy with their Lordships Resolution. All
that we have to wish for now is the safe Arrival of the Commodore and Captain Cheap: We are in Expectation of soon seeing
the former; but of the Captain we have as yet no Account.
However, we hope, when the Commodore shall arrive, that the
Character he will give of us will be of Service to us: He was
very well acquainted with the Behaviour of every Officer in his
Squadron, and will certainly give an Account of them accordingly."

Did Bulkeley really hope for the safe arrival of Cheap? He
probably expected more lenient treatment from Anson than he
could ever expect from Cheap. What if Captain Cheap should
still be alive, and after all, turn up in England to provide the
evidence? In his mind he must have thought this most unlikely
if not impossible. He had written the captain's obituary in his
journal, after leaving him ashore at Wager Island.

CHAPTER 12

WHEEL OF FORTUNE

THE LOSS of the barge was a shattering blow to Cheap and his associates. They were alone on a desolate coast with practically nothing to support them. Elliot the surgeon was so ill that he could not raise himself from the ground. He was dying of exhaustion and starvation. Perhaps Bulkeley would have had some suitable quip for such a situation. Gloomily the remaining four faced the same death suffered by the four marines so callously left ashore at Marine Bay.

In fact this was the turning point in their disastrous journey, and an indication of the inscrutable ways of Providence. Slowly they realized that the barge had been a burden that consumed all their energy and exposed them to the merciless forces of nature. As if to mark the ways of Providence it was by chance that Byron, while walking along the shore, suddenly saw a black image atop a huge wave, far out to sea. It seemed impossible that a canoe could live in such conditions, but it was in fact moving along the coast. Byron ran back to his companions who were so despondent as to be unwilling to take much notice. Gradually he persuaded them to hang up rags on a pole and attract attention. The canoe pulled in to a cove further along the coast. Here Byron and Cheap found Martin and his family. They immediately took Martin back to the surgeon who was almost too ill to speak.

The first question Martin asked concerned the whereabouts of the barge and his servant. Receiving no satisfactory answer he concluded that the latter had been murdered. He was with difficulty persuaded not to leave them. Providentially the servant escaped from the six deserters and returned to Martin some days later. The deserters were never seen again.

Martin was disappointed at the loss of the barge but agreed to carry out his side of the contract on being promised Byron's fowling piece and some recompense on arrival. The canoe was to be carried to a bay on the other side of the island from which Cheap and Byron would embark with Martin to collect some of his friends. Martin's wife and children were to be left behind with Hamilton, Campbell, and Elliot, as hostages.

Byron described the next few days in some detail, and it is apparent that his new experiences left a lasting impression. He was made to do much of the pulling in the canoe for two days, with nothing to eat but a few scraps. Cheap was better looked after. On arrival at a camp of six wigwams, Martin indicated that all the men of the camp, excepting two, were away on an expedition but would return in a few days. They would then go back to the assistance of their companions. Cheap was provided with shelter in a wigwam, but Byron, who was exhausted with fatigue and hunger, was left to fend for himself, and continued to be neglected by Martin. He thereupon crawled uninvited into one of the wigwams where, after an initial reluctance, the two women occupants warmed to him, and with food and attention endeavoured to make him comfortable. The Indians did not restrict themselves to one wife, and according to Campbell " take their own sisters and daughters in their commerce with women ". This fact is supported by Byron's account.

Byron wrote:

" In this wigwam into which I took the liberty to introduce myself, I found only two women, who, upon first seeing a figure they were not accustomed to, and such a figure too as I then made, were struck with astonishment. They were sitting by a fire, to which I approached without any apology. However inclined I might have been to make one, my ignorance of their language made it impossible to attempt it. One of these women appeared to be young, and very handsome for an Indian; the other old, and as frightful as it is possible to conceive any thing in human shape to be. Having stared at me some little time, they both went out; and I, without farther ceremony, sat me down by the fire to warm myself, and dry the rags I wore. Yet I cannot say my situation was very easy, as I expected every instant to see two or three men come in and thrust me out, if they did not deal with me in a rougher manner.

" Soon after the two women came in again, having, as I supposed, conferred with the Indian, our conductor; and appearing to be in great good humour, began to chatter and laugh immoderately. Perceiving the wet and cold condition I was in, they seemed to have compassion on me, and the old woman went out and brought some wood, with which she made a good fire; but my hunger being impatient, I could not forbear expressing my desire that they would extend their hospitality a little further, and bring me something to eat. They soon comprehended my meaning, and the younger beginning to rummage under some pieces of bark that lay in the corner of the wigwam, produced a fine large fish; this they presently put upon the fire to broil; and when it was just warm through, they made a sign for me to eat. They had no need to repeat the invitation; I fell to, and dispatched it in so short a time, that I was in hopes they would comprehend, without further tokens, that I was ready for another; but it was of no consequence, for their stock of eatables was entirely exhausted.

" After sitting some time in conference together, in which

conversation I could bear no part, the women made some
signs to me to lay down and go to sleep, first having strewed
some dry boughs upon the ground. I laid myself down, and
soon fell fast asleep; and about three or four hours after
awaking, I found myself covered with a bit of blanket, made
of the down of birds, which the women usually wear about
their waist. The young woman, who had carefully covered
me, whilst sleeping, with her own blanket, was lying close
by me: the old woman lay on the other side of her. The fire
was low, and almost burnt out; but as soon as they found
me awake they renewed it, by putting on more fuel. What
I had hitherto eat served only to sharpen my appetite; I
could not help, therefore, being earnest with them to get me
some more victuals. Having understood my necessities, they
talked together some little time; after which getting up, they
both went out, taking with them a couple of dogs, which they
train to assist them in fishing. After an hour's absence, they
came in trembling with cold, and their hair streaming with
water, and brought two fish; which having broiled, they gave
me the largest share; and then we all laid down as before to
rest."

This must have been bliss after months of exhaustion from
cold and hunger. But next morning Byron heard that the men
would soon be returning; "a hearing by no means pleasant to
me: I was, therefore, determined to enjoy myself as long as
they were absent, and make the most of the good fare I was
possessed of."

He even went to the extent of washing his shirt "which
might be said to be alive with vermin."

Fortune certainly smiled on him now, for he went fishing
with his hostesses who, in long and deep underwater dives filled
baskets with sea eggs, in spite of the cold sea. That night he
camped with them in their portable wigwam: "we reposed

ourselves as before." The following day they fished with a net into which a trained dog drove the fish. An excellent supper followed. But on the third day they returned to the camp at noon. There was a look of consternation on the face of the beautiful young Indian girl. The canoes of the Indian men had returned, and Martin was explaining the presence of Cheap and Byron and the help they required. He addressed himself particularly to a chief with a remarkably surly and stern countenance, who had an air of importance. Byron witnessed a sad incident.

Byron wrote:

"I now understood that the two Indian women with whom I had sojourned, were wives to this chieftain, though one was young enough to be his daughter; and as far as I could learn, did really stand in the different relations to him both of daughter and wife. It was easy to be perceived that all did not go well between them at this time; either that he was not satisfied with the answers that they returned him to his questions, or that he suspected some misconduct on their side; for presently after, breaking out into savage fury, he took the young one up in his arms, and threw her with violence against the stones; but his brutal resentment did not stop here, he beat her afterwards in a cruel manner. I could not see this treatment of my benefactress without the highest concern for her, and rage against the author of it; especially as the natural jealousy of these people gave occasion to think that it was on my account she suffered. I could hardly suppress the first emotions of my resentment, which prompted me to return him his barbarity in his own kind; but besides that this might have drawn upon her fresh marks of his severity, it was neither politic, nor indeed in my power, to have done it to any good purpose at this time."

Martin indicated to Cheap and Byron that it was time to return: the other Indians would join them in a few days. They found Campbell and Hamilton in a starving condition; for Martin's wife had been unable or unwilling to provide them with anything more than a few sea eggs, and they were without ammunition for wildfowling. Elliot was near to death. None except Cheap received food from Martin, though the needs of the others were greater. Cheap seemed proud of the distinction thus shown him, and encouraged it. The remainder were treated as slaves, more particularly the two midshipmen, for Elliot was now past caring, and Hamilton showed an independence of spirit.

The arrival of the Indians for the commencement of the journey to Chiloe was a welcome relief, particularly as they shared out a little seal. They also procured shag and cormorant by the process of going out to their perches on the rocks at night, dazzling them with lighted bark, and clubbing them as they fell into canoes. Seals could be taken by the accurate throw of a lance from a great distance. Byron's lady friends also continued to help him from time to time, but he points out that this was a hazardous affair, and remarks on the brutality of the Indians.

Byron says:

" Though I was not suffered to enter their wigwams, they would find opportunities of throwing in my way such scraps as they could secrete from their husband. The obligation I was under to them on this account is great, as the hazard they ran in conferring these favours was little less than death. The men, unrestrained by any laws or ties of conscience, in the management of their own families, exercise a most despotic authority over their wives, whom they consider in the same view they do any other part of their property, and dispose of them accordingly: even their com-

mon treatment of them is cruel; for though the toil and
hazard of procuring food lies entirely upon the women, yet
they are not suffered to touch any part of it till the husband
is satisfied; and then he assigns them their portion, which is
generally very scanty, and such as he has not a stomach for
himself."

It was about the middle of March 1742 that the journey
with the Indians began. After the passage of the autumnal
equinox winter would quickly follow; the winter solstice in mid
June would be with them in three months.

Barely had they set out before they were forced by bad
weather to return. "Here," says Alexander Campbell suc-
cinctly, "Mr. Elliot, Surgeon of his Majesty's Ship *Wager*,
departed this miserable Life". It seems almost certain that he
died of fatigue and starvation, perhaps without a morsel from
the man with whom he had shared a mess, and for whom he
must have provided much food by his shooting. Byron says,
"The weather coming on too bad for their canoes to keep the
sea, we landed again, without making great progress that day.
Here Mr. Elliot, our surgeon, died. At our first setting out, he
promised the fairest for holding out, being a very strong, active
young man: he had gone through an infinite deal of fatigue, as
Mr. Hamilton and he were the best shots amongst us, and
whilst our ammunition lasted never spared themselves, and in
a great measure provided for the rest; but he died the death
many others had done before him, being quite starved. We
scraped a hole for him in the sand, and buried him in the best
manner we could." Now there were four.

The *Wager* survivors were divided up by the Indians, presumably to avoid collusion and treachery, not allowing more
than one in each canoe. Byron and Campbell were made to
pull. Cheap was sufficiently distinguished to be exempt, and
Hamilton, being a soldier, could not be expected to pull. There

was little mercy from these Indians, and both Campbell and Byron complain of inhuman treatment and starvation. Martin appeared, from the habit of crossing himself, to have been influenced by the Spaniards, and was less pagan in religious behaviour than most of the other Indians. These, from time to time, would work themselves into a frenzy of religious madness, with groans and shrieks, burning and bloodletting, foaming at the mouth until they collapsed with exhaustion. Byron relates a tragic incident concerning Martin.

Byron says:

" He and his wife had gone off, at some distance from the shore, in their canoe, when she dived for sea-eggs; but not meeting with great success, they returned a good deal out of humour. A little boy of theirs, about three years old, whom they appeared to be doatingly fond of, watching for his father and mother's return, ran into the surf to meet them: the father handed a basket of sea-eggs to the child, which being too heavy for him to carry, he let it fall; upon which the father jumped out of the canoe, and catching the boy up in his arms, dashed him with the utmost violence against the stones. The poor little creature lay motionless and bleeding, and in that condition was taken up by the mother; but died soon after. She appeared inconsolable for some time; but the brute his father shewed little concern about it."

The progress northward cannot be exactly traced. The canoes crossed great bays, and were then dismantled for carrying across a neck of land to another bay, or were rowed upstream to a carrying place which was often through thick woods and swamps. Every man and woman except Cheap carried some item on these occasions. Byron complains at this stage of having " been three days at the oar without any kind of nourishment, but the wretched root . . . and we were devoured by vermin ". His clothes were in rags, and he had neither shoe nor stocking.

On one occasion he was left behind, without a morsel of food, and instructed by signs to await the arrival of other Indians. This was at a great lake, the opposite side of which appeared to be at the foot of the Cordilleras. On their arrival, the following day, the Indians gave him a small piece of seal which he gulped whole. Nevertheless he was brutally treated, kicked and beaten, and not permitted to shelter in the wigwams. For one offence, such as throwing away some empty shells, he was nearly killed when one Indian twisted a ragged handkerchief about his neck. Another seized his legs to throw him overboard. An old women came to his rescue. One begins to wonder if the men were jealous of his appeal to the women, but, Byron says, the following day his life was saved when a man snatched some poisonous berries he was about to eat.

Byron later joined his companions again. There was no expression of joy. Here there was a very large canoe belonging to their guide. Campbell says of this: " Our Canoe was large, yet there was nobody in her to row but the Indian, his Partner, us two, and the Indian Wife who steered. She was our Mistress, but not a very good one. Thus we lived mid March to early June 1742. We were naked and starved. Neither Tongue nor Pen can possibly express our Misery."

Byron however used his pen to describe the misery and the appalling condition into which Cheap had sunk. He was filthy, almost in a stupor, but still determined to cling to his scraps of seal. He appears to have been suffering from elephantiasis.

Byron says:

" I joined my companions again but don't remember that there was the least joy shewn on either side at meeting . . . Mr. Hamilton continued in the same canoe he had been in all along, and which still was to keep us company some way further, though many of the others had left us. This was dreadful hard work to such poor starved wretches as we were, to be slaving at the oar all day long in such a heavy boat; and this inhuman fellow would never give us a scrap to eat, excepting when he took so much seal that he could not contrive to carry it all away with him, which happened very seldom. After working like gally-slaves all day, towards night, when we landed, instead of taking any rest, Mr. Campbell and I were sometimes obliged to go miles along shore to get a few shell-fish; and just as we have made a little fire in order to dress them, he has commanded us into the boat again, and kept us rowing the whole night without ever landing. It is impossible for me to describe the miserable state we were reduced to: our bodies were so emaciated, that we hardly appeared the figures of men. It has often happened to me in the coldest night, both in hail and snow, where we had nothing but an open beach to lay down upon, in order to procure a little rest, that I have been obliged to pull off the few rags I had on, as it was impossible to get a moment's sleep with them on for the vermin that swarmed about them; though I used, as often as I had time, to take my clothes off, and putting them upon a large stone, beat them with another, in hopes of killing hundreds at once; for it was endless work to pick them off. What we suffered from this was ten times worse even than hunger. But we were clean in comparison to captain Cheap; for I could compare his body to nothing but an ant-hill, with thousands of those insects crawling over it; for he was now past attempting to rid himself in the least from this torment, as he had quite lost himself, not recollecting our names that were about him, or even his own. His beard was as long as a hermit's: that and his face being covered with train-oil and dirt, from having long accustomed himself to sleep upon a bag, by the way of pillow, in which he kept the pieces of stinking seal. This prudent method he took to prevent our getting at it whilst he slept. His legs were as big as mill-posts, though his body appeared to be nothing but skin and bone."

Byron describes the arrival on one occasion at Anna Pink Bay. This bay in 46° S is the spot where Anson's victualler the *Anna* had a year earlier, on the 18th May 1741, four days after *Wager* had driven ashore, found miraculously a small opening channel and a sheltered bay. Unlike the *Wager*, she was little damaged. After a refit of two months, she and her crew of sixteen sailed to rejoin Anson at Juan Fernandez. Anson's ships were at that time severely rationed for food. " Her arrival," wrote Walter, the chaplain of the *Centurion*, " gave us all the sincerest joy: for each ship's company was immediately restored to their full allowance of bread, and we were now freed from the apprehension of our provisions falling short before we could reach some amiable port; a calamity which in these seas is of all others the most irretrievable."

While the *Wager* survivors were at Anna Pink Bay, they were visited by a tribe of Indians whose language was very different from that of the guides, but they were able to make them understand that a ship with a red flag had been here for two months, though at this time they little realized that she was the little victualler of their squadron, that had accompanied them round the Horn.

It was here that a change of canoes again took place. That in which Hamilton had travelled had come to its journey's end, and was to return south. The guide indicated to Hamilton that he was now to join up with the other three in one canoe. To his credit, Hamilton refused; " the insolence of this fellow was to him insupportable ". He voluntarily chose to remain at Anna Pink Bay, to wait for some further opportunity. Cheap's party was now down to three.

By slow degrees, crossing from island to island, they travelled northward, until they reached what is now called the Corcovado Gulf. The entrance to this is about thirty miles across to the island of Chiloe, quite open to the ocean. It seemed almost three times this to our *Wager* survivors. The Indian chief was obviously apprehensive of danger, and waited two days for weather and sea to moderate. The prospect of crossing in a canoe composed of a few planks kept together by a kind of bindweed must have daunted the hardiest. Cheap was now so ill as to be almost past caring.

Wrote Byron:

" At last we reached an island about thirty leagues to the southward of Chiloe. Here we remained two days for a favourable opportunity to cross the bay, the very thought of which seemed to frighten our cacique out of his senses; and indeed, there was great reason for his apprehensions; for there ran a most dreadful hollow sea, dangerous, indeed, for any open boat whatever, but a thousand times more for such a crazy vessel as we were in. He at length mustered up resolution enough to attempt it, first having crossed himself for an hour together, and made a kind of lug-sail out of the bits of blankets they wore about them, sewed together with split supple jacks. We then put off, and a terrible passage we had. The bottom plank of the canoe was split, which opened upon every sea; and the water continually rushing over the gunnel, I may say that we were in a manner full the whole way over, though all hands were employed in baling without ceasing a moment. As we drew near the shore, the cacique was eager to land, having been terrified to that degree with this run, that if it had not been for us, every soul must have perished; for he had very near got in amongst the breakers, where the sea drove with such violence upon the rocks, that not even an Indian could have escaped, especially as it was in the night. We kept off till we got into smooth water, and landed upon the island of Chiloe; though in a part of it that was not inhabited. Here we staid all the next day, in a very heavy snow, to recover ourselves a little after our fatigue; but the cold was so excessive, having neither shoe nor stocking, we thought we should have lost our feet; and captain Cheap was so ill, that if he had had but a few leagues further to have gone without relief, he could not have held out. It pleased God now that our sufferings, in a great measure, were drawing to an end."

Their sufferings were indeed drawing to an end, and food was at hand. But their anxieties had scarce ended when new ones began, for they were now in Spanish territory. Cheap had managed to accomplish his northward passage to Chiloe, though not quite in the swashbuckling manner he had envisaged when endeavouring to persuade Bulkeley to abandon his plan for a southward passage. At this moment Bulkeley was in Brazil, neutral territory, awaiting passage to Europe.

After making a landfall, Cheap and his two midshipmen were conducted to an Indian village where they received great hospitality and kindness. Cheap was laid on a bed of sheepskins, close to a fire. A sheep was killed for roasting. Hot broth and cakes of barley meal were brought. The trio ate until they could eat no longer, and after a night of sleep by a fire, they spent the best part of the next day eating. Indian women brought them broth, eggs, and potatoes. The Indians here were well made, good featured, and tidy in their person. They had no shoes, but wore clothes of coloured stripes. They were a great improvement on the inhuman savages who had brought the trio to Chiloe, and seemed concerned that their guests might soon receive ill treatment from the Spaniards by whom they were themselves treated as slaves.

Very soon they were taken to Castro the capital, under a

Spanish guard consisting of a number of officers and men who seemed to regard their prisoners as a formidable enemy, though the enemy could barely stand. The prisoners were given a spread of cold ham and chicken on arrival at Castro, and then, still under guard, were lodged in a cell in the Jesuits College. They had beds to sleep on, and were given a clean shirt each, "which," says Byron, "was of infinite service to us; nor did eating at first give me half the satisfaction this treasure of an old shirt did."

The language barrier made understanding difficult. The weakness and starved appearance of the prisoners told their own story, and much use must have been made of sign language. Interpreters were available but were somewhat ineffectual. Cheap was sent for by the Father Superior, and a kind of conversation was carried on in Latin, though not very good on either side. The chief subject concerned any articles they had saved or which they might still have about them which could be given to the Jesuit father. Campbell had had a watch given to him by the dying Elliot, but had already been relieved of it on arrival in Chiloe, when approached by a Jesuit. The latter had however given him clothes in return. The corregidor of Castro, on hearing that the English were heretics, expressed a wish that they should be converted. One of the fathers told him that it was ludicrous to attempt to convert them now. There would be more inducement when they later got to Chile, where "diversions and entertainment would convert them soon enough". This was prophetic, certainly in the case of one of the prisoners.

After a week here, the prisoners were escorted to the governor of Chaco in the north of the island. They travelled on horseback, their guard consisting of thirty soldiers also on horseback. Byron as usual made a good impression with a lady hostess at a farmhouse on the way. She had two beautiful daughters, and sent a message to the governor at Chaco that she would like Byron to stay for a month at the farm at a later date.

At Chaco the prisoners were well received by the governor, with whom they frequently dined; they were guarded at night in their prison by a sentry. After two weeks they were given leave to walk in the town, and were often entertained to a meal by the inhabitants, who thought they could never eat enough after their months of deprivation.

They appear to have been strangely unenquiring or curious about their future, feeling perhaps astonished to be back in some sort of civilization after so many providential escapes: they were now bent on enjoying all that lay before them. It may have been an accepted thing that they would be prisoners for the duration of the war.

Three months after the prisoners' arrival, Lieutenant Hamilton was brought in by a party that had been sent by the governor to look for him. He was in wretched condition, but, like the other three, quickly recovered under the good living that was provided.

After six months in Chaco, in December 1742, the four prisoners heard of the arrival of the packet from Lima, a ship of 250 tons. This was normally an annual event, but there had been no packet in the previous year because of the news of Anson's arrival in the south seas. News of his squadron had spread alarm all along this coast. Pizarro's failure augmented this. The captain of the Lima ship was so alarmed to hear that English prisoners were allowed to roam the streets of Chaco that he complained to the governor that he feared they might board his ship and sail her away. This gives point to a remark made by Campbell praising Cheap's plan: " If the ship's company of the *Wager* had stood by their captain, they would have been masters of Chiloe, and of the Lima ship into the bargain." In spite of large numbers of soldiery, there were no guns or forts.

The governor took his prisoners with him on a tour which was an annual affair. Once again they found themselves in Chaco. The old lady with the two beautiful daughters begged the governor to allow Byron to go to her for a few weeks. " This was granted; and accordingly I went and passed about three weeks with her very happily, as she seemed to be as fond of me as if I had been her own son. She was very unwilling to part with me again; but as the governor was soon to return to Chaco, he sent for me, and I left my benefactress with regret." Byron makes no mention this time of the daughters. He was shortly to be involved a little deeper, but managed to extricate himself.

Byron continued:

" Amongst the houses we visited at Castro there was one belonging to an old priest, who was esteemed one of the richest persons upon the island. He had a niece, of whom he was extremely fond, and who was to inherit all he possessed. He had taken a great deal of pains with her education, and she was reckoned one of the most accomplished young ladies of Chiloe. Her person was good, though she could not be called a regular beauty. This young lady did me the honour to take more notice of me than I deserved, and proposed to her uncle to convert me, and afterwards begged his consent to marry me. As the old man doated upon her, he readily agreed to it; and accordingly on the next visit I made him, acquainted me with the young lady's proposal, and his approbation of it, taking me at the same time into a room where there were several chests and boxes, which he unlocked; first shewing me what a number of fine cloaths his niece had, and then his own wardrobe, which he said should be mine at his death. Amongst other things, he produced a piece of linen, which he said should immediately be made up into shirts for me. I own this last article was a great temptation to me; however, I had the resolution to withstand it, and made the best excuses I could for not accepting of the honour they intended me; for by this time I could speak Spanish well enough to make myself understood."

They returned to Chaco with the governor at the end of the tour. At the beginning of January 1743, about the time that Bulkeley arrived at Spithead, they were put on board the first ship to Valparaiso, as prisoners of war. On arrival at that port they were confined in the condemned cell in a dungeon of the fort. A sentry with fixed bayonet guarded their exit.

Their destiny now seemed to be as unpredictable as the dice in the wheel of fortune.

CHAPTER 13

SLAVERY OR STARVATION

ONE OF the eight left ashore by Bulkeley at Freshwater Bay in
Patagonia was midshipman Isaac Morris. The other seven were
Guy Broadwater, Samuel Cooper, Benjamin Smith, John Duck,
Joseph Clinch, John Andrews, and John Allen. The prospect
of getting away from this desolate place looked grim indeed,
for they were all weak and sickly, practically destitute of food,
and had only a limited amount of ammunition. The Indians
who lived here were reputed to be savage and hostile.

Bulkeley had stated that it was impossible for the *Speedwell* to remain on a lee shore. He may have been right in
refusing to hazard the schooner, but the narrative written by
Morris does not support this view.

" The wind blew fresh at east-south-east on the four-
teenth, and we saw our vessel stretching farther off. Soon
afterwards, we received, in a scuttled cask, a few necessaries,
with ammunition, and a letter to acquaint us of the risk
which the people ran in lying near the shore, and that
they were obliged to stand farther off for their own safety,
until the weather should be more favourable.

" Next morning we had fair weather, when we expected
the boat would have stretched in for the land; but, to our

great surprise, we saw her, with her ensign hoisted, sail from us. The moderate weather, with the wind off shore, gave her people a good opportunity of standing in again, if they had thought fit. Why they did not was best known to themselves; but the most probable reason we could give for such inhuman treatment was, that, by lessening the number of their crew, they might be better accommodated with room and provisions. Possibly they might apprehend inhabitants to be near us; if so, they could be none but Indians. We could not help looking on it as an act of the greatest cruelty, thus to desert us, under a false pretence of an utter impossibility of taking us on board with them.

" The dismal apprehensions which were created by such an unexpected blow appeared plainly in our countenance, and can be much easier imagined than described. We found ourselves on a wild desolate part of the world, fatigued, sickly, and destitute of provisions. However, we had arms and ammunition; and while these lasted, we made a tolerable shift for a livelihood. The nearest inhabited place, of which we knew, was Buenos Ayres, about three hundred miles to the north-west: but we were then miserably reduced by our tedious passage through the Straits of Magellan, and in a poor condition to undertake so hazardous a journey. Nothing remained but to commit ourselves to kind Providence, and make the best of our melancholy situation, until we became recruited."

After a month, living on seal which they killed with stones, they lay in a stock of food, and began their journey for the Spanish settlement in Buenos Ayres. They knew this lay some 300 miles to the northward. Their greatest fear was of savage Indians. They travelled sixty miles in two days and met nobody, but could find no fresh water. They decided to return to Freshwater Bay and wait for the wet season.

A second attempt in May also failed, this time through lack of food.

Arrived once more at their old quarters, they divided into two watches: one watch should scour the countryside for food on one day, and the other the next. They also swore an oath that they would keep together as far as was possible, and put up a struggle if attacked. They tamed two wild puppies, and bred from them. They did the same with wild pigs, and all lived happily together with the men in their home-made hut.

They were now tolerably comfortable. But with the approach of the winter solstice in June, and the sight of a tiger on one day, followed by the appearance of a lion on the next, they quickly decided on a third attempt to reach Buenos Ayres. This time they resolved to take provisions which would last a month. Divided into two parties of four, they searched far and near for food. Grim tragedy struck them.

Isaac Morris says:

" Early in the morning it was my duty, with Samuel Cooper, John Andrews, and John Duck, to go to the rocks. As our usual way of killing seals was with stones or clubs, we never carried muskets along with us. We had been out all day, and killed three; and having got within a stone-cast of our hut in the dusk of the evening, I perceived our dogs very busy at a small distance wagging their tails in a fondling manner. Being a-head of my companions, I passed on without much regarding it, thinking they had lighted on a dead colt; but on coming to the hut, I was quite confounded to find it rifled, and all our necessaries taken away. In the utmost consternation, I ran back to my companions, whom I saw standing where I had left the dogs; and they, seeing me eagerly hastening towards them, cried out, ' What's the matter, Isaac?' I told them our hut was pulled down, and every thing taken away. ' Aye,' said they, ' and something

Sir Joshua Reynolds.

11. John Byron, midshipman in the *Wager,* later vice-admiral nicknamed
Foul Weather Jack.

Minutes at a Court-Martial held on board his Maty's Ship Prince George at Spithead the 15 April 1746 for enquiring into the Cause of the Loss of his Maty's Ship the Wager, cast away on a Sunken Rock on the Coast of Patagonia in the South Seas on the 14 May 1741 pursuant to an Order from the Right Honoble the Lords Commrs of the Admiralty Dated 24 March 1745 Vizt)

Admiralty's Warrt 11th Octor 1744 Empowering Vice Admiral Steuart to hold Courts-Martial ————— Read.

Court Sworne.

Prisoners brought in.

Admiralty's Order 24 March 1745 ———— Read.

Captn Cheaps Narrative 11 April 1746 ——— Read.

· Captn Cheap: doe you Charge any Officer besides the Lieut with being in any degree Afcessary to the Loss of the Wager.

Noe Sir, I acquit them all of that.

John Jones late Maty of the Wager Sworne Deposition, read which he Confirms.

When did you see the Land first.

I did not see it, being sick in my Hammacoe, but I heard it was seen at 2 in the Afternoon. I reckoned that day we were 45 Leagues from the Shore.

Captn Cheap doe you think you could have carried your Topsails.

Yes, I thought soe when I ordered them to be sett, there are 17 Degrees of Variation in that part of the World, but we were certainly Embayed.

Captn Cheap how doe you reckon the Land lay there

(1)

Job.

12. A page from the Minutes of the Court-martial held on board H.M.S. *Prince George* at Spithead 15th April, 1746.

worse has happened, for yonder lie poor Guy Broadwater and Benjamin Smith murdered.' It was a most shocking sight: one had his throat cut, and the other was stabbed in the breast: they were hardly cold, so that we thought the murderers could not be far off; and were under no small apprehensions of sharing the like fate. Going to inspect the state of the hut more narrowly, we found every thing carried off; our powder, ball, and muskets gone; the fire extinguished; and not the least utensil left. Where to go, or what to do, we knew not: we durst not trust ourselves another night on this fatal spot, and yet were afraid to venture farther.

" At last we came to the resolution of proceeding to the next sandy bay, about a mile distant, and taking up our quarters there for the night. But, on arriving, we could find no shelter, not so much as a cliff to lie under, which obliged us to return to our old place, and pass the night at it, happen what would.

" Next morning, the dogs that belonged to our comrades stood on the top of the cliff barking at us, and would not come down, though we called them by their names; and it was with difficulty that we enticed them to come in the evening. What became of Joseph Clinch and John Allen we knew not, nor could we afterwards learn any account of them. It seemed most probable to us that the Indians had carried them off, and murdered the other two, who possibly might make some resistance, as we had all agreed to do in case of an attack. But had it been so, we might reasonably have expected to find some of their enemies killed, as our people had fire-arms with them. It was impossible, too, that this catastrophe could be the result of a quarrel among themselves, from the manner of their death; for the one was stabbed, and the other had his throat cut; both, very plainly, done with a knife, an implement of which none of us was in

G

possession. We buried our two murdered comrades in the best manner we could, by scraping away the light sand with our hands two feet deep, and raising a bed of it over their corpses."

Besides losing their four comrades in such violent and shocking fashion, the four survivors had lost everything. They were without arms, utensils, or the means of making a fire. What food they could acquire must be eaten raw. They were fearful of the prospect of starvation; and even more terrified at the knowledge of murderers in the neighbourhood. They started immediately for the third attempt to reach Buenos Ayres, accompanied by sixteen dogs and two pigs. They prayed for guidance, and set out along the sandy beach. After ten days they had reached swamps and bogs into which they sank at times up to their shoulders. Further progress became impossible. For the third time they returned to Freshwater Bay. They lived on raw meat; dog, pig, and a dead horse. They continued thus for three months, not straying far from their hut for fear of Indians, lions and tigers. In desperation, for want of a tool, they walked sixty miles to retrieve an old musket that John Duck remembered throwing away a year earlier. On return they beat half the length of the musket barrel flat with stones, and sharpened the edge on the rocks. Using this as a hatchet they intended converting the trunk of a fallen tree into a boat. They could have saved themselves the trouble. Once again they were overtaken by a crucial event. They had recently been fearful for their lives, but had given little thought to their freedom. Isaac Morris writes dramatically of the event.

" Two days after finishing our hatchet, it being my turn to stay in the hut, my three comrades went to a place which we called the Long Point, in quest of provisions. Towards evening I walked out to see if they were returning, when, to my astonishment, I discovered about a dozen of horses galloping down the sandy bay in the direction of our hut; and as they came nearer I plainly saw men on their backs, and that these were Indians. It was vain to fly: I imagined nothing but death approaching, and prepared to meet it with all the resolution I could muster up. I ran towards the strangers, and, falling on my knees, begged my life with all the signs of humility I could make, when I heard a voice saying, 'Don't be afraid, Isaac, we are all here'; words which revived me. The Indians alighted; and whilst some were intent on examining the hut, others stood with drawn knives ready to dispatch us, in case we made any resistance. When they had satisfied their curiosity, they gave three confused shouts, and immediately making us get up behind them, carried us away a few miles inland from the sea-shore, where there were about a dozen more of their companions with above four hundred horses taken in hunting. We were treated with great humanity: they killed a horse, kindled a fire, and roasted part of it; which, to us, who had been eating raw flesh three months, was most delicious entertainment. They also gave each of us a piece of an old blanket to cover our nakedness.

" I had been in great hazard of being left alone; for, when the Indians met with my three comrades, and were immediately hurrying them away to their place of rendezvous, they were with difficulty made to understand by signs, that there was one more belonging to their party a little way off; and then my comrades guided them to the hut, where I had the happiness of being taken prisoner."

Theirs was now the happiness of slaves. They had no more thinking to do. They went where they were taken; they were fed, clothed, and even housed in rough huts. They were treated with humanity. Their price was not high. In one place they were bought and sold four different times; first for a pair of spurs, second for a brass pan, third for ostrich feathers, and so on for trifles. Sometimes they were gambled for with dice. They travelled a thousand miles in a south-westerly direction, taking four months, arriving eventually at a town where the king of the Indians lived.

The king examined them, asking questions in Spanish. Morris knew a little Spanish. When the king heard that they were at war with the Spaniards, he ordered a horse to be killed and roasted for them, and a hut to be built for them. They were to remain here as slaves, carrying wood and water, and skinning horses. It was now May 1743. Another winter was approaching. Bulkeley and his companions had arrived in England four months earlier. Cheap and his companions Hamilton, Byron, and Campbell, were prisoners of war in Chile. These were the few survivors of the *Wager*, who had seen one after another of their shipmates depart through murder, drowning, starvation, or exhaustion.

Isaac Morris, together with his companions Samuel Cooper, John Andrews, and John Duck, were now slaves to the Indians, but seem to have revelled in their new-found existence. Winter was extreme, with snow often five or six feet deep. The Indians had captured many Spanish women. The king gave Morris and his companions a wife each.

At the end of 1743, in fine summer weather, after eight months as slaves, in a life blissful compared with the rigors they had previously suffered, Morris and his companions represented to the king that they wished to go to Buenos Ayres. Here, they said, they had friends who would recompense him handsomely for their redemption, if he allowed them to go. He was delighted to do so, for a price of ninety dollars per head; but refused to let poor John Duck go. The latter was a mulatto who had been born in London. Because of his colour the Indians felt that he should end his days with them.

The ransom for the three English slaves was paid by an Englishman in Montevideo. Morris writes, " We were greatly indebted to the president of the English Assiento house, Mr. Grey, from whose compassion and kind intercession we were redeemed from the hands of the Indians, as he offered to do it entirely at his own charge." Morris and his two companions were interviewed frequently by the governor of Buenos Ayres, who urged them to become catholics. This they refused. They were then sent as prisoners of war on board the *Asia*, which lay at Montevideo, on the north bank, about a hundred miles down river from Buenos Ayres. In retrospect it is possible that they would have preferred to be the slaves of the Indians.

The *Asia*, it will be remembered, had been Admiral Pizarro's flagship when his squadron raced Anson to be first in the South Sea. The *Asia*, with Pizarro, had had to return to Montevideo, having rolled out her masts. A second attempt was made by Pizarro the following year. Again the *Asia* lost her masts off Cape Horn. One ship of the Spanish squadron, the *Esperanza*, was successfully sailed round the Horn to Chile by Captain Mindinuetta, who had been captain of the *Guipuscoa* when she was lost. Pizarro then went overland to join her and assumed command early in 1743. This of course did not endear him to Mindinuetta. The *Asia* had returned to Montevideo after her second failure, and had lain there neglected ever since. There was a great shortage of hands among the Spaniards after the earlier disasters to Pizarro's ships. The *Asia* was in any case in no fit state to take the seas.

Now, early in 1745, Morris and his companions found themselves living as prisoners of war in the *Asia*, together with sixteen other English prisoners. The latter had been members of an English trader, the *Philip*, which the Spaniards had boarded in the River Plate two years earlier, under pretext of trading. They had murdered Penkethman the captain, and nine of the crew, and then took the vessel.

The prisoners cleaned ship and swabbed decks, and were kept under guard between decks when off duty. Their food was poor and scanty, and there were no wives for them in this port.

Morris, knowing the duties of a prisoner of war, escaped one night, and swam a quarter of a mile to the shore. He hid in a bush of thorns, practically naked, and in frosty weather. He was recaptured the next morning, taken on board the *Asia*, and for two weeks afterwards was punished by having his neck and heels put into the stocks, four hours every day. He and his companions were now regarded as potentially dangerous men. The guards were increased. All chance of escape had now been removed. All they could do was to be patient: to wait for the end of the war; and perhaps linger over happy memories of slavery, and their women and children left behind.

CHAPTER 14

PRISONERS OF WAR

WHILE MIDSHIPMAN Isaac Morris and his two companions were languishing as prisoners of war in the decaying Spanish ship *Asia*, Cheap was a prisoner in Valparaiso.

Cheap's arrival in Valparaiso caused quite a stir. The sentries who guarded him and his three companions were able to make a pretty penny by allowing the curious to see them. With the knowledge that Anson's squadron was making free in the Pacific, the governor must have felt no little pride at having under his care four dangerous English seamen of such odd and scraggy appearance.

Byron said:

" The Spanish captain waited upon the governor of the fort, and informed him that he had four English prisoners on board. We were ordered ashore in the afternoon, and were received as we got upon the beach, by a file of soldiers, with their bayonets fixed, who surrounded us, and then marched up to the fort, attended by a numerous mob. We were carried before the governor, whose house was full of officers. He was blind, asked a few questions, and then spoke of nothing but the strength of the garrison he commanded, and desired to know if we had observed that all the lower battery was

brass guns. We were immediately after, by his order, put
into the condemned hole. There was nothing but four bare
walls, excepting a heap of lime that filled one third of it, and
made the place swarm with fleas in such a manner that
we were presently covered with them. Some of admiral
Pizarro's soldiers were here in garrison that had been landed
from his ships at Buenos Ayres, as he could not get round
Cape Horn. A sentinel's box was placed at our door, and we
had always a soldier with his bayonet fixed, to prevent our
stirring out. The curiosity of the people was such, that our
prison was continually full from morning till night, by which
the soldiers made a pretty penny, as they took money from
every person for the sight. In a few days, captain Cheap and
Mr. Hamilton were ordered up to St. Jago, as they were
known to be officers by having saved their commissions; but
Mr. Campbell and I were to continue in prison. Captain
Cheap expressed great concern when he left us; he told me it
was what he had all along dreaded, that they would separate
us when we got into this country; but he assured me, if he
was permitted to speak to the president, that he would never
leave soliciting him till he obtained a grant for me to be sent
up to him. No sooner were they gone than we fared very
badly."

Byron and Campbell were now reduced to one meal a day,
consisting of a few potatoes mixed with hot water. The governor remarked that if it was insufficient they could starve. This
attitude invoked considerable sympathy. Everybody who came
to see these curious exhibits gave them something either of
food or of money. Their sentry was particularly moved, and
"never would receive a farthing from us," said Byron, " telling us we might still want it; and the whole time we were there,
which was some weeks, he laid aside half his daily pay to
supply us, though he had a wife and six children, and never

could have the least hope or expectation of any recompence."

They were in terror one night when a dreadful earthquake rocked the prison. They expected to be buried or crushed. Added to this horror was the sound of chains and imprecations from seventy fettered men condemned to the galleys, who were in an adjoining cell.

Shortly afterwards, Byron and Campbell were ordered to join Cheap and Hamilton in Santiago, ninety miles inland. They were escorted by a mule-driver who took such a fancy to Byron, because he helped to prevent the mules from straying, that he advised him very seriously against remaining in Santiago. It was a wicked city, he said, full of extravagance, vice, and folly, and Byron could soon become an expert mule-driver, leading a happy and innocent life. Byron thanked him, but said he would try the city first, and join the mule-driver if he did not like it. Santiago must have agreed with him, for he remained there with the others for all of 1743 and 1744.

They were comfortably lodged with a Scottish physician who did everything possible for their comfort. The president sent them an invitation to dine with him, to meet Admiral Pizarro and his officers. One of the latter made them a generous offer of money for new clothes. They were now on parole, and enjoyed themselves immensely. This is a story of men's actions and thoughts, and the ways of Providence, rather than a description of places visited, but it is appropriate to include some extracts from Byron's enthusiastic description of Santiago, and to realize what joy now followed to compensate for past sufferings.

Says Byron:

" This city is situated in about 33 degrees and 30 minutes, south latitude, at the west foot of the immense chain of mountains called the Cordilleras. It stands on a most beautiful plain of above thirty leagues extent. It was founded by don

Pedro de Baldivia, the conqueror of Chili. The plan of it was
marked out by him in squares, like Lima; and almost every
house belonging to people of any fashion, has a large court
before it, with great gates, and a garden behind. There is a
little rivulet, neatly faced with stone, runs through every
street; by which they can cool the streets, or water their
gardens, when they please. The whole town is extremely
well paved. Their gardens are full of noble orange-trees and
floripondies, with all sorts of flowers, which perfume the
houses, and even the whole city. Much about the middle of
it, is the great square, called the Plaça Real, or the Royal
Square; there are eight avenues leading into it. The west
side contains the cathedral and the bishop's palace; the north
side is the president's palace, the royal court, the council
house, and the prison; the south side is a row of piazzas, the
whole length of which are shops, and over it a gallery to see
the bull-feasts; the east side has some large houses belonging
to people of distinction; and in the middle is a large foun-
tain, with a brass bason.

" The climate of Chili is, I believe, the finest in the world.
What they call their winter does not last three months; and
even that is very moderate, as may be imagined by their
manner of building, for they have no chimneys in their
houses. All the rest of the year is delightful; for though from
ten or eleven in the morning till five in the afternoon, it is
very hot, yet the evenings and mornings are very cool and
pleasant; and in the hottest time of the year, it is from six
in the evening till two or three in the morning, that the
people of this country meet to divert themselves with music
and other entertainments, at which there is plenty of cool-
ing liquors, as they are well supplied with ice from the neighbouring Cordilleras. At these assemblies, many intrigues are
carried on; for they think of nothing else through the year.
Their fandangoes are very agreeable; the women dance

inimitably well, and very gracefully. They are all born with
an ear for music, and most of them have delightful voices;
and all play upon the guittar and harp. The latter, at first,
appears a very aukward instrument for a woman; yet that
prejudice is soon got over, and they far excell any other
nation upon it. They are extremely complaisant and polite;
and when asked either to play, dance, or sing, they do it
without a moment's hesitation, and that with an exceeding
good grace."

This complaisance pleased Byron very much. He was not
unobservant of their charms, or backward in returning their
gallantry.

" The women are remarkably handsome, and very extrava-
gant in their dress. Their hair, which is as thick as is possible
to be conceived, they wear of a vast length, without any
other ornaments upon the head than a few flowers; they
plait it behind in four plaits, and twist them round a bodkin,
at each end of which is a diamond rose. Their shifts are all
over lace, as is a little tight waistcoat they wear over them.
Their petticoats are open before, and lap over, and have
commonly three rows of very rich lace of gold or silver. In
winter, they have an upper waistcoat of cloth of gold or
silver, and in summer, of the finest linen, covered all over
with the finest Flanders lace. The sleeves of these are immensely wide. Over all this, when the air is cool, they have a
mantle, which is only of bays, of the finest colours, round
which there is abundance of lace. When they go abroad, they
wear a veil, which is so contrived that one eye is only seen.
Their feet are very small, and they value themselves as
much upon it as the Chinese do. Their shoes are pinked
and cut; their stockings silk, with gold and silver clocks; and
they love to have the end of an embroidered garter hang a

little below the petticoat. Their breasts and shoulders are
very naked; and, indeed, you may easily discern their whole
shape by their manner of dress. They have fine sparkling
eyes, ready wit, a great deal of good-nature, and a strong
disposition to gallantry.

"A lady lived next door to us, whose name was donna
Francisca Giron; and as my name sounded something like
it, she would have it that we were Parientes. She had a
daughter, a very fine young woman, who both played and
sung remarkably well: she was reckoned the finest voice in
St. Jago. They saw a great deal of company, and we were
welcome to her house whenever we pleased. We were a long
time in this country, but we passed it very agreeably." . . .
"One night in Lent, as I was standing close to the houses as
the procession went by, and having nothing but a thin waistcoat on under my cloak, and happening to have my arm out,
a lady came by, and gave me a pinch with so good a will,
that I thought she had taken the piece out; and indeed, I
carried the marks for a long time after. I durst not take the
least notice of this at the time; for had I made any disturbance, I should have been knocked on the head. This kind
lady immediately after mixed with the crowd, and I never
could find out who had done me that favour."

Campbell also comments on the attractions of the women.

"The Spaniards are very proud and dress extremely
gay; particularly the Women, who spend a great deal of
Money upon their Persons and Houses. They are a good Sort
of People, and very courteous to Strangers: Their Women
are also fond of Gentlemen from other Countries, and of
other Nations. The Dress of the fair Sex here is widely
different from that of the Spanish Women in Europe. They
wear no Stays, only a little Jacket, with large white Sleeves
to it. Their Petty-coats are not close all round like the

European Petty-coat; they are very short, one Part doubles over the other, and they tie it as low as Men button the Waist-band of their Breeches. They wear no Hoop, for the smaller they are below, the more in Fashion. Their Shoes have no Heels, and are all cut in Figures. Their Hair they dress in a very fine Taste, and wearing no Caps, it looks extremely handsome."

This life must have stood in great contrast with the starving days of canoe pulling, or the days when they were the principal exhibit in a dungeon.

Perhaps the most interesting item pertinent to this story is Byron's reference to meeting people who had been passengers in Spanish ships captured by Anson. There is no doubt that Anson's humanity in dealing with prisoners did much towards increasing the goodwill between Englishman and Spaniard far and wide in the South American continent.

" We found many Spaniards here that had been taken by commodore Anson, and had been for some time prisoners on board the *Centurion*. They all spoke in the highest terms of the kind treatment they had received; and it is natural to imagine, that it was chiefly owing to that laudable example of humanity our reception here was so good. They had never had anything but privateers and buccaneers amongst them before, who handled their prisoners very roughly; so that the Spaniards in general, both of Peru and Chili, had the greatest dread of being taken by the English; but some of them told us, that they were so happy on board the *Centurion*, that they should not have been sorry if the commodore had taken them with him to England."

While in Santiago, Cheap's party were able to draw money and live in style. They were also offered a generous present of

2,000 dollars by don Manuel de Guiror, one of Pizarro's officers, who had no desire to be repaid. As Pizarro was very short of officers, it is likely that he hoped to persuade the *Wager* survivors to join the Spanish Navy; Cheap would be the first to be aware of this hope. Cheap accepted an advance of 600 dollars, but not as a present. He insisted that it should be drawn on the English consul in Lisbon. Cheap gave both Hamilton and Byron a quarter of this, 150 dollars each; but to Campbell he gave only one eighth. Campbell was furious at this unequal treatment. Reports current at this time stated that Campbell had married or intended to marry a young Spanish woman, and would embrace the Roman Catholic faith. This was regarded as rank heresy by Englishment at this time, and was contrary to the rules of the Navy. After a year in Santiago, Cheap was offered the chance of drawing more money. This he did, but emphatically refused to let Campbell have any. A rift developed which could not be repaired. Campbell left his three companions.

Towards the end of two years, the president at Santiago sent for Cheap to say that a French ship was at Valparaiso, bound for Spain. He offered the four Englishmen a passage. All accepted but Campbell, who preferred to travel overland to Buenos Ayres with four officers of Pizarro's fleet to join a Spanish ship.

Cheap, Hamilton, and Byron embarked in the French frigate *Lys* at Valparaiso on the 20th December 1744. Before embarking, Byron sought out the soldier who had been so good to him two years earlier, and made him an unexpected present.

Their voyage was to be eventful. In the first place, Britain was now at war with France as well as with Spain. Very soon the *Lys* sprang a dangerous leak and had to put back to Valparaiso for repairs. On the 1st March 1745 she again sailed. She made a good passage round the Horn, and reached the island of Tobago before the end of June. The navigation from

here onwards into the Caribbean Sea was somewhat extraordinary; but even more extraordinary was the behaviour of
the crew at the prospect of being taken by a British ship.
Says Byron:

"On the 29th of June, in the morning, we made the
island of Tobago, and then shaped a course for Martinico;
and on the first of July, by our reckonings, expected to see
it, but were disappointed. This was imputed to the currents,
which, whether they had set the ship to the eastward or
westward, nobody could tell; but upon looking over the
charts, it was imagined, if the current had driven her to the
westward, it must have been among the Granadillos, which
was thought impossible without seeing any of them, as they
are so near together, and a most dangerous place for rocks.
It was then concluded we were to the eastward, and accordingly we steered S.W. by W. but having run this course for
above thirty leagues, and no land appearing, it was resolved
to stand to the northward till we should gain the latitude
of Porto Rico, and on the fourth in the evening we made
that island; so that it was now certain the ship had been
hustled through the Granadillos in the night, which was,
without doubt, as extraordinary a passage as ever ship made.

"It was now resolved to go between the islands of Porto
Rico and St. Domingo for Cape François, therefore we lay
to that night. In the morning, we made sail along shore; and
about ten o'clock, as I was walking the quarter-deck, captain
Cheap came out of the cabin, and told me he had just seen
a beef-barrel go by the ship; that he was sure it had but
lately been thrown overboard, and that he would venture any
wager we saw an English cruizer before long. In about half
an hour after, we saw two sail to leeward, from off the
quarter-deck; for they kept no look out from the mast head,
and we presently observed they were in chace of us. The

French and Spaniards on board, now began to grow a good deal alarmed, when it fell stark calm; but not before the ships had neared us so much, that we plainly discerned them to be English men of war; the one a two-decker, the other a twenty-gun ship. The French had now thoughts, when a breeze should spring up, of running the ship on shore upon Porto Rico; but when they came to consider what a set of banditti inhabited that island, and that in all probability they would have their throats cut for the sake of plundering the wreck, they were resolved to take their chance, and stand to the northward between the two islands.

" In the evening, a fresh breeze sprung up, and we shaped a course accordingly. The two ships had it presently afterwards, and neared us amazingly fast. Now every body on board gave themselves up; the officers were busy in their cabins, filling their pockets with what was most valuable; the men put on their best cloaths, and many of them came to me with little lumps of gold, desiring I would take them, as they said they had much rather I should benefit by them, whom they were acquainted with, than those that chaced them. I told them there was time enough, though I thought they were as surely taken as if the English had been already on board. A fine moonlight night came on, and we expected every moment to see the ships along-side of us; but we saw nothing of them in the night, and to our great astonishment, in the morning no ships were to be seen even from the mast-head. Thus did these two cruizers lose one of the richest prizes, by not chacing an hour or two longer. There were near two millions of dollars on board, besides a valuable cargo."

The *Lys* narrowly missed being taken off San Domingo. Byron also comments on the remarkable fact that there was not one sick man on board during the whole of the passage to San

Domingo, yet on arrival there "many were taken ill and three or four died."

Towards the end of August the *Lys* sailed from San Domingo with a large convoy of fifty merchantmen escorted by a French squadron. Neither the commodore nor any French officer took the least notice of the English prisoners of war, who were allowed ashore every day.

The discipline of the commodore, l'Etanducre, was severe, and the cruel punishment inflicted on an offending captain, who allowed his ship to get out of station, exceptional. Nevertheless the punishment had the desired effect. Not a ship of the convoy was taken. Byron's description of the event is worth recounting.

Says Byron:

"On the sixth of September we put to sea, in company with the five men of war, and about fifty sail of merchantmen. On the eighth we made the Cayco Grande; and the next day a Jamaica privateer, a large fine sloop, hove in sight, keeping a little to windward of the convoy, resolving to pick up one or two of them in the night, if possible. This obliged monsieur L'Etanducre to send a frigate to speak to all the convoy, and order them to keep close to him in the night; which they did, and in such a manner, that sometimes seven or eight of them were on board one another together; by which they received much damage; and to repair which, the whole squadron was obliged to lay to sometimes for a whole day. The privateer kept her station, jogging on with the fleet.

"At last, the commodore ordered two of his best-going ships to chace her. She appeared to take no notice of them till they were pretty near her, and then would make sail and be out of sight presently. The chacing ships no sooner returned, than the privateer was in company again. As by this every night some accident happened to some of the convoy by keeping so close together, a fine ship of thirty guns, belonging to Marseilles, hauled out a little to windward of the rest of the fleet; which L'Etanducre perceiving in the morning, ordered the frigate to bring the captain of her on board of him; and then making a signal for all the convoy to close to him, he fired a gun, and hoisted a red flag at the ensign staff; and immediately after the captain of the merchantman was run up to the main-yard-arm, and from thence ducked three times. He was then sent on board his ship again, with orders to keep his colours flying the whole day, in order to distinguish him from the rest.

" One day, the ship we were in happened to be out of her station, by sailing so heavily, when the commodore made the signal to speak to our captain, who seemed frightened out of his wits. When we came near him, he began with the grossest abuse, threatening our captain, that if ever he was out of his station again, he would serve him as he had done the other. This rigid discipline, however, preserved the convoy; for though the privateer kept company a long time, she was not so fortunate as to meet with the reward of her perseverance."

On the 31st October, the *Lys* came to an anchor in Brest Road, and having a valuable cargo on board, was towed into the harbour next morning, and lashed alongside one of the men-of-war. The money she contained, amounting to two millions of dollars, was soon landed, and the officers and men, being impatient to get on shore, left nobody on board except the three English prisoners, and a man or two to look after the ship. Some of the French officers sent them food, but there was no regular allowance, and they would, according to Byron, have starved without this generosity. There was no light or heating, nor had they warm clothes. Every night, from five onwards, they were obliged to sit in the dark. Not a single officer came to call on Cheap.

Eventually an order came for their release, but it was nearly six months before they were able to embark for England. This they did from Morlaix, in a Dutch ship. On the 9th April 1746, they were off Dover, and reminded the Dutchman of his promise to land them at Dover. He said he would, but the next morning they found themselves off the coast of France. At this moment an English man-of-war appeared to windward, bore down on the Dutchman, and sent a boat with an officer. The ship proved to be H.M.S. *Squirrel*, whose captain sent Cheap, Hamilton, and Byron to Dover in one of his cutters. On landing at Dover the three set out immediately for Canterbury. Cheap was so tired by the time they got there that he was unable to proceed further that night. He was still tired the next morning, so it was agreed that he and Hamilton should take a post-chaise while Byron rode. They found themselves short of money and were unable to buy anything to eat. Hunger seemed to pursue them to the end of their journey.

Byron concludes his narrative, written long after this, in 1768, with his unexpected arrival in London.

" My proportion fell so short, that it was, by calculation, barely, enough to pay for horses, without a farthing for eating a bit upon the road, or even for the very turnpikes. Those I was obliged to defraud, by riding as hard as I could through them all, not paying the least regard to the man, who called out to stop me. The want of refreshment I bore as well as I could. When I got to the Borough, I took a coach and drove to Marlborough-street, where my friends had lived when I left England; but when I came there, I found the house shut up. Having been absent so many years, and in all that time never having heard a word from home, I knew not who was dead, or who was living, or where to go next; or even how to pay the coachman. I recollected a linen-draper's shop, not far from thence, which our family had used. I therefore drove there next, and making myself known, they paid the coachman. I then enquired after our family, and was told my sister had married lord Carlisle, and was at that time in Soho-square. I immediately walked to the house, and knocked at the door; but the porter not liking my figure, which was half French, half Spanish, with the addition of a large pair of boots covered with dirt, he was going to shut the door in my face; but I prevailed with him to let me come in.

" I need not acquaint my readers with what surprise and joy my sister received me. She immediately furnished me with money sufficient to appear like the rest of my country-men; till that time I could not be properly said to have finished all the extraordinary scenes which a series of unfortunate adventures had kept me in for the space of five years and upwards."

Of the twenty who had left Wager Island with Cheap in the barge on the 15th December 1741, three only now returned to their native land, having taken four years and four months over the journey. Campbell was still on his way, preferring to travel under Spanish jurisdiction.

With Cheap's unexpected arrival in England, for he had long been given up for dead, a court martial was ordered to enquire into the loss of the *Wager*. The news of his arrival must have given Mr. Bulkeley and Mr. Cummins a severe turn. It was like hearing of somebody returning from the dead. Their *Voyage to the South Seas* 1740-1741 was selling well. Until this moment they must have felt like public heroes. Now there were grim thoughts of the noose at the yard-arm.

CHAPTER 15

ANOTHER MUTINY

WE SAW that Alexander Campbell left Cheap at Santiago where the prisoners were living on the fat of the land, on the grounds that he had been unfairly treated. Cheap would not let him have his share of the money advanced for them.

Campbell refused to travel to Valparaiso with Cheap to embark in the *Lys* for France. Instead, he joined four of Pizarro's officers on the 20th January 1745 and went overland to Buenos Ayres. This was a hazardous journey, with mules, over precipitous mountains and long narrow and winding paths. One mule slipped from the path and was dashed to pieces on rocks below; two were frozen to death, and twenty died of starvation or thirst. Both water and vegetation were scarce. Campbell and the officers rode on mules, but Admiral Pizarro drove in a wagon drawn by oxen. The journey lasted seven weeks.

On arrival at Buenos Ayres, Campbell was invited to dine with the governor. This was the man who had treated Isaac Morris and his two companions in such an uncivil manner upon their redemption from the Indians. When they had repeatedly refused to be converted to Roman Catholicism he had sent them as prisoners of war to the *Asia* lying off Montevideo.

She was now fitting out for a passage to Europe with Admiral Pizarro.

Campbell was reputed already to have been converted and was allowed his liberty. Nevertheless the governor of Buenos Ayres had him twice confined in a fort for periods of several weeks. In August 1745, five months after his arrival, the governor sent him to Montevideo. Here he was treated with great attention, being visited by the officers of the Spanish men-of-war lying in harbour, among whom were two Irish captains, one Scotch captain, and one English lieutenant. Cheap's impression that Campbell may have offered his services at some time to the Spaniards may be understood. His treatment here was in great contrast to that dealt out to his fellow midshipman Isaac Morris. He embarked in the *Asia* on the 13th October 1745 bound for Europe with Pizarro, presumably as one of the hands sent on board to help make up the general shortage.

Also sent on board were eleven Indians whom the Spaniards had taken in a skirmish. They were ultimately destined for the galleys.

The four *Wager* survivors now on board were Alexander Campbell, Isaac Morris, Samuel Cooper, and John Andrews. Even now they were not permitted to travel without further incident, in this case a small matter of mutiny. Dandy Kidd's prophecy was still being worked out. The affair is best told in accordance with Isaac Morris's narrative, since he was a witness. It emphasizes beautifully the prevailing attitudes between Spaniard, Indian, and Englishman.

"In the latter end of October 1745, we sailed from Monte Video in the *Asia*, bound for Spain; and in three days an incident happened on board, which had nearly proved fatal to the whole crew.

"About nine at night, we were alarmed with the cry of

mutiny, and so indeed it proved; but such a mutiny as never would have been suspected by any of the ship's crew, or perhaps credited by posterity, if a number of persons were not living to attest the fact. The Indians, above mentioned, were a chief named Orellana, and ten of his followers, who belonged to a very powerful tribe, which had committed great ravages in the neighbourhood of Buenos Ayres. Now on board the *Asia,* they were treated with much insolence and barbarity by the Spaniards, the meanest officers among whom were accustomed to beat them on the slightest pretences, and sometimes only to shew their superiority. Orellana and his followers, though apparently patient and submissive, meditated a severe revenge. He endeavoured to converse with such of the English as understood the Spanish language, and seemed very desirous of learning how many of them were on board, and which they were. Aware of their being as hostile to the Spaniards as himself, he certainly meant to disclose his purpose, and induce them to embark in the plan he had formed for avenging himself and regaining his liberty. But, not finding them so precipitate and vindictive as he expected, after distantly sounding them, he proceeded no farther in respect to their participation, but resolved to trust his enterprise to himself and his ten faithful followers.

" The necessary arrangements being made, the Indians provided themselves with the sharp pointed knives which were in common use in the ship, and also were secretly employed in cutting out thongs from raw hides, to the ends of which they fixed the double-headed shot of the small quarter-deck guns. This, when swung round their heads, is a dangerous weapon, and, as already observed, they are extremely expert with it. An outrage committed on the chief himself, precipitated the execution of his daring enterprise; for one of the officers, a brutal fellow, having órdered him aloft, of which he was incapable of performance, then, under pretence of disobedience, cruelly beat him, and left him bleeding on the deck.

"Within a day or two afterwards, Orellana and his followers about nine in the evening, while many of the principal officers were enjoying the coolness of the air on the quarter-deck, came all together on the quarter-deck, and drew towards the door of the great cabin. They were immediately reprimanded by the boatswain, who ordered them to be gone. On this Orellana spoke to his followers in their native langauge, when four of them retired, two towards each gangway, while he himself, and the remaining six, seemed to be slowly quitting the quarter-deck. When the Indians detched had taken possession of the gangway, Orellana gave the war whoop, which is the harshest and most terrific yell that can be conceived. Instantly the whole drew their knives, and brandished the double headed shot which had been prepared, and, immediately falling on the Spaniards, laid nearly forty of them at their feet. About twenty of these were killed on the spot, and the remainder disabled. Many of the officers, at the commencement of the tumult, pushed into the great cabin, where they put out the lights and barricaded the door; and, of those who had escaped the first fury of the Indians, some endeavoured to escape one way and some another, but most of them ascended the main-shrouds, and sheltered themselves either in the tops or the rigging. Although the attack was made on the quarter-deck only, the watch in the forecastle, finding the communication cut off, and terrified by the wounds of the few who had forced their way along to them for refuge, and besides, being ignorant of who and what were their enemies, also run up the rigging of the foremast and bowsprit.

"Thus did eleven Indians, with unexampled courage and resolution, almost instantaneously make themselves master of the quarter-deck of a sixty-six-gun ship, manned with nearly five hundred men, and continue some time in peaceable possession of it. The officers and crew, who had escaped into different parts of the ship, were long anxious only for their own safety, and incapable of forming any plan for quelling the insurrection. The yells of the Indians, indeed, the groans of the wounded, and the confused clamours of the crew, all heightened by the obscurity prevailing, greatly magnified the danger at first. The Spaniards, likewise, sensible of the disaffection of the impressed men, and, at the same time, conscious of the barbarity their prisoners had experienced, believed that it was a general conspiracy, and that their own destruction was inevitable.

" But the tumult considerably subsided when the Indians had completely cleared the quarter-deck, for those who had escaped were kept silent by dread, and the Indians were incapable of pursuing them to renew the disorder. When Orellana saw himself master of the quarter-deck, he broke open the arm-chest, which, on a slight suspicion of mutiny, had been placed there a few days preceding, as a place of greater security. Here he expected to find cutlasses sufficient for himself and his companions, in the employment of which they were extremely skilful; and with these, it was supposed, he meant to make his way to the great cabin. But, to his great disappointment, it contained nothing except fire-arms, which were of no use to him, at least they concealed the cutlasses under them. By this time, Pizarro, the admiral, and his companions in the great cabin, were able to hold conversation through the windows and port-holes with those in the gun-room and between decks, and thence learned, that the English, who were chiefly suspected, had not intermeddled in the mutiny, and were all safe; and they also found, that the only participators were Orellana and his people. Pizarro, therefore, resolved to attack them on the quarter-deck, before the discontented should join them; and, collecting together whatever arms were in the cabin, distributed them to his companions. They had pistols, but neither powder nor ball; however, in consequence of the correspondence established with the gun-room, they lowered down a bucket from the cabin, and, by that means, received a quantity of pistol-cartridges out of one of the gun-room ports. They then partly opened the cabin door, and fired some shot among the Indians on the quarter-deck at first without effect. At length, Mindinuetta had the good fortune to shoot Orellana dead on the spot, on which his faithful companions, abandoning all thoughts of further resistance, leaped into the sea, where every man perished. Thus was the insurrection quelled, and the ship regained, after being two hours in the possession of this gallant chief and his unfortunate countrymen. To the whole of the affair I was witness.

" The admiral finding that none of the English had engaged in the insurrection, treated them with a little more lenity for a few days, and endeavoured, though fruitlessly, to persuade them, with great promises of preferment, to enter into the Spanish service."

The last paragraph adds support to Campbell's contention that Cheap was guilty of a false accusation concerning his services to the Spaniards.

Off the coast of Portugal the Spaniards were greatly alarmed at the sight of some ships, and immediately put Campbell, as also the other prisoners, into confinement. The *Asia* had 5,000,000 dollars on board, with a weak and sickly crew to protect them; therefore, the Spaniards had sufficient grounds for apprehension, which kept them three days and nights under arms.

Campbell was ordered to Madrid on arrival and was questioned about Anson's voyage. He states that he refused any information, for he had none, and also refused to enter into Spanish service.

Morris and his companions, together with the other English prisoners, were sent ashore on arrival late in February 1746, chained together. They were confined with only bread and water for fifteen days in a prison. They were then moved from prison to prison over a period of fourteen weeks until a court order released them to be sent to Portugal for embarkation. They arrived in London on the 5th July 1746, three survivors of the eight who had been so ruthlessly left by Bulkeley on the desolate coast at Freshwater Bay.

Campbell arrived in London at the beginning of May 1746, shortly after Cheap's arrival. He presented himself at the Admiralty, but because of his change of religion, which he does not dispute, he was disqualified from further employment.

His book was published in 1747, " dress'd " as he said, " in the plain unsophisticated language of an honest Tar, whose principal View in publishing is to clear his Character from a very gross Calumny. Most of the Hardships I suffered in following the Fortunes of Captain Cheap were the Consequence of my voluntary Attachment to that Gentleman. In Reward for this the Captain has approved himself the greatest Enemy I have in the World . . . His ungenerous Usage of me, forced me to quit his Company, and embark for Europe in a Spanish Ship, rather than go there with him in a French one."

Campbell remarks bitterly that since their return Cheap had received command of a 40 gun man-of-war, and Byron a 20 gun ship. During his absence Byron had been promoted lieutenant. He was promoted captain on the 30th December 1746. It is amusing to read that Byron was then given the frigate *Syren*. Any serving or retired naval officer will tell you that it is a naval custom to play havoc with names, and it is not unusual, for example, to appoint two, or even three, officers of an unusual name or similarly sounding names, all at the same

time, if possible to the same ship, just to add to the confusion
and the merriment.

Campbell concludes his book:

" From Plymouth I went to Portsmouth in the same Ship
and proceeded directly to London where I arrived in the
beginning of May 1746; and informed the Lords of Admiralty of my Arrival by a Petition to Their Lordships. Speaking at the same time with Mr. Corbet, Secretary to Admiralty, I found to my great Surprise, that their Lordships had
been told by Captain Cheap that I was in the Spanish service! That this was a false Aspersion, the Publick will hardly
require any other Proof than the reading the foregoing
Narrative. If I had been in the Spanish service, how could
I have acquir'd a Passport from a Minister of Spain, and
how could I likewise arrive here in England so soon after the
Captain? Upon the whole, I hope that what I have here
wrote will be sufficient to satsfy the Publick of my Inno-
cense, and clear me of what is so wrongfully laid to my
Charge."

Campbell was never again employed in the Royal Navy, and
received no pay beyond the day on which *Wager* was wrecked.
His case became a great discussion among the naval officers of
the day, who felt great sympathy for him.

CHAPTER 16

TRIAL AT SPITHEAD

ON ARRIVAL at Spithead in H.M.S. *Stirling Castle* at the beginning of 1743, Bulkeley and Cummins were detained on board for two weeks. Baynes the lieutenant had arrived before them and had made a report to the Admiralty in order to exonerate himself. As in the case of the lieutenant's remarks to sundry people in Lisbon, his report to their Lordships reflected adversely on the behaviour of Bulkeley and Cummins. When the case had been examined by a local court of enquiry it was decided that there should be no trial until the return of either Commodore Anson or Captain Cheap. When Anson returned in 1744 after his four year voyage round the world, it was thought proper that a trial should be held only if Cheap returned. The 1743 court of enquiry had also recommended that until the case was clearer as a result of a trial, no arrears of wages should be paid, and none of the *Wager* survivors should be employed in the Royal Navy.

Bulkeley thereupon wrote to their Lordships asking permission to publish his journal:

" My Lords
   We are offer'd a considerable Sum by the Booksellers of London, for the Copy of our Journal, to publish it to the World; notwithstanding Money is a great Temptation to

People in our Circumstances, still we are determined to abide by your Lordships Resolutions."

A reply was sent by one of the Admiralty messengers. " The journal is your own and Their Lordships are not concerned with it. You may do as you will."

The journal was then published, in London, at a price of three shillings and sixpence.

The first reaction from many who read it was that the mutineers should be hanged, for they had stolen crown property in the form of the longboat and had deserted the captain. There were also other opinions.

" There was one great good Man," said Bulkeley, " that gave his Judgment in our Favour, so far as to say, She was not the King's Long-boat." The arguments savour of a salty old sea-lawyer such as the gunner himself. The reasons given were that the longboat had been retrieved from the wreck at the express order of the captain; his faithful followers had then, in compliance again with the captain's orders, sawn the longboat in two, thus destroying the King's property. But by the goodness of the kind carpenter, together with ready assistance from the good " people ", wood had been procured from the island trees, sawn into planks, beams, and knees, and the wreck of the longboat, destroyed at the behest of the captain, had been reconstructed into a serviceable vessel of twenty-three tons. The fact that pay had ceased when the *Wager* was lost was also brought forward by the " great good Man " as an extenuating circumstance; and instances of precedent were quoted such as the captain of H.M.S. *Ruby* who had been seized by officers and men for murdering his brother.

Bulkeley was without a job until the summer of 1745 when London merchants offered him the command of an old ship for her passage from Plymouth to London. She was to become a privateer. He and his crew of forty men were given a certificate of exemption from impressment for a period of six weeks. The certificate is of particular interest as it bears the signature of Anson, who had recently joined the board of Admiralty.

Bulkeley describes the passage in this ship: she had been the 40 gun man-of-war *Saphire*, and though now with only an armament of ten guns, she still had her gun ports. Two French privateers, each with 117 men, unfortunately approached him off the Start, whereupon he ran out his ten guns, fired a single shot, and hoisted his colours. The privateers were quite unmoved. Bulkeley then ordered the lower gun ports to be hauled up, and immediately fired another shot. This had the desired effect. The privateers, now believing *Saphire* to be a warship, at once tacked away.

Bulkeley of course had this affair published in the *St. James Evening Post*. His fame was rising. He must have felt that it should not be long before he would be re-employed by the Admiralty. It was now 1745; four years since he had left Cheap ashore on Wager Island.

Imagine his surprise on reading a newspaper nine months later, to see an advertisement ordering all survivors of the *Wager* now in England to repair on board H.M.S. *Prince George* at Spithead. Cheap had returned. The Lords of the Admiralty had ordered a court martial to enquire into the loss of H.M.S. *Wager*. Officers and men were to give depositions.

If Bulkeley now tried to shrug off thoughts of the yard-arm he was not given much consolation by current gossip. His thoughts are best appreciated by reading his own words. Wrote Bulkeley:

"One of the Proctors of Doctors-Commons ask'd me what News now our Captain was come home? I told him I was going to Portsmouth to the Court-Martial: He then ask'd me if I knew nothing more than the Advertisement for the Court-Martial? I hold him no; at which he told me, that the Monday before the Advertisement was published, there were four Messengers dispatch'd from the Marshal of the Admiralty, in order to take up the Lieutenant, Boatswain, Myself and Carpenter.

"On this I reply'd if that is Fact, I will go and deliver my self up to the Marshal here in Town; finding me fix'd in my resolution, he desired me to go and dine at the Paul's-Head Tavern in St. Paul's Church-Yard, where the Deputy Marshal was to dine that Day, accordingly I went, and after Dinner apply'd to him, desiring to know his Opinion in regard to the Officers of the *Wager,* as their Captain was come home; for that I had a near relation which was an Officer that came in that Long-boat to the Brazil, and it would give me Concern if he should suffer: His Answer was, that he believ'd we should be hang'd; to which I replied, for God's Sake for what, for not being drown'd? And is a Murderer at last come Home to be their Accuser? I have carefully perused the Journal, and can't conceive that they have been guilty of Piracy, Mutiny, nor any Thing else to deserve it. It looks to me, if so, that their Adversaries have taken up Arms against the Power of the Almightly, for delivering them. At which he said, Sir, they have been guilty of such Things to Captain Cheap whilst a Prisoner, that I believe the Gunner and Carpenter will be hang'd, if no Body else.

"As I was not known to him, on these words, I told him, then I was one of the Men that must suffer, for that I was the unfortunate Gunner of the *Wager*: After he was convinced, he told me, I was then become his Prisoner; he had me to his House, where I was confined until the rest of the Officers were brought up to Town, which, as soon as they came up, he wrote to their Lordships to inform them, that he had us all in Custody; but that I had delivered my self up to him here in Town; desiring their Lordships farther Directions concerning us.

" The Answer received was, to send us to Portsmouth and there to deliver us up on Board Admiral Steward (*Prince George*), to take a receipt, and to take particular Care that the Gunner and Carpenter did not make their escape. After on Board of Admiral Steward, we were told we were to be hang'd, nay, not a Letter came from any of our Friends, but there were these Words mentioned, you are to be hang'd.

" When the Captain came down to Portsmouth, some of my Friends waited on him, desiring to know what he had to alledge against us? His Answer was, Gentlemen, I have nothing to say for nor against the Villains, until the Day of Tryal, and then it is not in my Power to be off from hanging them. This Expression occasioned the whole Place to believe it would be so. On the Sunday following we were had up to Prayers, where there was a great Congregation, the Text was taken out of the Psalms, Them that go down to the Deep, and occupy their Business in great Waters, see the Works of the Lord."

The trial was to take place on the following Tuesday. Bulkeley was allowed the privilege of pen, ink, and paper, until the day of the trial, and was informed that " no Man after Sentence of Death should be indulged with it on any Account."

On the Monday, the Deputy Judge Advocate came on board to take the depositions. When it came to Bulkeley's turn the gunner complained of being kept prisoner without knowing the charge. He assumed he was charged by Cheap, and wished to know what the accusation was. He must have been shocked as well as relieved to hear that the court-martial was being held only to know how the ship was lost. The captain had alleged that the loss of the ship was due to the lieutenant, who had failed to carry out his orders to set the maintopsail and let go the anchor. He made no other charges.

H

Depositions were taken on Monday the 14th April 1746 and are recorded here by kind permission of the Public Record Office. They are fascinating since they are eye-witness accounts of those grim hours that preceded the loss of the *Wager*.

The mate John Jones had been ill in his hammock for days, yet came quickly on deck and took charge of the steering by sheets and braces when the rudder had gone. His testimony and that of Byron are those of the real seaman, and help considerably in establishing the final track and resting place of the *Wager*. Jones thought it had not been possible to set the main-topsail; but Byron and Hamilton supported the captain's view that it could have been set. Cheap was of the opinion that with the topsail set the *Wager* would have pointed higher, made less leeway, and cleared the bay.

A seaman John George and the Boatswain were both quite definite that the topsail could not have been set, nor could the ship have carried it. Bulkeley and Cummins both agreed with this view. Bulkeley describes how it took three hours to sway up the foreyard, set the foresail, and wear the ship with her head pointing southward. He remarks on the violence of the gale, and Cummins says it blew a hurricane.

The depositions are as follows and lead on to the minutes of the court-martial which took place on Tuesday the 15th April 1746 on board the *Prince George*. The president of the court was the Commander-in-Chief at Spithead, Vice Admiral of the Red Squadron, James Stewart, and the officers of the court were twelve officers of captain's rank, together with the Deputy Judge Advocate.

Depositions taken 14th April 1746 for enquiring into the Loss of his Maty's late Ship the *Wager* on the 14 May 1741 on the Coast of Patagonia. Pursuant to an Order from the Right Honoble. the Lords Commissioners of the Admtry dated 24th Mar. 1745 Viz.

John Jones late Mate of his Maty's Ship the *Wager*. Sworne Deposeth Viz. On the 14th May 1741 between the Hours of four and five in the morning, the above mention'd Ship Struck on a Rock or Shoal; I then being in my Hammacoe, and had not been out of it, to do any duty for Several days before; but when I came on the Deck found the Fore and Main Course satt, it then blowing very hard, and had our men been all well, whereas wee had not above six men in a Watch to the best of my remembrance, in my humble Opinion we were not able to carry any more Sail; our mizon mast being gone; wee always with our Foresail satt carried our Helm a Lee. I looked at the Compass and found after she got off the Shoal that she lay up to W., and I told them she lay with her head off Shore. The Carpenters mate came and said that there was $6\frac{1}{2}$ foot of water in the hold, wee had our Starboard tacks aboard, and the Wind Variable from the N. to the N.W. the Lieut. proposed letting goe the Anchor, but I told him there was not room to bring the Ship up and if wee shou'd swing clear of the Rocks, she must sink as the Water increased so much on us. I went to Capt. Cheap, who was then in the Surgeons Cabbin, and had the Evening before by a fall very much hurt his Shoulder, I think I have heard the Docter say it was Dislocated which render'd him incapable to give his necessary Orders, he told me that if the people's lives were saved, he had no regard to his Own, the second or third time she struck she broke the Rudder after which accident we were forced to back and fill her to keep clear of the Shoals and I believe the Currant satt true through them or else 'twere impossible for the Ship to come where she sunk.

Sworne by me   JNO. JONES
GEO. ATKINS
Dep. Jud. Adv.

Honoble. John Byron Mid. Sworne Deposeth Viz.

May 13th at 8 a.m. when I came upon Deck, I saw several bunches of Rock Weed pass by the Ship, upon which I called to the Carpenter who was by me and shew'd him them, He told me he believed he had seen the Land and had shew'd it the Lieut.   May the 14th at ½ past 2 p.m. saw the Land bearing N.N.W. dist. 4 Leagues, wee were then laying too under a Reef mainsail with the Larboard tack aboard. and the Fore Yard down; upon which the Captn. wore Ship, and layed her head to the Westward, the Wind at N.N.W. The Captn. going forward to give Directions for the fixing of New Strapps to the Geer Blocks, they being broke, and four of our Starboard forechain plates; He fell down the After hold all the grattings being unlaid, and dislocated his Arm. He was brought up and layed in the Surgeons Cabbin, as being thought by the Surgeon more proper than his Own for the Reducing his Arm; as soon as he came a little to himself, he sent for the Lieut. and hearing the Wind was at N.W.B.N. he ordered him to sett the Topsails and keep all hands upon Deck all night, as Captn. has often told me. At ½ past 4 a.m. the Ship struck, but having received no Damage the Officers upon Deck was immediately for loosing the Topsails, but it then being too late, the Captn. ordered them to let go the Anchor, but it not being clear, wee drove upon a second Reef, which broke the head of our Rudder, and had 7 foot water in the hold. So afterwards Steering with our head sails, till we stuck fast on a Bank near the Island we got ashore upon. I do think that with the Strength wee had, wee could have satt our Topsails and hawled the Sheets home.

Sworne by me   JOHN BYRON
GEO. ATKINS
Dep. Jud. Adv.

Thomas Hamilton Lieut. of Marines Sworne Deposeth Viz.

Some days before our Shipwreck I was told wee were in or near the Lattitude of our Rendezvous the Island of Sogoras. Wee lay too o'th'nights and made Sail in the day. On the 13th May I heard the Officers talking of Sea weeds which they saw and 3 p.m. of the 14th was told they saw Land, and had wore the Ship, and stood to the Westward, I went upon Deck and saw the Land upon our Wea. Bow, bearing about N.W. 4 or 5 Leagues as I imagine. The Captn. was upon Deck and uneasie about the Rigging of the Foremast being disabled, he gave Orders about it and at last went forward himself; He fell down the after hatchway, pitched upon head and Shoulders; both were much bruised, and his left Shoulder put out, soe that the head of the Bone came down below his Armpit. After the Shoulder was reduced with infinite difficulty and torture to the Captn. as soon as he recovered himself and was a little easier, he sent for the Lieut. but I know not what passed, the Surgeon gave the Captn. a Composing Cordial, and he fell asleep. About 9 or 10 All was quiet and noe Officer came to the Captn. nor I heard of no apprehension of danger, but about 4 a.m. the stroke of the Ship upon the Rocks awaked me, I ran to the Captn. he bid me send the Lieut. not finding him, I returned, and the Captn. bid me order to lett go the Anchor, it was not clear. Wee struck again, and satt fast 'til the Tyde rising hove us off. I think it was here wee broke our Rother, and our head sails and a strong tyde carried us clear; when we were just upon the Rocks almost touching. At last wee satt fast on a Small Island. I understood from the Captn. that our Misfortune was owing to the Lieut. not setting the Topsails as Ordered, and which I believe was the truth, for I never heard it contradicted.

Sworne by me   THO. HAMILTON
GEO. ATKINS
Dep. Jud. Adv.

John George Mariner late belonging to the *Wager* Sworne
Deposeth Viz.

On the 14th May 1741 It was my watch upon Deck, when
about 4 o'th'clock a.m. the Ship struck upon a Rock on the
coast of Patagonia. It blew very hard right on the Shore, and
wee had but 8 men in the Watch and those very weak. Wee
had our Courses satt and the Ship cripled very much with that
Sail, but was as much in my Opinion as she could bear, but wee
were forced to carry what sail wee could, to endeavour to claw
it off the Shore and I doe think wee were too weakly handed
to have satt the Topsails and hawl'd the Sheets home, but if
wee cou'd have done it, I don't think the Ship cou'd have
carried them.

Sworne by me   JOHN GEORGE
GEO. ATKINS
Dep. Jud. Adv.

John King Boatswain Sworne Deposeth Viz.

On the 14th of May 1741 between 4 and 5 a.m. it blowing
very fresh and wee under our Courses the Ship ran upon a
Sunken Rock from whence she beat to a Small Island and there
lay fast. I know of no Order for setting our Topsails, but had
wee had Orders to sett the Maintopsail I am of Opinion the
Ship wou'd not have carried him, there was such a gale of
Wind. I think the Ship cou'd not bear him sat, nor had we
Strength enough I think to do it. At this time the Capn. had
put out his Shoulder and was not upon Deck.

Sworne by me   JOHN KING
GEO. ATKINS
Dep. Jud. Adv.

John Bulkeley Gunner Sworne Deposeth Viz.

May the 14th at 2 p.m. being on the Fore Yard assisting
in handing the Fore sail saw the Land bearing N.W.½N., at

the sight of which I acquainted Captn. Cheap, on which he instantly gave Orders to sway the Fore yard up, satt the Sail and wore the Ship to the So'ward which wee were three Hours about, the Captn. seeing the weakness of the People and want of Strength, he coming forward to assist himself fell off the Ladder and unhappily Dislocated his Shoulder. At 8 o'Clock of the same Evening the Captn. sent for the Lieut. and myself, and said Gentlemen you are senciable of the Danger the Ship is in and the necessity of making Sail being on a Lee Shore; therefore desire you will use your utmost endeavour to croud her off, and if possible set the Maintopsail; but the Violence of the Gale wou'd not permit of making more Sail without indangering the Ship. At 4 a.m. the Master and Self Relieved the Lieut., he having had the Middle Watch, about $\frac{3}{4}$ of an hour after the Ship Struck: at which time wee cou'd not deserne half her Length for the Storme of Wind and Rain; the Ship's Striking, the Captn. sent several times up with Orders to lett go the Anchor, which was Impossable to be done; the Ship in a Short time after Bilged and grounded where it was impossible ever to get her off, wee could not if the wea. had permitted have satt our Topsails for want of Strength, for in the two Watches wee could muster no more than 13 hands Petty Officer's and all.

Sworne by me	JNO. BULKELEY
GEO. ATKINS	Gunner
Dep. Jud. Adv.	

John Cummins Carpent. Sworne Deposeth Viz.

On the 13th May 1741 about nine in the morning I sent to inspect the Chain Plates on the Starboard side, after going on the Forecastle, saw the Land, and Shewed it to the men of the Forecastle, and immediately acquainted the Lieut. with it. He not allowing it to be Land because the bearing was N.N.W. I answered May we not be imbayed, the Hon. John Byron answered true Carpent. About 4 in the Afternoon the Captn. going down the Ladder of the Qr. Deck fell down and dislocated his Shoulder, and was laid in the Surgeons Cabbin; About eight at Night the Captn. sent to me to Acquaint me I must take the Middle Watch with the Lieut. Was called out at 12 o'Clock went on Deck, but dismall dark; pump'd Ship at Seven Glasses. At 4 the Gunner Relieved the Lieut. About ½ past being between Sleep and waking felt a Shock as tho. the Sea took the Ship under the Main Chains, Immediately the Gunner acquainted me the Ship struck, I got out of Bed called to my Mate to Step in the Well and see what water; Answered no Water, I was for letting go the Anchor, Mr. Jones Mate answered if you let go the Anchor we shall perish, the Ship rann till about half past five than satt fast. I hear'd nothing of setting the Topsails but am of Opinion, wee had not Strength enough to have satt them and hawled home the Sheets nor wou'd the mast have bore the Sail for it blew a Hurricane.

Sworne by me   JN. CUMMINS
GEO. ATKINS
Dep. Jud. Adv.

MINUTES at a Court-Martial held on board his Maty's Ship *Prince George* at Spithead the 15th April 1746 for enquiring into the Cause of the Loss of his Maty's Ship the *Wager*, cast away on a Sunken Rock on the Coast of Patagonia in the South-Seas on the 14th May 1741 Pursuant to an Order from the Right Honoble. The Lords Commrs. of the Admtry Dated 24th March 1745 Viz.

Admiralty's Warrt. 11th Octor. 1744 Empowering Vice Admiral Steuart to hold Courts-Martial . . . Read.

Court Sworne.

Prisoners brought in.

Admiralty's Order 24th March 1745 . . . Read.

Captn. Cheaps Narrative 11th April 1746 . . . Read.

Captn. Cheap: doe you Charge any Officer besides the Lieut. with being in any degree accessary to the Loss of the *Wager*.

Noe Sir. I acquit them all of that.

John Jones late Mate of the *Wager* Sworne Deposition, read which he confirms.

When did you see the Land first.

I did not see it, being sick in my Hammacoe, but I heard it was seen at 2 in the afternoon. I reckoned that day wee were 45 Leagues from the Shore.

Captn. Cheap doe you think you could have carried your Toptails.

Yes, I thought soe when I ordered them to be satt, there are 17 Degrees of Variation in that part of the World, but we were certainly Embayed.

Captn. Cheap how doe you reckon the Land lay there.

North and South. Jones S.W.B.S., N.E.B.N. from the Streights of Magellan to the place where wee were lost.

The 13th May, what Lattitude did you judge your Selves in.

46 and 40 to the best of my remembrance.

Was there any dispute among the Officers about the Course you steer'd.

Yes, I heard some of the Officers the Lieut. and Gunner and others uneasie at Steering for Segona, for fear wee shou'd fall in with a Lee Shore, therefore wee wished to have gone to Juan Fernandez.

Captn. Cheap says by his reckoning they were 55 Leagues from the Shore and all the Officers except the Mate made it farther, some even ninety.

What was the Last Land you made before you was lost.

Sometime about the beginning of April wee made Land, which Frazier calls the Passage of the Sta. Barbara. Wee had an Observation two days before we were lost.

Was you desirous to make the Land.

Yes, the Land of Segora, but this was to the S.ward of it. What time did the Ship strike.

Between 4 and 5 a.m.

Was every thing done for the Preservation of the Ship and the Peoples Lives.

Yes, every thing was done.

Capt. Cheap asks Did you remember that the Carpenter told the Lieut. He saw the Land the 13th.

Yes, I heard the Carpent. say soe, after the Ship was lost.

Did you ever hear any reason given why the Captn. was not acquainted with your seeing the Land.

I cannot tell, I never heard any reason only that it could not be the Land because it bore N.N.W.

Did you ever hear any body say that they hove the Lead after you wore the Ship.

Noe, I never heard of it.

Lieut. Baynes asks Jones if he does not remember that on the 1st May the wind being fair for Juan Fernandez, which wee could have fetched if wee had not lay by 3 or 4 days with the Wind Westerly, S.S.W. I asked the Captn. why he would not goe thither, and Captn. Cheap said his Randezvous was at Segora, and there he would go if possible.

Did you know the Randezvous before that time.

Noe, it never was Publick.

Jones says in Answer, that was the time he speaks off before.

Captn. Cheap. After you told the Lieut. the Randezvous was at Segora, How did the Lieut. behave then.

I can lay nothing to his Charge after that, he Obeyed my Orders.

Honoble. John Byron Sworne, Deposition read which he confirms.

Did you tell the Captn. that the Carpenter had seen the Land.

Noe, I did not think it my Place.

Did you ever tell the Lieut.

I cannot say whether I did or not.

Did you endeavour to make more sail after the Fore-yard was swayed up.

We satt our Foresail, but never attempted to sett the Topsails. Our Yard was Swayed up about 7 or 8 p.m. before wee Struck.

When you put the Ship about did you see any Bay within you.

Yes a very deep Bay, but wee had but just Entered it.

After you wore did you ever know or hear whether the Lead was hove.

Yes, I do think there were Soundings, but I cannot remember them. Captn. Cheap says Campbell the Mid. told him there was noe water in 20 fathm. of Line.

Did the Ship go off from the Shore after you wore.

I believe not. I think she went wholly to Leeward.

Doe you think the Ship wou'd have bore her Topsails.

Yes; with all the Reefs in. I doe think she wou'd at least, it should have been tryed, I think.

Thomas Hamilton Lieut. of Marines sworne, Deposition read which he confirms.

After you wore Ship did you see or know, whether they hove the Lead.

Noe, I know not, nor did I hear the Captns. Orders to the Lieut. to sett the Topsails. I have heard some of the People say that the Lieut. disobeyed the Captain's Orders by not setting the Topsails and saved their Lives.

John George Mariner Sworne Deposition read which he confirms.

Did you ever know, or see, or hear that the Lead was hove when you wore the Ship.

Noe.

Why do you think you could not carry your Topsails.

Because there was a great Sea, Violent Squals of Wind, and the Ship lay Gunnel too wth. Reef Courses.

Could the Ship at any time have carried her Topsails when you first wore, 'til she was lost.

Noe, it blew a Hurricane of Wind, but it was my first Voyage, and I cant say much, but her Gunnel was even with the Water, and I dont think she could bear more Sail.

John King Boatsn. Sworne, Deposition read which he confirms.

Did you ever hear the Lead was hove from your wearing the Ship to your Strikeing.

I cant remember the Lead ever was hove til we had Struck, then wee hove the Lead and had 14 fathom water.

Could the Lead have been hove and you not hear'd of it or known it.

Noe, certainly it could not, for I was then upon Deck.

Did you ever hear the Deepsea Line ordered to be Stretched forward after you wore.

Noe I never did.

Did you ever hear that the Captn. Ordered the Lieut. to sett the Topsails.

The Lieut. came upon Deck, said the Captn. had ordered if it was possible to sett the Topsails. I said it was impossible to loose them in the Brails, they wou'd have Splitt to Peices, nor could the Ship carry them, nor had wee any Strength. Wee had not above 3 Seamen in One and 4 in 'tother Watch besides Marines.

How many Marines had you in a Watch.

I dont know.

How many Persons had you in each Watch Marines and Seamen.

16 in Both Watches, as well as I remember.

Have you any thing to say against your Captn, of remissness or Neglect, or being any ways deserving Censure for the Loss of the Ship.

Noe, the Captn. behaved very well. I have nothing to say against him or any other Officer.

Was you upon Deck when you wore Ship or was you in the Sick List.

Yes, I was upon Deck, assisted in fitting the Jeer Blocks, swaying the Fore Yard up, saw the Captain in the Steeridge, when he had reced his hurt, and was upon Deck when the Ship struck, had done my Duty two or three days.

John Bulkeley Gunner Sworne, Deposition read which he confirms.

Did you ever hear any Directions for Stretching the Deepsea Line or was the Lead hove when you made the Land N.W.$\frac{1}{2}$N.

Noe.

Why did you not heave the Lead.

The Master was in the Watch with me, and it was his Business.

After the Ship Struck upon the first Rock and went off again how did you keep her.

Upon a Wind close hawled till wee Struck again which broke our Tiller, then wee steer'd with our Sails, and she ran ashore the 3rd time before the wind.

How came you not to let go your anchor.

The Cable was foul.

Captn. Cheap says the Cable was Cross the Catthead.

How long after you Struck the first time was it before you Struck the 2nd time.

Half an hour.

Doe you know if the Lieut. acquainted the Captn. from time to time of the bearings and of all the transactions.

It was so dark noe bearings could be seen. I don't know what he did with the other transactions.

Was the Boatswain upon Deck, and did he keep all hands upon Deck.

Yes.

Have you any thing to Object to the Conduct of the Captn. or Officers, or to his Proceedings in all respects for the good and preservation of the Ship and Crew.

I believe not, I can lay nothing to the Charge of any Officer.

Did you ever hear any reason given for not heaving the Lead.

Noe never, I believe it was forgot.

Doe you believe the Ship could at any time, from the

time of wearing to her Striking have carried even her maintopsail.

I think she could not till 12 at Night then my watch was out.

John Cummins Carpent. Sworne Deposition read which he confirms.

Mr. Baynes how came you not to acquaint the Captn. that the Carpenter saw Land.

I did not think it was Land, it looked like dark, between two heavy clouds, which very soon disappear'd. The Carpent. says the Sight of it was soon gone, tho' it must be the Land.

Did you hear the Lead ordered to be hove.

Noe, not 'til after we had Struck.

Lieut. Baynes is asked how he came not to cast the Lead.

He says he could not believe it was Land, it so soon disappear'd, and by his reckoning they were 70 Leags. off.

Have you any thing to lay to the Charge of the Captn. or any of the Officers, for neglecting the Preservation of the Ship.

Noe.

Mr. Baynes how came you not to have your Cable clear.

They were bent about a fortnight before wee came in Sight of Land, and I know not how the Cable came over the Catthead.

After the Ship had beat over the first Reef of Rocks why did you not let goe an Anchor.

I was for it, but Mr. Jones the Mate said wee shou'd all Perish if wee did, nor doe I think there was trust to be put to the Cables. Captn. Cheap says the Best

Bower had been bent not above nine or tenn days before.

After you first Struck how long might it be before you came upon the 2nd Reef of Rocks.

An hour I believe, but upon the first Rock wee Struck twice very soon after one the other, and the Rother after that could not be traversed, soe that wee were obliged to Steer with our Sails.

Mr. Baynes when you was Obliged to Steer with your Sails how came you not to hawl the Mainsail up.

Wee did at last, but wee were a long while about it.

Lieut. Fielding of Fraziers Marines Sworne.

Doe you know any thing of the *Wager* at the time of her going ashore, or before it.

I know nothing of it, more than that the Ship was in a terrible condition, there could not be above 3 Soldiers in each watch I think, they were all down with the Scurvy. I heard some of the People say they saw the Land, and looked where they did, but could not see it, nor can I say any thing to the matter.

The President tells Lieut. Baynes he has heard what his Captain's Charge was, and what was said by the Several Evidences. What have you to say in your Defence.

I never could sett the Topsails it blew so very hard. I did not believe it was Land that the Carpent, saw, otherwise I wou'd have certainly told the Captain. As to having the Lead, the Captn. and Master were then upon Deck and they did not Order it, and neither from the Signs of the Land, nor from my Own Reckoning could I suppose it to be Land, therefore it did not come into my thoughts to heave the Lead.

Withdraw every Body and the Court debated the Sentence.

GEO. ATKINS

Dep. Jud. Adv.

At a Court-Martial held on board his Majty: Ship *Prince George* at Spithead, the 15th April 1746 pursuant to an Order from the Rt. Honble the Lords Commers. of the Admiralty 24th Mrch 1745 viz.

PRESENT

Jas. Steuart Esqure. Vice-Admiral of the Redd Squadron of his Majty. Fleet and Comander in Chief of All his Majty. Ships and Vessels at Spithead and in Portsmth. Harbour.

President.

Comodore Chas. Windham Esqre.   Captns. Chas. Watson

Captns. Solo. Gideon   Thos. Philpott

Thos. Harrison   Wm. Parry

Edwd. Rich   Timthy. Nucella

Clark Gayton   Thos. Stanhope

Jno. Hume   Robt. Harland

All duly Sworne according to Act of Parliament.

The Court proceeded to enquire into the Cause of the Loss of his Majty. late Ship the *Wager* on the 14th May 1741 upon a sunken Rock on the Coast of Patagonia, & having heard Captn. Cheaps Narrative read, as well as what Lieut. Robt. Baynes had to say in his own Defence, the Depositions of such of the Officers & Crew of the said Ship as could be mett with, & what they had all to say on the Occasion & maturely considered the same, were unanimously of Opinion, that Captn. David Cheap had done his duty, & used all means in his power to have preserv'd his Majty. Ship *Wager* under his Comand. & as he says he has noe Charge to lay against any of the

Officers of the said Ship, save only against Lieut. Baynes; therefore the Court doe acquit him the said Captn. Cheap & all the Officers & Ships Company, except the said Lieut. Baynes. & they are hereby acquitted accordingly, for the Loss of the said Ship *Wager*. And the Court haveing maturely Considered the Case of Lieut. Baynes, are unanimously of Opinion that he was to blame in not acquainting the Captain when the Carpenter told him, he thought he saw the Land, in never heaving the Lead, nor letting goe the Anchor, but in regard to the weakly condition of the Ship, the Cable being foul, and but thirteen sickly hands to clear it, as well as the little reason he appear'd to have not to believe it could have been the Land, wch. the Carpenter fancied he saw, either from it's Appearance, or from the Distance, his own, & the general reckonings of the Ship, made them from the Land. Therefore the Court do adjudge him the said Robt. Baynes to be acquitted for the Loss of the said Ship *Wager*, but, to be reprimanded by the President, for such omission, & he is hereby acquitted accordingly, & ordered to be reprimanded.

Jas. Steuart

Charles Windham

Chas. Watson

Solon. Gideon

Thos. Philpott

Thos. Harrison

Willm. Parry

E. Rich

Timthy. Nucella

Clark Gayton

Thos. Stanhope

Jno. Hume

R. Harland

GEO. ATKINS
Dep. Jud. Adv.

The Court were unanimous in acquitting Cheap and his officers over the loss of the ship, but Baynes was reprimanded on the charge of not informing the captain when land was sighted, and for not letting go the anchor when ordered. No further charge was laid against any officer. Never was there a word of mutiny. It is apparent that Bulkeley expected some such charge when confined in the *Prince George* and it is obvious that many others did. It was in order that he should be able to prepare his defence that he specifically asked why he was being kept prisoner. Doubtless he had in mind a counter charge of murder against Cheap for the shooting of midshipman Cozens. And it is certain that Cheap himself realized the position, and agreed to drop the charge of mutiny which he had so repeatedly threatened when on Wager Island. Perhaps a word from the Board of Admiralty had suggested that it was inadvisable for a number of reasons, some of which are mentioned in my concluding chapter.

Soon after the court-martial Bulkeley made a personal call at the Admiralty to ask for his pay, for he received no reply to his written application. He saw one of the Lords in person, and was asked "How dare you presume to touch a Gentleman's character in so public a manner as you have done?" His Lordship was referring to the book. "Do you think that Captain Cheap has nothing to say in vindication of his character? He will no doubt call you to account. We have not heard as yet what he has to charge you with. Therefore no wages until a hearing from him."

Bulkeley was alarmed at such a possibility still existing, and thereupon suggested that as he had been honourably acquitted, the matter should be dropped. He also wrote a letter to his Lordship as follows:

" My Lord,
    As your Lordship's Goodness was pleased to tell me Yesterday, that no Wages could be paid, nor any Thing else done for me, until a Hearing from Captain Cheap; therefore do most humbly pray and beseech your Lordship, to inter-

cede with their Lordships, if there is to be a second Tryal, that I may not be kept in Suspence, being prepared for every Thing that Captain Cheap has to alledge against me; praying Leave to subscribe myself,

Your Lordships most dutiful and
Obedient humble Servant,
J.B.

" On this Letter," says Bulkeley, " their Lordships were pleased to order the Wages to be paid to the Time the Ship was lost." The matter was now closed. The threat of hanging was no more. The noose had been removed. Bulkeley expressed righteous joy.

Shortly afterwards Bulkeley was offered the command of the cutter *Royal George,* and being the man he was, declined it. He thought her too small to keep the sea, " which " he says " was verify'd in her Cruise, for she founder'd in the Bay of Biscay, and every Man in her was drowned." Bulkeley was right and had escaped once again.

CHAPTER 17

RECAPITULATION

IT HAS been said that the *Wager* mutiny was no mutiny. This fallacy appears to be based on the fact that nobody was convicted of mutiny at the court-martial held in April 1746 concerning the loss of H.M.S. *Wager*.

But it is necessary to consider the facts prevailing at the time. In Bulkeley's own words, he the gunner, and Cummins the carpenter were convinced " we were to be hang'd for Piracy in coming away with the King's long-boat without the Capt. and also for mutinying." The Admiralty messenger sent out for Bulkeley's arrest said, " I believe the Gunner and Carpenter will be hang'd if no Body else." Bulkeley writes before the court-martial, " not a letter came from any of our friends, but there were these words mentioned, ' You are to be hang'd! ' "

Mutiny is insurrection against constituted authority, and particularly applies to authority granted in naval or military service. There is no question that Baynes, Bulkeley, and Cummins, together with their " licentious crew " as the Hon John Byron called them, not only directly disobeyed their captain, appointed to the command of the *Wager* by Their Lordships of the Admiralty, but also subjected him to bodily assault and made him prisoner.

The reason that nobody was convicted of mutiny was that Their Lordships knew that such a conviction would be unpopular with the country. Things were bad with the Navy in April 1746. Their Lordships were out of favour. One of the reasons for their unpopularity was their harsh treatment of Admiral Vernon, a popular figure with the public. Bulkeley and Cummins dedicated their first edition to him. Vernon had circulated pamphlets which were extremely critical of the administration; they called attention to current abuses and neglect of the Navy. In December 1745 he was ordered to strike his flag. He retaliated with two more vicious pamphlets. In April 1746 he was summoned before Their Lordships, and his name was struck off the flaglist without any trial being allowed.

The defence that the mutineers offered for their behaviour was that the captain's authority must automatically cease with the loss of the ship. It was also pointed out by the ringleaders that pay ceased at the same time. They therefore owed allegiance to no-one. This was a dangerous attitude. Existence of such a misconception could lead, in time of enemy action or other hazard, to anticipation that the ship was already taken or lost, when greater zeal and united resolution might save the ship. Anson realized the danger, and corrected this misconception. As a Lord Commissioner he removed any further doubt in 1747. An Act was passed " for extending the discipline of the Navy to crews of His Majesty's ships, wrecked, lost, or taken, and continuing to receive their wages upon certain conditions."

The survivors of the *Wager* were extremely lucky not to be convicted of mutiny. They owe their acquittal not only to the unpopularity of the Board, but to the strength of public opinion, and also to the fact that their miraculous escapes had caught the public fancy, particularly as described in Bulkeley's book, first published in London in 1743. Authorship was shared nominally with John Cummins, the carpenter, but he took little part in the writing of it. It is likely that the gunner, always the sea-lawyer, and the brains and main driving force against the intentions of the captain, wished Cummins to share something of the responsibility for the insurrection and all those actions which were intended to look justifiable when written as " daily transactions " by Bulkeley.

Anson completed his world voyage in June 1744, and his fame grew rapidly. Anyone associated with the voyage was immediately befriended by the British public. Interest and enthusiasm were stirred by the many narratives that were published. It seemed unbelievable that men could survive such hardships and misfortunes. The public were ready to shut an eye to misdemeanour, and welcome all sailors as romantic heroes, and this applied as much to the *Wager* men as to those of the *Centurion*. They had survived in spite of neglect of ships, corruption in dockyards, and weak administration.

Bulkeley's book served its purpose. The reader of it will find it difficult to exonerate Cheap from the accusation of murder made by the mutineers. Certainly he cuts a poor figure at times: inhuman and stupid. Yet one cannot help being sorry for the loneliness that accompanied his continual aloofness, and admire his steadfast purpose and loyalty in the face of adversity, particularly when all looked hopeless. Cheap was appointed to the *Lark* and took a valuable prize which enabled him to marry in 1748. He died in 1752.

Byron's book, not published until 1768, paints a good picture of Cheap, and we are able to follow adventures which he shared with the captain he admired: adventures which led to a conclusion that must have stirred fearful anxiety in Bulkeley's mind, the prospect of hanging from the yard-arm getting nearer every day.

Yet a different version is found in Campbell's book, published in 1747 as a sequel to Bulkeley's account, and intended to refute the story that he left Cheap and Byron while in South America because he married a Spanish girl and offered his services to the Spaniards.

The other two stories by *Wager* survivors were published in 1751. That by Isaac Morris, midshipman, adds little to our conception of either Bulkeley or Cheap, but graphically describes his own adventurous escape from what seemed certain death when he and his seven shipmates were deserted by Bulkeley at Freshwater Bay on the barren coast of Patagonia. The " affecting narrative " by the cooper of the *Wager*, John Young, is probably the best book of all. It follows very closely the pattern of Bulkeley's account, but in some ways gives us a better picture of both Bulkeley and Cheap, which I have attempted to reproduce in this book. The cooper pathetically describes his golden dreams on setting out on the expedition with Anson: " I flatter'd myself with nothing less than a Fortune sufficient to buy a Peerage ". He ends with an account of his imprisonment on arrival in England, and a refusal on the part of Their Lordships to pay his back wages. " The Grief we expressed at this Disappointment was proportionate to the Hope we had conceived."

On reading all these stories it is not difficult to appreciate the conviction with which Samuel Johnson in 1759 made his dictum, " No man will be a sailor who has contrivance enough to get himself into a jail; for being in a ship is being in jail, with a chance of being drowned."

CHAPTER 18

CONCLUSION

SOME EXPLANATION is necessary of my rough track of the *Wager* before shipwreck, because this differs radically from that shown in Burney's narrative in Volume V of his *Voyages and Discoveries in the South Seas*, 1817.

From the depositions and the testimony given at the court-martial in 1746 it is clear that the wind was of gale force between west and north-west and that there was a tremendous in-draught into the gulf of Peñas. It is also clear that owing to both drift and excessive leeway to the eastward, the *Wager* was unable to make good anything better than a southerly course, though her head lay to the south-west.

This could lead her, after the operation of wearing ship which took three hours, direct to the island which is marked on modern charts as Isla Wager. Burney assumed a continuation of the wind from between south and south-east, which *Wager* had had for several days. But Byron and Jones both gave north-west in their testimony at the court-martial. The Peninsula de Tres Montes on which, according to Burney, the *Wager* was wrecked, had not been properly surveyed when Burney wrote his narrative. It was known only that there was a great promontory extending as a northern flank to the gulf of Peñas. Its western extremity was uncertain, as was the delineation of the islands which lie on the southern flank of the gulf, one of which was to prove a storm-tossed resting place for the stricken *Wager*.

The *Wager* really seems to have been doomed. She had been purchased by the Admiralty at the end of 1739, and had begun her fatal journey a few months later in September 1740. In her short active naval life she had had three captains: Dandy Kidd, the Honourable George Murray, and finally David Cheap. Her end came as a combination of misfortunes: loss of mizzen-mast; crazy rigging; sickly crew; parting of the forehalyard blocks; captain's disablement; landfall in a bay not recorded on charts, with an in-draught of wind and sea; and the final approach to a lee shore in the black of night with a gale blowing on shore and visibility down to a few yards. The absence of any one of these might have saved her.

One cannot help thinking of the curse referred to by Dandy Kidd as he lay dying in the captain's cabin in H.M.S. *Pearl*. Nevertheless had the Almighty not shown mercy in settling the *Wager* providentially near land, and in providing miraculous deliverance on so many occasions recorded in this book, there would have been no survivors to tell the tale. And what a tale!

THE END

BIBLIOGRAPHY

Bulkeley and Cummins: *A Voyage to the South Seas* 1740-
1741
First edition, London 1743.
Reprinted Harrap 1927.

Burney, James: *Voyages and Discoveries in the South Sea,*
Vol. V.
London, 1817.

Byron, John: The narrative containing an account of the great
distresses suffered by himself and his companions on the
coast of Patagonia, 1740-1746, and the loss of the *Wager*
Man of War.
London, 1768.

Campbell, Alexander: Sequel to A Voyage to the South Seas,
or the Adventures of Captain Cheap, the Hon. Mr. Byron,
Lieut. Hamilton, Alexander Campbell, and others, late of
H.M.S. *Wager.*
London, 1747.

Morris, Isaac: A Narrative of the Dangers and Difficulties
which befell Isaac Morris, a midshipman of the *Wager,* and
seven more of the crew belonging to the *Wager.*
London, 1751.

Murray, Arthur (Viscount Elibank): *An Episode in the Spanish
War* 1739-1744.
Seeley, Service & Co., Ltd.
London, 1952.

Pack, S. W. C.: *Admiral Lord Anson.*

Cassel, 1960.

Walter, Richard: *Anson's Voyage Round the World* 1740-1744.

Dent, London, 1942.

Young, John: An affecting narrative of the unfortunate voyage and catastrophe of H.M.S. *Wager,* one of Commodore Anson's squadron in the South Sea Expedition.

London, 1751.

INDEX